KEYSTONE CORRUPTION

A PENNSYLVANIA INSIDER'S VIEW OF A STATE GONE WRONG

D1622740

Brad Bumsted

Best,

Brad

Camino Books, Inc.

Philadelphia

Manufactured in the United States of America
1 2 3 4   16   15   14   13

Library of Congress Cataloging-in-Publication Data

Bumsted, Brad.
    Keystone corruption: a Pennsylvania insider's view of a state gone wrong / Brad Bumsted.
        pages cm
    Includes bibliographical references.
    ISBN 978-1-933822-80-8 (alkaline paper)
1. Political corruption — Pennsylvania — History. 2. Political culture — Pennsylvania
— History. 3. Politicians — Pennsylvania — Biography. 4. Legislators — Pennsylvania
— Biography. 5. Pennsylvania General Assembly — History. 6. Pennsylvania — Politics
and government — 1951-. 7. Pennsylvania — Politics and government — 1865-
1950. 8. Pennsylvania — Biography. I. Title.

    F155.B86 2013
    364.1'323 — dc23   2013008606

ISBN 978-1-933822-80-8
ISBN 978-1-933822-81-5 (ebook)

Interior design: Jerilyn Bockorick
Front cover design: Natalie Cake

This book is available at a special discount on bulk purchases for promotional, business, and educational use.

Publisher
Camino Books, Inc
P.O. Box 59026
Philadelphia, PA 19102
www.caminobooks.com

Contents

Acknowledgments

My deep thanks go to four women who made this book possible: my wife, Gail; my daughter, Lindsey; my mother, Barbara; and my longtime partner at the *The Pittsburgh Tribune-Review* on many stories, Debra Erdley.

Special thanks go to historian Robert B. Swift, the state capitol reporter for Times Shamrock newspapers, who graciously provided clips and documents he'd hoarded over the years. He also proved to be a loyal reader, editor, contributor, and a collaborator on ideas. This book would not have been possible without his encouragement and his critiques. We shared something. We both lived through and reported on the era of supreme leadership power in the General Assembly and the downfall of those leaders.

Natalie Cake, a most talented photographer, designed the cover panel for this book. Her contribution is truly appreciated.

The *Tribune-Review* gave me the green light to use *Trib* photos. The Harrisburg *Patriot-News*, which plays a prominent role in this story, graciously provided photos. My thanks to Sandy Tolliver, deputy managing news editor, who did skillful edits of many chapters. Debra Erdley also edited key chapters. When Sari Heidenreich was a capitol newsroom intern, I noticed that she was good at copy editing. Now with ABC-27 TV in Harrisburg, she helped me in editing the manuscript. I also wish to thank Edward Jutkowitz and Brad Fisher of Camino Books for their enthusiastic support of my idea for *Keystone Corruption*.

Former FBI Special Agent Kathleen MacAfee was an invaluable resource, and I am grateful for her assistance. House Republican Caucus spokesman Stephen Miskin was helpful to me as well.

My *Trib* colleague Bobby Kerlik played a special role in the chapter on the Orie sisters. That chapter is based in part on his trial reporting, on other stories we did together, and on his advice.

A friend and author, William G. Williams, helped get me started. Author Bill Morris, who has dedicated his life to writing, was an inspiration to me in writing this book.

Several prosecutors, defense attorneys, and legislative aides, provided technical advice and valuable information. They can't be named because of their position and/or proximity to the cases or the defendants. Numerous others in the state capitol newsroom, though unnamed here, are nevertheless remembered for their help.

I am indebted to former Representative Frank LaGrotta, who shared his memoirs, deepest thoughts and still-open wounds. My daughter, Lindsey, took photographs and helped me frame ideas and concepts.

The world's not perfect and neither am I. Any mistakes herein are my own.

Prologue

G. TERRY MADONNA

Pennsylvania has long been the home of political chicanery. In *Keystone Corruption*, veteran journalist Brad Bumsted writes succinctly and superbly about the major political corruption cases that unfolded in the 20th and early 21st centuries, with an emphasis on those officials in state government that used state resources for personal or political gain. Much of the volume is devoted to the series of prosecutions, brought by the state's attorney general, often referred to as "Bonusgate," a generic but limiting term that describes the awarding of state-paid bonuses to legislative employees for their political work using state resources.

What led to the largest number of prosecutions for public corruption in the state's history can be traced to several important changes in the political environment. The first and the most systemic was the decline of county political organizations and the courthouse gangs that dominated state politics since the end of the Civil War. These local organizations dictated the choice of legislative candidates, raised the resources to fund the campaigns, and managed all aspects of the campaigns. By the 1980s, these organizations had atrophied to the extent that the functions of those campaigns were slowly transferred to the leaders of the legislative caucuses.

Entering the new millennium, full-service campaign operations in some cases became an integral part of the caucus legislative campaign committees and their leaders. What especially motivated the transition was the evolution of the part-time legislature starting in the 1970s to a full-time one, with rising salaries, pensions, health care benefits, and a huge growth in legislative staff.

One important event that occurred in 2005 was pivotal in the expansion in the use of state resources in legislative elections. In July 2005, the legislature voted to increase its salaries by 16 to 54 percent. The public reaction was immediate and visceral. In the following year's legislative elections, 54 incumbent members of the legislature retired or were defeated. The top two Senate leaders and the number-two Democratic leader in the House lost their seats.

Trial testimony indicated that legislative leaders, concerned about subsequent defeats for themselves or House colleagues in 2006, doubled down in the use of the state resources they devoted to their campaigns after ramping up in the two previous cycles. Newspaper accounts of the extensive use of legislative staffers in campaigns led to the state's attorney general launching an investigation and convening grand juries that led to the prosecutions.

Brad Bumsted is an awarding-winning reporter who has covered Pennsylvania government and politics for more than 30 years, early in his career for several state newspapers and Gannett News Service. Currently, he is the state capitol reporter for *The Pittsburgh Tribune-Review* and has covered most of Pennsylvania's high-profile corruption trials in recent years. In 2004, he co-authored *Murder Is the Charge* with attorney William Costopoulos, a true account covering the investigation and eventual acquittal of a former mayor of York, Pennsylvania, who had been charged with murder while serving on the city's police force during the infamous race riots in 1969. Brad Bumsted also appears on many Pennsylvania television and radio programs where he is a much sought-after commentator.

Introduction

As Jerry Sandusky was led off in handcuffs, I felt nauseous. Not because he was arrested, but because he was charged with molesting 10 young boys over a 15-year period. Sandusky was the legendary defensive coordinator who helped the Nittany Lions earn a reputation as "Linebacker U." He used his reputation and the imprimatur of Penn State, even as an ex-coach, to gain trust with victims and their families. His arrest in November 2011 rocked the campus and the state.

More worried about negative news stories if Sandusky's activities were exposed, top university officials failed to protect children for more than a decade from the serial child rapist, according to a university-commissioned report by Louis Freeh, a former FBI director.

They "concealed Sandusky's activities from the board of trustees, the university community, and law enforcement authorities. They exhibited a striking lack of empathy for Sandusky's victims," the Freeh report concluded.

How could Penn State have allowed it to happen? The head-turning at Penn State to protect the institution and the football program has also taken place for decades in Pennsylvania government.

Corruption has festered like a cancer in Pennsylvania, at least since the Civil War. Corruption comes in waves, then subsides, and finally returns. The citizens are always losing, their tax dollars squandered by politicians who begin as caring, conscientious lawmakers who are eventually corrupted by the system.

In Luzerne County, two corrupt judges took bribes and railroaded juvenile offenders. The "Kids for Cash" scandal that unraveled in 2008 was just another symptom of the toxicity beneath Pennsylvania's political soil.

Politicians in Harrisburg stole almost $14 million of Pennsylvanians' tax money from approximately 2000 to 2006 to finance their campaigns and personal needs. It happened because people don't speak out. Politicians didn't challenge corrupt leaders. Voters turned their heads. In a way you can't blame them. For decades, incumbents have stacked the deck. The Sandusky revelations may have been Pennsylvania's version of Colombia's notorious Jamundi Massacre. Internal corruption doesn't just occur in certain parts of Latin America.

Hugh Bronstein, a veteran of Pennsylvania's Capitol Newsroom with UPI, covered the 2006 Jamundi Massacre in which Colombian soldiers on the payroll of drug lords gunned down 10 members of an elite, U.S.-trained anti-narcotics police force in an ambush.

In Bogota, as a correspondent for Reuters, Bronstein saw corruption at its worst.

He stopped by my house on Harrisburg's West Shore in December 2010. He came armed with some kick-ass coffee, his usual quick wit, and an insightful question. Dressed casually in a vest and jeans, Hugh was between assignments in Central and South America.

Bronstein left Harrisburg for a job with the *Morning Call* in Allentown in 1992. Four years later, he went to Reuters in New York City. On the business beat in New York, he eventually landed an assignment for Reuters in Colombia. Hugh returned over the holidays in 2010 to visit his parents, who live near me. He was moving on to a post in Buenos Aires for Reuters after a stint in Ecuador. He also reported out of Venezuela for a month in 2011.

I was pleasantly surprised when Hugh showed up at my door on an evening near Christmas with a pound of Colombian coffee. The real stuff, not the coffee they sell to Americanos, he told me.

Hugh had followed some of the Pennsylvania news about the state House Democrats' Bonusgate scandal and Senator Vincent Fumo, who was cited as likely among the most corrupt politicians in America in a *Reader's Digest* story. And Hugh was curious. What was this "corruption" they were talking about? Both Pennsylvania cases involved the use of taxpayers' resources: for campaigns during Bonusgate and for Fumo's political and personal needs. Hugh seemed to be asking: Is there more, or is that it?

Where Bronstein had worked in Bogota, corruption meant government officials taking bribes or cops on the payroll of the cartels. He covered corruption in Colombia that in his words "makes Fumo look like Mr. Rogers."

Imagine this from Bronstein's September 29, 2007 story: With a month to go before ballots were cast, the Colombian government says there were 69 political murders in this campaign season, including 27 candidates, 13 town council members, five campaign volunteers, and a campaign manager. Many were political murders related to the drug trade.

Bronstein's laser-like question caught me off guard. It focused on the essence of Bonusgate and other political corruption in Pennsylvania. I thought about it a long time.

It made me wonder: Why is using public resources for campaigns a crime? And why does corruption in Pennsylvania seem as prevalent as its crummy highways?

His explanation for the casual inquiry, when I contacted him a year later, made enormous sense. The reason the U.S. is not Colombia, Bronstein noted, is because "we stop corruption at the statehouse level." He added, "In Pennsylvania you write the Fumo stories so you don't have to write the Jamundi stories." By focusing on corruption at the local level, which the United States generally does and many other countries do not, the press helps people keep from becoming jaded, and that helps stop corruption from growing.

Based on his travels, Hugh believes many people in the rest of the world don't know you are not supposed to be corrupt. He is glad that he grew up in a country where people stop at stop signs, even when there are no police around.

Corresponding from Chile in 2011, Bronstein wrote that the worst part was the way people just turned their heads. "And I must say that was the worst of what I saw in Colombia, the way people shrugged off horrible, bloody, outrageous stories of corruption like Jamundi. Once corruption is allowed to be seen as business as usual, civic culture is gone."

I believe Hugh's theory applies to Pennsylvania. For the most part, we're stamping out corruption at the local and state level before it grows or gets worse. Then the cancer grows back.

We are not stopping corruption totally at the statehouse level, as evidenced by national scandals like Abscam and the Jack Abramoff lobbying schemes. But for the most part, we aren't shooting politicians in the street. The Kids for Cash and the Sandusky scandals stunned us because the victims were children. Some of them may never totally recover.

But corruption is part of Pennsylvania's long history. As corruption continues, democracy is damaged. The cycle repeats itself and the voters become more cynical. They don't bother voting. The bottom line is that all too often we tolerate Pennsylvania's culture of corruption.

(The opinions expressed in this book are those of the author and are not necessarily those of *The Pittsburgh Tribune-Review*.)

KEYSTONE CORRUPTION

1

Fish Stinks from the Head

August 31, 2011

Former House Speaker John M. Perzel was trapped. Moments before, he had pleaded guilty to eight felonies, and now he was being pursued by a dozen reporters and several TV cameramen down a dingy hallway in the Dauphin County Courthouse. Microphones were thrust forward like weapons. Reporters continued to pepper him with questions. TV reporters in particular seemed to have a stock set of questions: "Are you sorry? What do you say to the taxpayers? How do you feel?" Perzel and his two attorneys, Brian McMonagle and Fortunato Perri, stood with their backs to the media, waiting for an elevator. When they shifted left, the pack shifted left. They were surrounded, and they were saying nothing. Finally, an elevator door opened across the hallway. The speaker and his lawyers made a dash for it. With the door still open, I locked eyes with Perzel for the first time. He looked like a wounded animal. His head was cocked slightly to the right. What I saw in his eyes was pain, an intense pain about his life's turn.

Sure, I thought he should go to prison. But no human being should have to hurt like this. It was almost as if his entire life, all he had been, all he could have been, was lost in the moment.

I had known John Perzel since his rise to power and at his peak. He was the most powerful Republican lawmaker in Pennsylvania from 1995 through January 2007. He was cunning and ruthless. He was glib and spat words out faster than most humans can think. He worked hard for everything he had, including his job as a maitre d' at an Italian restaurant in Philadelphia. His downfall came when he reached for even more.

1

Perzel oversaw the theft of $10 million in state money for computer equipment and programs designed to help Republicans including himself win re-election.

If a computer could do it, he wanted it. If the programs could apply to campaigns, he bought them. In all cases, the taxpayer paid for it. A former top aide would later tell me that the speaker saw no difference between John Perzel the candidate and John Perzel the public official.

"Guilty, your honor," Perzel told Dauphin County Judge Richard Lewis, moments before the scene at the elevator on August 31, 2011. Perzel and his lawyers all wore dark, pin-stripe suits. The stripe was subtler in Perzel's suit. He had on a white shirt and a blue tie with a light pattern. His once dark hair was now gray, whitened no doubt by the stress of the past three years when he was under investigation and indictment.

Perzel wasn't putting money in his own pocket, though a statewide grand jury presentment said he had a scheme to do so. It was about power, pure and simple. It was about holding onto his office and keeping the majority at all costs. It was also about punishing his enemies, including Republican legislators who stood up to him. He also had a scheme to use the new gadgetry to run for governor.

Holding a majority in the 203-member House was key. The majority controlled the flow of legislation, committee assignments, and jobs. It meant the best offices. The majority equaled power.

There was a win-at-all-costs mentality among leaders in the highly partisan Pennsylvania General Assembly. Each political caucus in each chamber has its own staff, equipment, web pages, and re-election machine.

PLEA DEAL

Facing 82 criminal counts, John Perzel had reached a "cooperative" plea agreement with the Commonwealth of Pennsylvania. He was now a state witness against three remaining co-defendants. He would soon be on a very short leash held by his new handlers in the Attorney General's office. Attorney Brian J. McMonagle realized that nothing should interfere with that. Nothing should jeopardize his client's deal, least of all getting into an ugly exchange with reporters. Since he had been charged in November 2009, Perzel had harshly criticized the Attorney General's investigation. If he went to trial, he was prepared to invoke a scorched earth approach to take down other Republicans.

The strategy employed by McMonagle, one of the best criminal defense lawyers in the state, was to say nothing to reporters. Perzel's track record in dealing with media on the whole was not good. Since the 2005 pay raise he helped push through, it was disastrous. So nothing would be said. How much of the remainder of his life would be spent outside prison depended on it.

MASSIVE MISAPPROPRIATION

Perzel and the other crooks who stole a combined $14 million from Pennsylvania taxpayers deserved to be locked up for a long time. Still I was conflicted about them. I respected some of these men and admired their ability as legislators. A few I knew quite well. For better or worse, most of them were part of my life since 1983.

By 2012, eight top legislative leaders had pleaded guilty or been convicted at trial of crimes that essentially involved using public resources for campaigns. The convictions came over a span of four years, from 2009 to 2012, and resulted from prosecutions by the Pennsylvania Attorney General's Office, the U.S. Attorney for the Eastern District of Pennsylvania, the U.S. Attorney for the Middle District of Pennsylvania, and the Allegheny County District Attorney's Office. It was unprecedented in Pennsylvania history. At least in modern times, it was also unique among state legislatures across the nation.

"I am not aware of any state that got rid of its leaders because of corruption, as Pennsylvania has," said Robert Stern, former president of the Center for Governmental Studies in Los Angeles. But Stern and other ethics experts say there is no single place or institution that keeps statistics on the number of convicted leaders. Certainly, some states with FBI sting operations had more legislators charged at one time.

It is difficult to compare because Pennsylvania has more legislative leaders (30) than most other states, given the size of its House and Senate (253 members), noted Alan Rosenthal, professor of public policy at the Eagleton Institute for Politics at Rutgers University. Each political party in the House and Senate has seven leaders (28 in total), and each chamber has a presiding officer, the speaker and president pro tempore.

In all, 38 public officials with ties to the capitol were charged with public corruption by federal, state, and local prosecutors from 2007 through mid-2012. Thirty-five people pleaded guilty or were convicted at trial. These were largely ex-lawmakers, a few sitting legislators, and legislative aides, but also included allegations against a Supreme Court justice. The common theme was using public resources for campaigns.

Separately, in Northeastern Pennsylvania, 29 local officials, judges, and contractors were charged with crimes stemming from public corruption investigations since 2009. Bribery-related charges were a common thread. (In addition, two senators were charged, and they are counted among the 38 above with ties to the capitol.)

LEGAL THIEVERY

In Pennsylvania, the crimes that leaders committed from approximately 2000 through 2006 would make just about anyone furious. But the legal thievery they were never charged with was even more maddening. Pennsylvania legislative leaders over the past decade had squandered millions more on high-end restaurant meals, luxury cars, drivers, political polls, catered dinners for rank-and-file members, and liberal policies for lawmakers to collect per diems (averaging $162 in mid-2012) for food and lodging even when they were wined and dined by lobbyists or ate catered meals. In 2007–08, the House Clerk's Office spent almost $250,000 on catered meals, from elaborate spreads to pizza. They had redundant print shops for the Republicans and Democrats to publish constituent newsletters adorned with their pictures and tantamount to campaign mailers. They had TV studios to put out look-alike news shows for cable TV.

Legislators spent untold millions of taxpayers' dollars on legal incumbency protection programs — including glossy news releases, newsletters, blast email, and a special legislative office catering to constituents who needed documents from the state Department of Transportation. Millions more were spent over the past decade on "public service announcements" — slick TV spots featuring the incumbents. They spent about $100 million a year on WAMs (walking around money outlays) — a program that allowed legislative leaders to earmark lawmakers' pet projects for goodwill in their districts. Depending on how you defined it, discretionary money totaled $300 to $400 million.

In the 1990s, former Republican governor Tom Ridge swore he'd get rid of WAMs. But they came raging back like a stage-four cancer. Even while he was governor, a new strain of WAMs surfaced that were called "Ridgies."

The top leaders — John Perzel; Philadelphia Senator Vincent Fumo, ranking Democrat on the Senate Appropriation Committee; and another powerful Philly leader, Representative Dwight Evans, a Democrat — each controlled millions of dollars a year for projects. There was a $1 million WAM for Evans' jazz festival at a time when his spokeswoman was denying there were any WAMs in the budget, according to a July 2010 column by *Philadelphia Inquirer* columnist Karen Heller. Fumo obtained $2.2 million in grants in 1992 for a Columbus Day festival, which included a trip to Italy for Fumo and other officials to bring renowned tenor Luciano Pavarotti to Philadelphia. This was reported in a 2004 *Tribune-Review* story by Richard Gazarik.

A $900,000 grant was awarded to the Business Institute for International Development in Allegheny County. No one had ever heard of it. There was no phone number and no staff for the institute. It turns out that the institute's address was the home address of former Democratic senator Mike Dawida, then a lame duck Allegheny County commissioner, as revealed by *Tribune-Review* reporters Debra Erdley and Rich Gazarik in 1999. Apparently, the ex-senator was planning a start-up company. Dawida turned down the grant after a public outcry. Lawmakers played this cute game, often claiming they didn't know the term, asking "What are WAMs?"

A RIGGED SYSTEM

All of this was in addition to the $10 million that House Republicans were using illegally in state tax money to pay for campaign computer programs aimed at boosting their chances at the polls. We did not know about it until it was uncovered by a grand jury. And then there was the $1.4 million bonus program by House Democrats to reward staffers who worked on campaigns with illegal bonuses. Or the estimated $2 million in tax money spent illegally by Senate powerbroker Vincent Fumo for his personal and political needs, such as hiring a private detective to spy on his enemies, using state workers to develop his gentleman's farm, and putting friends on the state payroll who did little or no work.

Former House Democratic Whip Mike Veon, from Beaver County, and former House Speaker Bill DeWeese, Democrat of Greene County, had state-paid staffers whose primary duty was to raise campaign money. Fumo had several people raising money on staff. Pennsylvania had never enacted publicly financed campaigns. But they might as well have because legislative elections in Pennsylvania were rigged in favor of the incumbents.

John Perzel would later brag in court about his fund-raising prowess. From 2000 to 2007, he raised $17 million in campaign money for himself, the state Republican Party, and the House Republican Campaign Committee. Despite that pile of cash, he used tax money to pay for sophisticated computer programs to help Republican House candidates. Why? Because it's hard to raise money, but it's easy to charge an account at your fingertips. And stockpiling the campaign cash provided a sense of security for incumbents.

There were other methods. From 2005 to 2011, the legislative payroll increased 22 percent to $119.5 million, a *Tribune-Review* investigation found. People who worked on campaigns often landed state jobs with legislators. The huge staff came into play in Bonusgate, in which Veon and his minions used House Democratic staffers to work on campaigns and rewarded them with secret bonuses. Republicans and Democrats illegally sent House staffers to work on a special election in the Lehigh Valley. The Democrats outdid themselves with 170 staffers in that one election, according to a grand jury finding.

The real crime was the hostile environment created for hundreds of challengers and people who didn't even bother to run for the state House and Senate because they knew the odds were too steep. About nine of 10 incumbents typically won re-election until leaders reached too far with the middle-of-the-night, 16 to 54 percent pay boost in 2005.

"These kinds of cases where public officials have been found to use government-paid staff, facilities, funds, and equipment in aid of manipulating or trying to control the electoral process is basically a fundamental assault on the whole democratic process," John Contino, executive director of the State Ethics Commission, testi-fied at a federal court hearing for Fumo in 2011. Challengers would tell you "if the incumbent has an army of government-paid campaign workers to assist them, it's virtually impossible to challenge them in a democratic process," Contino added.

In reapportionment every 10 years, politicians further insulated incumbents of their own party and increased the already long odds for challengers by drawing district lines to their liking. A close call for John Perzel in the 2000 election prompted him the following year to draw a Northeast Philadelphia district that would appear to make him legislator for life. That narrow election victory sparked the paranoia that led to Perzel's constant need for the latest computer gizmos he thought would institutionalize the Republican majority. Only being led off in handcuffs ruined his winning streak at the polls that began in 1978 and ended in 2010.

Without ever giving their consent, Pennsylvanians paid for all of the incum-bency protection and perks lawmakers used to reward themselves. That really made me angry.

GOLDEN PARACHUTES

Under a legislator-friendly state pension law — which legislators hiked by 50 percent for themselves in 2001 — lawmakers with lengthy service typically retired with annual pensions from $50,000 to more than $100,000. John Perzel's was almost $86,000. He had engineered the 2001 pension boost that went bust when the markets crashed in 2008 and 2009.

Vincent Fumo, a multi-millionaire, was slated for more than $100,000 annu-ally in state pension money, based on 30 years' service, until the time of his convic-tion. Lawmakers' base salary, aided by automatic annual cost-of-living increases, was $82,012 in 2011. It was typically one of the top two or three legislative base salaries in the nation. Legislators could retire at age 55, whereas most other state workers reach full benefits at 65, according to a 50-state survey by *USA Today* in September 2011. It was an insurance policy. The elections were made as uncom-petitive as possible. But if the worst happened and legislators lost their seats, they would be rewarded well. In 1968, the year I graduated from high school, lawmak-ers' salaries were $7,200. In those days, they had no secretaries or phones.

Perks piled up over the years. While their constituents struggled through the worst recession since the Great Depression, legislators retired with free lifetime health care. In fact, health care for still-serving legislators was free until 2006 in the Senate and 2011 in the House, when members were required to pay one per-cent of their salary toward their state-provided health care costs. One percent.

A BEAST

The Pennsylvania legislature with 253 members is the largest full-time state legislature in the nation. Only New Hampshire's part-time legislature has more at 424, and they're paid $200 every two years. On average, it costs about $300 million a year to operate the Pennsylvania General Assembly, though that number was inflated to build up a multi-million-dollar surplus that leaders used as a slush fund.

It wasn't really a full-time job. That notion was a sham. These guys were typically in session 80 days a year, but they would say they were working hard for constituents when they weren't in Harrisburg. Working hard to get re-elected was more like it. The total number of House session days was 72 in 2006, 115 in 2007, 72 in 2008, and 147 in 2009, the year of the 101-day budget crisis. A statewide grand jury noted that in 2006, 2007, and 2008, there were no session days in August. In 2006 and 2008, there were no session days in December.

A MUSHROOM FARM

A John or Jane Doe interested in serving in the state House or Senate faced a difficult task getting records about the incumbent. For decades, the state's open records law didn't apply to the legislature. They provided records based on their own rules. The legislature purposely sanctioned and condoned one of the weakest right-to-know laws in the nation until 2008, when it was beefed up, but still only partially covered the legislature.

Going to the House or Senate Clerk's office to get records on legislators' expenses was like a trip to the Kremlin. Under their rules, the written request had to be filed in person. That meant a reporter, say in Easton or Erie, could not mail in a request. Then unbeknownst to the requestor, the request was sent to the legislators before they even began compiling the records. It would take weeks, sometimes up to two months, to fill large requests. For years, most records could not be copied. One had to sit in the clerk's office under the watchful eye of a bureaucrat to review the records and copy them by hand.

Bob Zausner, when he worked in Harrisburg for *The Philadelphia Inquirer,* often said he thought it would be a good story if a reporter from Philadelphia they didn't know would come to the clerk's offices posing as a tourist in a T-shirt, with camera in tow, asking for his legislator's records. Then he or she would record each step of the obfuscation.

So you can see my quandary. For years, before the investigations began in 2007, I wondered whether the truth would ever come out about this institution that operated like an organized crime family. Reporters, those with persistence, would occasionally poke small holes in the body armor. But no one could connect the dots because of the defenses they'd erected. Like mushroom growers, they got their best results in darkness.

Anyone who spoke out of school about the sweet deal legislators had would be executed — not with a bullet, but with scorn and revulsion from their colleagues. Ask former state representative John Kennedy, a Cumberland County Republican, who refused to take a pension and publicly criticized the perks and per diems in the 1980s. He was a pariah in the state House and left politics to go back to the business world.

Sure, I admired the deal-making ability of Vincent Fumo, a Philadelphia Democrat. No one built coalitions better than John Perzel. Mike Veon was a student of the game and highly competent. Bill DeWeese was the consummate player, a wannabe orator who memorized multi-syllable words to impress his audiences. He was, however, highly likeable and one of the true characters of the past three decades of Pennsylvania political history.

LIMITED ADMISSION

It was with ambivalence that I sat through John Perzel's hearing when he pleaded guilty to eight felonies on August 31, 2011. His rise to power was remarkable and his fall from grace was stunningly tragic. But the fateful day when he pleaded guilty was about survival for the always-hustling former dishwasher and maitre d'.

Shortly before they made the mad dash across the hallway to catch the open elevator, Brian McMonagle, as he was peppered with questions, half-turned to reporters, saying he would be issuing a statement. "When…Where's the statement?" reporters asked. It would be emailed to reporters covering the case, he said. "You'll get the statement," McMonagle assured them. On behalf of the law firm, Bellevue Communications had sent the emailed statement from Perzel at 1:23 p.m. after the plea agreement was finalized:

> "I said from the start of this case that I would fight the charges against me, and I have done so for nearly every day of the last two years. It is a fight that has taken an enormous toll on my family and the friends who have been so steadfast in their support.
>
> "I have decided today that my fight has come to an end. The truth is that as the legislative leader of my caucus, I oversaw the spending of millions of dollars in taxpayer funds, and I bear the responsibility for the improprieties that occurred in the spending of those dollars. It was up to me to see that taxpayer funds were spent only for the betterment of the people of Pennsylvania, and not for my political benefit of that of my party.
>
> "To the people of Pennsylvania, to the voters who put their trust in me for the 32 years that I had the privilege of serving the 172nd District, and to my family and friends, I want to express my profound regret for my actions. You had a right to expect better from me, and I am sorry that I let you down."

It was a remarkable statement. It was an admission of wrongdoing and failed responsibility. Still, Perzel didn't specifically state that he did it. As the legislator was fond of saying to those close to him: "Fish stinks from the head." Indeed, in his case, it did.

John Perzel was the second person in 34 years who held the office of speaker to be convicted of a crime. In 1977, Herbert Fineman, a Philadelphia Democrat, was convicted of obstruction of justice while sitting as speaker. Another ex-speaker, Bill DeWeese, was awaiting trial on felony charges as Perzel pled guilty. DeWeese was found guilty of five felonies in February 2012, and became the third speaker convicted in more than three decades.

As former speakers, Perzel and DeWeese, became friendly over the phone as they prepared for trial. Once adversaries, they had a lot in common. The criminal charges against them and their mutual animosity toward Governor Tom Corbett, who as attorney general investigated and filed charges against both of them, forged a bond. All along, Perzel was telling DeWeese that he would fight the charges. I believe he would have but for his wheelchair-bound wife Sheryl's multiple sclerosis. If Perzel were convicted at trial, he would likely spend the rest of his life behind bars. If he pleaded guilty and cooperated with the prosecutors, he had a shot at doing a few years minimum. The two would eventually share a cell at Camp Hill State Correctional Institution. Like many another Pennsylvania politician, I believe Perzel and DeWeese were not convinced that they really had done anything wrong.

BULL ELEPHANT

The criminal cases against John Perzel and Bill DeWeese were an outgrowth of a larger scandal that rocked the Pennsylvania political scene. I started calling it Bonusgate in columns in early 2007. It caught on to such an extent that prosecutors, judges, and defendants adopted the term.

Perzel's case had nothing to do with bonuses. Neither did DeWeese's. But DeWeese's fate was tied to the award of illegal bonuses for campaign work in the House Democratic Caucus as assuredly as if he were a defendant in the bonus-related cases.

The pure bonus case was against Mike Veon, a Democrat from Beaver County. Veon was DeWeese's right-hand man for more than a decade. In time, he became "The Man" in the House Democratic Caucus.

If Veon was the lion, Perzel was the bull elephant fearing no other beast. The election of Democratic Governor Ed Rendell in November 2002 secured Perzel's place as the real king of the jungle. But on this day, the bull elephant was mortally wounded.

The convictions of Veon and DeWeese are on appeal.

Next: How it started.

2

A Crooked Path

August 5, 1907

The capitol building itself is a monument to graft. It is regarded as one of the most beautiful state capitols in the country. It is an awesome place to work. But the building dedicated by President Teddy Roosevelt on October 4, 1906 was a place where corruption festered throughout the 20th century. It is a foundation for understanding the scandals of the period from 2007 to 2012.

The bronze entrance doors to the capitol include "portrait heads representing two governors, prominent government officials, contractors, and an artist," according to an official description provided by capitol tour guides.

What that description fails to mention is that two of the people so honored were conspirators in the scandal that jacked the price of the capitol from four to 13 million dollars: Auditor General Dr. William P. Snyder, the Chester County Republican chairman, and Joseph M. Huston, the architect. They were among five people convicted of the fraud. Huston's likeness, fittingly, is over the keyhole. Two corrupt political bosses from the era, Matthew Quay and Boies Penrose, also have their likenesses on the door. They weren't touched in the scandal.

There's a statue of Penrose a few hundred yards from the capitol in a park across from Strawberry Square. In a hard-hitting 1978 series on the legislature, *The Philadelphia Inquirer* wrote that while the Penrose statue shows him with a hand in his pocket, historians questioned the accuracy because he usually had his hand in everyone else's pockets. Quay fared somewhat better for posterity. A marble statue of him overlooks the stairway leading to the Senate chamber.

Quay, Penrose, and their predecessor, Simon Cameron, "willfully used public funds, kickbacks, and corporate donations to finance campaigns (and enhance their own wealth), and with an estimated 20,000 federal and state patronage jobs in their control, they assembled an army of political faithful ward healers," say historians Randall W. Miller and William Pencak in their book, *Pennsylvania: A History of the Commonwealth.*

Penrose was never implicated in the graft scandal, but he is credited with inventing the "squeeze bill" before elections, historian Paul Beers wrote in a book about Pennsylvania politics. Leadership threatens to move a bill affecting a certain industry. The industry officials open their wallets. The bill is then blocked by leaders who never intended to pass it anyway. Penrose was corrupt but he wasn't a thief like Quay, Beers believed. Penrose was on the rise and would take over complete control of the Republican machine in 1904 upon Quay's death. They were both U.S. senators and former state legislators.

All or most of the effort by the bosses in raising booty and having loyal payroll workers was directed toward the ballot box. They delivered the Republican vote. In turn, they secured their power and influence.

Matthew Quay was a "political racketeer," while Boies Penrose was a "Machiavelli," wrote Penrose's biographer, Walter Davenport. Quay was also a scholar and a national political figure. Much like J. Edgar Hoover, Quay had files with political dirt on legislators — "Quay's coffins"— and was not adverse to blackmailing lawmakers to garner votes.

SYSTEMIC GRAFT

After the original state capitol burned in 1887, a replacement effort left only a partial structure in place after funding ran out at the turn of the century. Under a new set of plans with Joseph Huston as the architect, the new building came in — on budget — at four million dollars. But that didn't count the furnishings. With the furnishings added, it should have been nine million dollars, but soared to 13 million because of excessive profits taken by the contractor and, supposedly, the architect. When the final price tag was revealed, Pennsylvanians were outraged.

Like many scandals, the driving force behind this one was politics. In a sea of Republicans where the political machine delivered GOP votes for president, state, and local officers, it was rare indeed when Democrat William H. Berry was elected state treasurer in 1905. He was the only Democrat elected statewide in a span of almost four decades through the early 1930s.

In his new office, Berry noticed that $1,800 worth of paneling had been billed at $15,000, a $60 sofa cost $552, and a $500 ceiling cost $5,500. Berry blew the whistle.

The furnishings were the same throughout the capitol. The inflated prices were often five times the actual cost of the items supplied by Philadelphia furnishings contractor John H. Sanderson. Tubs used for umbrellas cost Sanderson $14 and he charged the state $73.60. They became known as "Sanderson tubs." A chandelier that cost $2,500 should have cost less than $200. Sanderson collected $72 for "specially designed Colonial andirons" for fireplace logs that actually cost $23 a pair.

Fourteen people were indicted in connection with the scandal. On December 8, 1908, architect Huston was convicted. Earlier that year, four others — Sanderson; former Auditor General William Snyder; James Shumaker, the superintendent of buildings and grounds; and former state treasurer William L. Mathues — were also found guilty. Henry B. Cassel, a former congressman who owned a construction company, was acquitted.

BIG GUYS UNTOUCHED

"Not a single important politician went to jail," wrote Robert Douglas Bowden in his biography of Penrose. Quay was still alive when the project was launched. The capitol was under construction from 1902 to 1906. The prevailing historical view is that the contractors and some lower-rung public officials got greedy. In my view, it's difficult to believe that graft of this magnitude would take place under the nose of the master thief Quay or the boss Penrose without their knowing about it. Think of it this way: In the heyday of organized crime in the 20th century, a thief just couldn't begin stealing or setting up illegal gambling operations in a neighborhood controlled by the Mob. To do so was a death sentence.

Construction of the capitol was big money at the turn of the century. The contracts allowed materials to be purchased per pound or per foot, which contributed to the latitude suppliers had in inflating prices.

Matthew Quay was the boss in 1898 when planning for the capitol project got under way. Quay's cousin, Samuel W. Pennypacker, served as governor from 1903 to 1907. Quay and Pennypacker were Civil War veterans. Pennypacker was handpicked by his cousin. Quay, who had a "fishy" eye that didn't move, was a Medal of Honor winner for returning to the ranks before the battle of Fredericksburg, after his tour of duty had expired.

Pennypacker would staunchly defend the capitol construction project in a book released after the trials. The governor who preceded him, Bill Stone, was Quay's man as well.

FALL GUYS?

There is no doubt that crimes took place. But were the defendants who stood trial set up to take the fall? Joseph Huston would serve only six months in prison and the case against him had been thin. John Sanderson and William Mathues died before sentencing. They were among five defendants who died before trial or sentencing. There were reports of defendants going insane and some committing suicide. Paul Beers reported up to three suicides. The record is hazy on the defendants' demise.

A commission that investigated the graft scandal noted that large payments had been made by contractors to banks across the state and in Washington, D.C. Investigators suggested that the huge capitol overcharges were used by "organization politicians" to cover up a state treasury deficit caused by worthless notes that had been accepted by state treasurers, this according to a *New York Times* story from August 4, 1907.

"Large deposits were made by the contractors in Washington, D.C. to banks and institutions in scattered parts of the state," the story noted. "From these deposits it was suggested payments were made to political leaders."

"It has been suggested by the investigators that the 1000 percent profits and stupendous overcharges were used by the organization politicians to cover up a treasury deficit and went to pay worthless political notes which had been accepted by state treasurers since the time of Matthew S. Quay," *The Times* asserted. Quay had been state treasurer in the late 1800s.

Quay was involved in a treasury scandal in March 1898 after the People's Bank of Philadelphia, which handled most of Quay's stock transactions and was a favored repository for tax money by state treasurers, closed its doors. In the wake of the bankruptcy, a clerk who personally handled Quay's accounts killed himself, according to biographer James A. Kehl. Quay was a gambler who liked to speculate on utility stocks.

The information was trumpeted in the closing weeks of the 1898 elections by Quay's opponents, chiefly John Wannamaker, a spokesman for the anti-Quay forces. Kehl discussed this period in his book, *Boss Rule in the Gilded Age*. On October 3, Quay was indicted for misappropriating state funds. He was acquitted in a high-profile trial the following year. His acquittal was aided by a judge's ruling that rejected use of a memo Quay had sent to his unfortunate clerk, saying, "If you buy and carry a thousand Met for me, I'll shake the plum tree." That meant dipping into the treasury to cover any losses.

A COVER UP?

Politically connected banks apparently did certify false notes to cover state treasury deficits. These were "later made good by deposits from the Capitol graft revenues," the foregoing *New York Times* story stated. The article noted that investigators considered this information "well-informed speculation" but still considered it of the "greatest import."

Investigators for the legislative commission speculated that the inflated prices were used for income to cover the treasury shortfalls or for campaigns. But Attorney General Moses Hampton Todd, a political appointee, said that a portion of the report needed to be "suppressed." Todd said it would be investigated. Efforts to locate the suppressed portion of the report were unsuccessful.

Boies Penrose, or "Big Grizzly" as he was called, was boss when the Capitol was completed. His biographer, Walter Davenport, concluded in 1931 that Penrose had to know about the graft. But Davenport also wrote that it may never be known whether he had a direct hand in the scandal.

"How far Penrose was involved we don't know," Davenport wrote in *Power and Glory: The Life of Boise Penrose.* "Perhaps we never shall. We can only assume, with every right of presumption, that Penrose, the dictator, knew about it long, long before his enemies awoke. He couldn't very well have helped knowing it. But he had the intelligence to remain aloof — probably sneering at the participants and even their victims, the actual designers and builders."

Another Penrose biographer, Robert Douglas Bowden, stated that Penrose claimed he never made money out of politics. "He was always scornful of Quay and his sort for profiting by the petty graft in contracts and the like. Franchises, contracts, gambling with state funds, small bribes and things of that kind furnished the source of Quay's wealth," Bowden wrote in *Boies Penrose: Symbol of an Era.*

In 1910, the state dropped the charges against those convicted in the graft scandal following restitution of $1.1 million. That's about one-fourth of the total inflated prices for furnishings. Where did the rest of the money go and did the big bosses insulate themselves to such a degree that they could not be touched in the investigation? Were any of the deaths tied to protection of the top culprits? What happened to the attorney general's investigation and to the suppressed documents? How much went back into the state treasury? Did money from the graft scandal fuel Republican campaigns? Were politicians' pockets lined?

My belief is that since the furnishings came into play at the latter end of the project, Quay was probably too sick by then to orchestrate grand theft. He died two years before the official opening. Quay and Penrose at one point lived together in a Harrisburg apartment suite. My hunch is that Quay had dipped into the treasury once too often for campaigns or stock speculation, and Penrose was covering Quay's tracks by paying back the treasury.

It fits with Paul Beers' theory that Penrose wasn't a petty thief. He was helping out a friend and his beloved Republican Party.

If this suppressed portion of the investigation hit close to the truth, what did that mean? State treasury funds were used to pay inflated prices to contractors, who turned it back to politicians to deposit in the treasury? Why was there a shortfall in the treasury to begin with? Had that money been "borrowed" — in other words stolen? In any case, the building of the state capitol was a scam like scores of events to follow.

THE SHIFT TO LOCAL BOSSES

There were waves of corruption after the early political bosses stole tax money to finance the election machinery and line their pockets. On the statewide level, corruption hit the scoreboard in 1938 with charges of graft and macing that would rock Governor George H. Earle III's administration. In the end, his highways secretary was convicted and served 60 days of a one-year prison sentence. The Pittsburgh city treasurer and another minor official were fined.

State political bosses pretty much died with Penrose. After "Big Grizzly," power tended to be consolidated into county organizations. Chief among them was the Delaware County "war board" headed by state Senator John J. McClure, a convicted felon, who ran the county GOP organization. He had been sentenced to 18 months in prison for bootlegging but never served a day behind bars, thanks to the repeal of Prohibition. The "war board" was a super-committee of 10 to 15 members who made the real decisions in the county.

McClure was later indicted for conspiracy in the sale of a waterworks to a private outfit, but was ultimately acquitted. He delivered Republican vote totals for statewide elections and presidential contests. In Harrisburg, he chaired the Senate Finance Committee and favored the interests of shipbuilders and utilities. McClure was the boss of Delaware County for more than five decades until his death in 1965.

Corruption of the legal and marginal variety can be worse than the crimes. Through the 1950s and '60s, lobbyists for Sun Oil Company and the Pennsylvania Railroad had reserved seats on the Senate floor. Other lobbyists were free to roam the area. Former Senate President Pro Tempore Martin Murray threw all lobbyists off the floor in 1970, according to former state senator Franklin Kury's 2011 political biography, *Clean Politics, Clean Streams*. The Senate was in the grip of Senate President Pro Tempore Harvey M. Taylor, a Republican who served there from 1941 to 1964. He also was state Republican Party Chairman and de facto boss of Dauphin County. While still in office, a new bridge from Harrisburg to its West Shore was named after him. It is still called the Harvey Taylor Bridge.

A Harrisburg insurance broker, Taylor used state insurance contracts as the source of his power. He brokered all state insurance on property and vehicles, and brought in about $450,000 annually in commissions. According to former Democratic governor George M. Leader, he gave the money to Republican senators, House GOP leaders, and Republican statewide candidates. Leader confirmed the account he gave to Kury, who reported it in *Clean Politics, Clean Streams*.

"Anybody who wanted anything in Pennsylvania, for years, they had to go to Harvey," Leader said in an interview. "He distributed the money as political patronage to legislators and senators."

"He always said he didn't take any commissions," Leader added. Taylor could say that because he was giving the money away, not putting it in his pocket, the former governor pointed out. The money from state insurance commissions consolidated Taylor's hold on the Senate and the movement of bills through the General Assembly. Taylor was not charged with any crimes. In Leader's view, "Harvey could control almost everything that went through the legislature."

Taylor's alleged scam with insurance contracts may have been legal then, but it would fall under the current conflict of interest statute today. The same actions by a Senate leader today would certainly draw the scrutiny of law enforcement, if not an indictment.

Harvey Taylor was state Republican chairman, the boss of Dauphin County, pro tempore of the Senate, and served on the General State Authority, which oversaw state property. Using the money to consolidate his power and apparently to help GOP campaigns is no different than the actions of Quay and Penrose on through to Perzel in the modern era. Taylor "loved winning elections, raising money, dispensing patronage and contracts, making appointments, holding incessant meetings, whispering in ears, and running the show," historian Paul Beers has written.

During the Leader administration in the 1950s, the Manu-Mine scandal stole the headlines. The scandal was centered at the turnpike commission. The Manu-Mine Research and Development Company fraudulently inflated prices for filling abandoned mines on the Northeast Extension of the Pennsylvania Turnpike. The president of the company and a turnpike commissioner were convicted. Leader was attacked politically for the nine-million-dollar scandal, though he was not personally responsible.

Now onto the era of corruption from the 1970s through the early 21st century for which I had an insider's view.

3

The Shapp Merry-Go-Round

January 17, 1976

In late 1975, Democratic governor Milton Shapp called muckraking journalist Jack Anderson in Washington, D.C. and complained that he was the victim of a "political investigation" by U.S. Assistant Attorney General Dick Thornburgh. Thornburgh had previously been the U.S. Attorney in Pittsburgh, where he was responsible for indicting and convicting dozens of local and state Democratic and some Republican public officials. Shapp felt Thornburgh, a Republican, was headline-grabbing at his expense. He wanted Anderson to check it out.

Anderson took Shapp up on the challenge and sent reporter Marc Smolonsky to Pennsylvania. In his Washington Merry-Go-Round column published on January 17, 1976 in *The Washington Post,* Anderson reported that he found "systematic corruption, including organized crime links, throughout the Shapp administration." During Shapp's tenure as governor, 57 state officials had been indicted by grand juries, Anderson reported. Another indictment was pending against a top Shapp loyalist at the turnpike commission, Egidio Cerelli. He would be convicted of extortion in 1978 after an earlier mistrial. There were also 21 state and federal investigations into Pennsylvania government pending at that time, Anderson noted. One might conclude from this that as many as 79 people were indicted or convicted.

In the Shapp era, executive branch employees as well as legislators were convicted. According to historian Paul Beers, Shapp attributed the total number of 60 persons who were indicted or convicted in his administration to Thornburgh's campaign. Shapp claimed that number represented a low percentage of the 107,000 state employees. That seems like sorry logic.

Beers is more precise. In the eight years that Shapp was governor, seven legislators and 11 high party officials were convicted. But that doesn't count agency corruption; state agencies are under the governor's control. He cited officials "fired, indicted or convicted" at the Departments of Public Welfare, Transportation, Revenue, Property and Supplies, and the Bureau of Occupational Affairs. Beers reported 42 officials indicted and 28 convicted in county PennDOT units for illegally forcing employees to contribute to the Democratic Party or extorting money in exchange for contracts and 17 Philadelphia caseworkers fired for fraud in the Department of Public Welfare.

A Pennsylvania Crime Commission report in 1978 blamed both political parties for using PennDOT as a fund-raising mechanism by demanding kickbacks of five to 10 percent off the top of contracts and two percent of the salary of patronage hires, the Associated Press reported. That story referred to 34 officials convicted or indicted in PennDOT scandals with 26 having been convicted as of 1978.

At the statewide level, for varying crimes, those convicted included Property and Supplies secretary Frank C. Hilton, Revenue secretary George Mowod, Adjutant General Harry Mier, and state police commissioner James Barger, the latter for lying to a grand jury.

In a 1977 speech to a GOP group in Mt. Lebanon, Dick Thornburgh called it a "severe integrity crisis" facing Pennsylvania.

"An epidemic of corruption and shoddy government from top to bottom has affected our state of late," Thornburgh noted. "High administration officials have been convicted of criminal offenses involving bribery, extortion and fraud. Others have been obliged to resign in disgrace upon disclosure of irregularities in the conduct of their office. And little seems to be being done about it in Harrisburg."

Thornburgh added that in March 1977, Watergate investigator Sam Dash assessed the Shapp administration as displaying "a conspicuous lack of commitment to investigating official corruption." The Shapp administration has been called the most corrupt Pennsylvania governing body in modern history. The interesting thing is that Shapp pushed through substantial new policy including a state income tax, creating a consumer advocate for the Public Utility Commission's rate cases, no-fault auto insurance, and a Department of Aging. He was never personally tied to any corruption. For me, the nexus of Shapp, Thornburgh, and Jack Anderson was important during my formative years as a young reporter at the *Chambersburg Public Opinion* and later at the *Valley News Dispatch* in Tarentum.

Shapp had been governor while I was in college and later when I held my first reporting job at the *Public Opinion*. In fact, I met him when the *Public Opinion* sent another reporter, Pete Gigliotti, and me to Shapp's first open cabinet meeting under the recently enacted Sunshine Law. Even as a cub reporter, I realized it was a dog-and-pony show. The cabinet members' lines were scripted. Among other appetizers, they served roasted chicken livers wrapped in bacon to the press. Two years into my first job, I thought nothing about journalistic ethics. We hadn't had lunch. I imagine now that the taxpayers picked up the tab. But I never thought to ask.

For such a smart man, the diminutive Shapp was wholly unimpressive. His thinning hair was plastered back. He had zero charisma, but was approachable and easy to talk to. He fawned over reporters at his "open cabinet meeting." The governor aggressively promoted himself.

A wealthy businessman, Shapp ran on beating the machine, the Democratic Party of Pennsylvania. By eventually self-imploding, the machine beat down his reputation. While he brought many independent people into his cabinet, the convictions of lower-rung employees from the highway sheds, most of them with Democratic Party ties, contributed heavily to an atmosphere of corruption.

I'm sure that Milton Shapp did feel persecuted by Dick Thornburgh. Thornburgh went after public corruption with zest. In 1978, he rode that reputation to the governor's mansion, just as Tom Corbett would 32 years later.

* * *

As a young reporter, the guy I most wanted to emulate was Jack Anderson. I loved his stuff. The Mormon columnist was fearless. The last place a politician wanted to be was in one of his columns, though at times he did some obvious stroking to develop sources. Anderson had this brilliant technique when exposing wrongdoing by a politician. He'd begin the column with effusive praise, citing the good works and accomplishments of one of his targets. Halfway through, he'd rip into the guy. Who could say he hadn't been fair? He'd given the guy his due upfront. Anderson won the Pulitzer Prize in 1972. His unabashed advocacy and his wheeling and dealing behind the scenes I would learn about much later in one of his books.

Jack Anderson was a Washington hand for Drew Pearson starting in 1945, decades before Bob Woodward and Carl Bernstein became household words. In 1977, Anderson had tipped off someone at Gannett News Service about Thornburgh running for Pennsylvania governor. The tip came to me via my editor in Chambersburg, Bob Collins. I called Anderson, who was helpful. I believe Thornburgh had resigned his position in Washington by then because I reached him at his home in Pittsburgh. I wrote a front-page story about it. The status of Pennsylvania gubernatorial candidates was not much fodder for a national column.

Anderson had already checked out Thornburgh, and I suspect he had a soft spot for a crime fighter. I called Jack about a few other things and he was always forthcoming. I was proud of this connection, and I kept his phone number on a list of frequently called people taped to my desk (as if the two of us were tight).

Later, in 1978, working in Pittsburgh for the *Valley News Dispatch*, I covered several Thornburgh campaign events. I remember how accessible he was as a candidate. I used to call him at his house early in the morning. His number was listed in the phone book. Reporters would claim Thornburgh was just the opposite as governor. He was "aloof," his critics would say, and inaccessible to the press. In the midst of the recession in 1982, Thornburgh only narrowly won re-election. I caught up with him again in 1983 when I was sent to Harrisburg as a reporter for Gannett and he was beginning his second term.

While Thornburgh was still a fed, Shapp's good friend Egidio Cerelli, the turnpike commissioner and Westmoreland Democratic Party chairman, was accused of extorting campaign money from state highway workers. In the same federal building where Thornburgh tried cases and got grand juries to issue indictments, Cerelli was convicted in 1978, along with two PennDOT officials, of shaking down PennDOT workers for $8,300 in campaign contributions. It seemed a paltry sum even by 1970 standards, but Cerelli was a big name in politics. It is also likely to be only one slice of a bigger picture, the portion the government was able to prove. Fittingly, it was the year Thornburgh won the governor's race.

The 1978 conviction was a retrial after a mistrial two years earlier. I was there for most days of the retrial, covering the story for the *Valley News*. Each day, I would talk to Cerelli a little in the hallway. I came to like him. He was very friendly and genuine, an authentic character and old-time pol. He was sentenced to three years in prison.

Five years after his release, Cerelli told an interviewer that he was only soliciting a political contribution. According to his 1991 obituary in the *Pittsburgh Post-Gazette*, Cerelli had said, "It happened 100 years ago. It will happen 100 years from now." His comment was dead on.

*   *   *

When Thornburgh was at the Justice Department in Washington as the head of the Attorney General's criminal division, a young assistant district attorney in Allegheny County named Tom Corbett admired his work. As Pennsylvania Attorney General in 2007, Corbett would launch the Bonusgate and later the Computergate investigations. Corbett served as U.S. Attorney for the Western District of Pennsylvania when Thornburgh headed the Justice Department.

During the Fumo case, Bonusgate, Computergate, the Northeastern corruption events, and the case against the three Orie sisters in Allegheny County from 2007 through 2012, it seemed like the corruption meter was going haywire with 38 Democrats and Republicans in state government — including former and sitting leaders — charged by state, federal, and local prosecutors. But these events didn't touch the corruption eruption during Shapp's administration, regardless of the exact total. What was different is that Bonusgate and Computergate stemmed from investigations solely of legislative corruption. Another major difference is that legislative staffers, as well as lawmakers, were charged in the bonus and computer scandals.

The next four chapters will examine executive branch employees — three independent "row" officers who broke the law.

4

The Bum Steer

April 10, 1984

Al Benedict was the best liar I ever met. He was also corrupt, charming, and charismatic. The former Auditor General of Pennsylvania, the state's fiscal watchdog, was hounded throughout much of his tenure by rumors — and later the indictment of his top aide, John Kerr — for selling state jobs. Kerr was charged with 223 counts for a $200,000 job-selling scheme in December 1983. At his arraignment, Kerr had dismissed the government's case as a "political fabrication." He was convicted in June 1984 of 139 of the charges. Benedict was not charged.

The widely held belief was that if the government could convict Kerr, they would flip him and take down Benedict. But Benedict served two terms (1977–84), eight years as auditor general. The attorney general's investigators and the feds never touched him while he was in office.

"Big Al" is what they called him. He was a former newscaster from Erie. He did the weather and then tried politics. The party faithful loved this guy. He really wanted to be governor. With his velvety baritone voice, Al Benedict could have been a country and western star. He was six feet, three inches tall; he was handsome and projected warmth and confidence.

I stood by him at a Democratic State Committee meeting on a Friday night in 1984 at a hotel just outside the city of Harrisburg. Benedict, then 54, was standing outside a reception room, greeting the guests. Blue-haired ladies trooped by and practically swooned over Al. He had "schmoozing" down to an art form. He'd clamp one hand under your arm, and with a firm grip shake hands. He had that gift of making people believe their concerns were the most important thing in the world. This was his arena and his crowd, the state party people, many of whom he probably employed. It was after the cocktail hour and Benedict had tipped a few. He made no secret of the fact that he would like to be governor some day. And that ambition would eventually trigger his downfall.

It took money, lots of it, to run for governor, and Benedict was using the auditor general's office to sell state jobs and to solicit bribes. Kerr and Michael Hanna Sr., two of his lieutenants, headed up the job-selling effort that began in 1978. Hanna, the former Washington County DA, died before he could be tried. He cooperated with prosecutors, however, and his testimony was presented at Kerr's trial by his son, Michael Hanna Jr.

The cost of a job or promotion was typically $3,000 to $5,000. A raise for incumbent employees could be $1,000 or $2,000. They could be hit for $6,000, $7,000, and even $10,000, according to a statewide grand jury.

You didn't have to speak English to work for Al Benedict. Authorities knew something was up when the auditor who showed up to do a local police/fire pension fund only spoke Greek. One of his relatives, who bought a job, brought the foreign-speaking auditor in on the action. You sure as heck didn't need auditing experience. Just cash.

Those buying state jobs had occupations ranging from a salesman or barber to a restaurant manager. State jobs were coveted because of the benefits. Great time off with pension and health care. The money was collected in western Pennsylvania by Nick Saittis, a supervisor in the liquor audit office in Pittsburgh.

Saittis paid $3,500 for his own job and in 1981, he pleaded guilty to bribery and conspiracy. He testified against John Kerr at trial. He was sentenced to 11½ to 23 months in prison.

"From a foundation built upon the political patronage system which has long existed within our government, greedy hands and corrupt minds soon turned the power to dole out jobs within the Auditor General's office into a scheme to bilk cash from those who sought such political employment," the Kerr grand jury stated, adding that Kerr continued selling jobs while he was under investigation.

Having run out his string as Auditor General, Al Benedict tried to extend his political life by running for treasurer in 1984. John Kerr, his top aide, was under indictment when Benedict ran in the primary. Benedict denied knowledge of job-selling to anyone who would listen. He knew nothing about it. He seemed sincere as hell. But there was blood in the water, and four people challenged Benedict in the Democratic primary for a nomination that should have been his for the taking. He was the number-one issue. Because of the corruption current, it was a closely watched race. Normally, it would have garnered little attention statewide.

While working as the Harrisburg reporter for Gannett News Service, I traveled with Benedict via commercial airline to a series of political stops in Pittsburgh, including an AFL-CIO event. He took me to the suite of Julius Uehlein, president of the Pennsylvania AFL-CIO, in the Hilton downtown. I do not know whether he told Uehlein we were coming, or if it was a spontaneous visit. In any case, Uehlein, a soft-spoken and intelligent man with thick glasses and slicked-back hair in an expensive suit, seemed sheepish about the meeting with Benedict and me. Benedict, after all, was tainted by the indictment of Kerr, his right-hand man.

Al Benedict was showing off. He was demonstrating to Uehlein that he was important enough to have a reporter following him on the campaign trail despite the controversy. The truth is that the corruption allegations swirling around Benedict made him the story. Normally, a candidate for treasurer would never have warranted that type of coverage, which is usually reserved for gubernatorial or U.S. Senate candidates. Benedict was also trying to impress me by suggesting that one of the state's most influential labor leaders was backing him. Uehlein never said he was endorsing Benedict, but he said supportive things about him in the hotel suite.

On the U.S. Air flight back to Harrisburg, Benedict sat beside me and gave me about a 45-minute interview. A cloud of smoke covered our seating area. We were both puffing away on cigarettes. Marlboro Lights in my case. Al may have been smoking Marlboro "reds." A smoking ban on flights was still four years in the future.

Al denied any knowledge of the job-selling scheme, expressed confidence in Kerr's innocence, and claimed his office would be completely vindicated. He looked me right in the eye as he spoke. He never blinked. I think he said, "I swear." But Al admitted that he was a practitioner of patronage — rewarding friends and supporters with jobs. Even in 1984, that was an outrageous statement — candid, for sure — but it showed that Benedict was part of the old breed of politicians.

That was the story I filed for Gannett newspapers: *The Valley News Dispatch* in Tarentum, *The Public Opinion* in Chambersburg, and *The Reporter* in Lansdale. Benedict was a dinosaur, openly promoting patronage but steadfastly denying he sold state jobs.

Four Democrats were challenging Al. For all intents and purposes, Benedict was the incumbent. His opponents made integrity the issue. Arlene Lotman, a Montgomery County attorney, really went after him. Catherine Baker Knoll, who had worked for Milton Shapp and had a political job in Allegheny County, was one of the two southwestern Pennsylvania candidates with Beaver County Prothonotary Michael Jackson and Al Smith, a member of the Democratic State Committee from York County

Where to station myself on election night? I had no doubt I needed to be in Erie, Benedict's hometown. I made arrangements and drove from my home, then in York County, to Erie. It was a brutal drive on Pennsylvania's crappy roads. I stayed in a budget hotel and showed up at Benedict's election headquarters, a bar called The Bum Steer. It looked like I was in a crowd of bookies and low-rung criminals. They were field auditors, of course, and Big Al was working the crowd and exercising his elbow.

The Bum Steer in Erie was hopping on primary election night, the drinks were flowing, and by midnight Benedict was half-sloshed. He was fielding calls on a pay phone from the Associated Press and other news outlets about the evening's results. He finally conceded the race to Knoll and it was over. We hung around the bar for hours. I was exercising my elbow by then as well, because I was no longer reporting. Benedict had conceded, and I was off-duty. A despondent Benedict spoke of his dreams of becoming governor.

Catherine Baker Knoll, of course, would later be able to copyright her fly-beneath-the-radar campaign. It was part rope-a-dope and part duck-and-cover. No substantive interviews or editorial boards. Visits to friendly events, nursing homes, and party picnics. Keep throwing your name on the ballot. Let people think, if they want, that you're a feminist with the use of Baker Knoll. It would eventually work. But not that night.

Sitting at a table with Benedict and two others, a man came over, handing Al a piece of paper. It was about 4:00 a.m. Benedict had won! Somewhere, as the story went, late precincts came in to carry him over the top. Benedict was ecstatic. He had pulled it off! I'd love to see those actual precinct counts today.

I had to grab coffee and head back to the hotel where I was staying and sketch out a story I would dictate in a few hours. There were no laptops or iPads, no cell phones or email.

Benedict was the Democratic nominee for treasurer and would face incumbent Republican R. Budd Dwyer in November. No one else in the media knew it. There are exclusives and there are exclusives. But not usually on the results of one single election.

It was worth the night at the Bum Steer and the seven-hour drive home from Erie with a hangover.

In no time at all, Al Benedict and Budd Dwyer were sliming each other. I remember one morning when Benedict and Dwyer had back-to-back news conferences accusing each other of malfeasance. Benedict, as auditor general, was conducting his own "investigation" of the state contract award by Dwyer to an obscure California company called Computer Technology Associates (CTA) to collect overpaid Social Security taxes by state employees. Influence peddling and kickbacks, Benedict claimed, were at the heart of the contract. A federal grand jury investigation was under way. Dwyer returned fire with job-selling allegations and the indictment of Benedict's top aide, John Kerr.

The stage was set in an upscale California community where John Torquato Jr. and CTA, a front company for Torquato's deals, both resided. A CTA employee named Janice Kinkaid had seen how he was bribing officials in Pennsylvania to get work. After falling out with Torquato, she went to Benedict with the goods.

Big Al must have thought that heaven had blessed him twice. He pulled out the come-from-behind primary victory, and then Kinkaid had served up Dwyer, who by then had awarded CTA a contract and was listed in Torquato's records as the target of a $300,000 bribe.

Benedict took CTA straight to the FBI. Battered by the job-selling scandal, he faced an uphill battle against Dwyer and needed something to try and knock him out. CTA was the ticket! The main actor in CTA was Torquato. He was the son of a former Democratic pol, John Torquato Sr., a Cambria County party boss who was prosecuted in the 1970s.

When Benedict attacked Dwyer on CTA, he did so with the personal knowledge that the feds knew all about Dwyer's involvement in CTA.

Jim Cuddy Jr., then a reporter for *The Pittsburgh Press* and now managing editor of the *Tribune-Review*, writing about a conference call "debate" between Benedict and Dwyer on KDKA radio in October 1984, summed it up best: "Any likelihood that the campaign for state treasurer would somehow rise out of the mud seems much more remote following a radio confrontation between incumbent R. Budd Dwyer and Democratic challenger Al Benedict. Only the antagonists' refusal to meet face-to-face saved the maintenance crew at KDKA radio from a costly cleanup following the hour-long broadcast last night." Benedict was damaged goods, and Dwyer eventually won the 1984 election by about 300,000 votes.

Given Al Benedict's loss, the glory on that night at the Bum Steer was short-lived. Benedict quietly left office. He must have wondered later how it was that by 1986, Dwyer was charged and convicted and he wasn't. Benedict had insulated himself quite well. But his conscience bothered him a lot. As he walked past the federal building on many occasions, he thought about going in and spilling his guts. But he didn't.

The breakthrough for investigators came when they turned John Kerr. Kerr wore a wire to record conversations with Benedict. In November 1986, while Kerr was still free on bail pending the outcome of his appeal, he agreed to cooperate. He was debriefed for hundreds of hours by federal and state agents. Kerr concealed a wire and recorded his meetings with Benedict and others for eight months.

The unusual joint investigation by James West, the U.S. Attorney for the Middle District, and Attorney General LeRoy Zimmerman caught most of the Harrisburg press corps completely off-guard. On January 14, 1988, they announced the filing of federal racketeering and tax charges against Big Al.

Benedict engaged in "a pattern of racketeering activity" as Auditor General. The indictment charged that he:

- Took a $2,500 cash bribe from a Philadelphia politician to promote an employee in his agency.
- Caused a $6,000 bribe to be paid to a legislator for a supplemental budget appropriation for his office.

- Took a $10,000 bribe through Kerr from people in the mushroom industry to oppose legislation against their interests.
- Committed another act of bribery in 1982 in exchange for a job.
- Took a $5,000 cash bribe in 1983 for awarding a contract.
- Took $15,000 in campaign money from a Wall Street investment banking firm to award two $90,000 no-bid contracts.
- Accepted a $2,500 cash bribe to award a contract.
- Took $5,000 in cash to award another state contract.
- Conspired with Kerr between 1976 and 1984 to sell state jobs.
- Paid wages to a "ghost employee" in the Auditor General's office.
- Failed to report $11,500 in taxable income in 1984 and understated his taxes by $4,000.

Big Al pleaded guilty the same day. "I did wrong here and I am prepared to pay the price," he told reporters in the lobby of the federal building in Williamsport. He would serve two years in prison. Just a year before, Al's nemesis, R. Budd Dwyer, shot himself in the head at a news conference the day before sentencing on corruption charges arising from the CTA scandal.

In typical Benedict fashion, with that edge to the end, he said in response to a reporter who asked if he planned to repay the taxpayers, "What do you want me to do, blow my brains out?" Pure Al Benedict there.

I wondered then and again in 2012, was Dwyer actually guilty?

5

"No, Budd, Don't"

January 22, 1987

The news from Williamsport cut through the party like high-voltage current. Reporters from the capitol newsroom were holding their annual Christmas party in the capitol rotunda. Pennsylvania had enacted tougher drunk driving laws in 1983 and 1984. Reporters in the Pennsylvania Legislative Correspondents Association wanted just a low-key affair. The idea was to move away from the old parties in the capitol newsroom when the Liquor Control Board and the liquor companies donated dozens of bottles of spirits and wine, and they were consumed by the press and the pols alike. As usual, many of the state's most powerful political leaders, including Governor Dick Thornburgh, mingled with reporters in a rare, informal, off-the-record session. Then it came.

The verdict: R. Budd Dwyer — guilty!

The Republican state treasurer and former state GOP Chairman Bob Asher were convicted of bribery in the scandal involving Computer Technology Associates. Budd Dwyer was found guilty by a jury of agreeing to take a $300,000 bribe to award a contract to CTA, a California computer company owned by John Torquato Jr. Harrisburg attorney William T. Smith, the Dauphin County Republican chairman and Torquato's partner, offered the bribe. Dwyer was convicted of conspiracy to commit bribery, mail fraud, interstate transportation in aid of racketeering, and perjury. Torquato's company was awarded the no-bid contract by Dwyer to recover overpayments of Social Security taxes by school districts. CTA stood to make $4.7 million. Dwyer continued to insist on his innocence.

* * *

On January 22, 1987, John L. Taylor, a veteran state capitol reporter, was on his first assignment as a deputy press secretary for the new governor, Robert P. Casey. At the behest of Casey's press secretary, Bob Grotevant, Taylor was sent to cover Budd Dwyer's expected resignation at a news conference. He was sent to brief the governor's office so that Casey could name an interim successor.

It was a blustery day in Harrisburg. The pavement and cars were already covered with snow. Heavy snowfall was predicted. As a former reporter for *The Pittsburgh Press* and the Associated Press, Taylor had pretty much seen it all. He had, for instance, covered the mayhem in the streets at the Democratic National Convention in 1968. The native Oklahoman didn't easily get rattled. I know that because I sat across from Taylor in my first year or two in Harrisburg. I peppered him with questions about the legislature and state politics on most days.

Bob Casey, a devout Roman Catholic and pro-life advocate from Scranton, was sworn in just four days earlier. Years later, pols and press alike would use the term "Casey Democrat" to describe a Democrat who opposed abortion and supported gun owners' rights, but backed traditional Democratic values of education funding and environmental protection. It was a particularly good mix for Western Pennsylvania politicians.

John Taylor joined the governor's press office in Dick Thornburgh's final years in office. A nonpartisan pro, he would remain in the press office through Casey's tenure and after that the administrations of Republican governors Tom Ridge and Mark Schweiker.

When he arrived in the treasurer's office in the Finance Building late in the morning of the 22nd, Taylor was handed a 20-page statement by Dwyer's press secretary, Duke Horshock. As reporters often do with court opinions, Taylor flipped to the last page. It was missing. The last line of the 19th page read, "I have successfully participated in eight primary elections," ending with a comma. The 20th page was a favorable editorial published on December 29, 1986 by *The Meadville Tribune*, Dwyer's hometown paper.

There was no answer about Dwyer's stepping down.

Taylor was muttering to himself about what he believed was sheer incompetence by Dwyer's office. They forgot to include the final page that would likely say he was resigning. Taylor never dreamed it was intentional. So with about 25 reporters, he had to sit through the entire news conference to get the answer.

"Greg, what's he doing?" Tony Romeo of Radio Pennsylvania asked Gregg Penny, a Dwyer press aide. "I don't know," Penny replied.

The night before, Steve Drachler, then of the *Morning Call*, mentioned the news conference to Romeo at a Hershey Bears' game. Romeo didn't know about it. Apparently, only certain reporters were invited. Dwyer's staff evidently convinced him he could not do that. He had to invite everyone.

Romeo believes that Dwyer wanted to include only certain reporters he disliked, such as those who most aggressively pursued the CTA story — like Drachler. There is no way to know for sure what Dwyer's intent really was, Romeo admitted.

As Dwyer droned on, Taylor considered leaving and calling back later. Dwyer was obviously going to resign, but he knew a reporter who had been burned by writing a story based on prepared remarks when the senator involved became ill and never actually delivered them. And Taylor still had a reporter's instinct to get the news firsthand. So he stayed. At one point, as TV crews began packing up their equipment, Dwyer told them they might not want to leave just yet.

Dwyer read his rambling statement but never got to the final page. He took a large manila envelope from his briefcase and pulled out a .357 magnum handgun. Holding the gun in his right hand while his left hand was raised with fingers outstretched as if to hold back anyone who would rush him, Dwyer was trying to make one final comment, "When I... this will... ."

It took almost three seconds for most people in the room to grasp what they were actually seeing: a statewide elected official waving a powerful handgun in front of a group of reporters. Paul Vathis, a Pulitzer Prize-winning AP photographer, thought Dwyer was reaching into the envelope for handouts about his resignation.

"No, no, Budd, don't. Budd, no, no, please. Budd, don't do this," reporters and his staff shouted.

"Listen to me," Dwyer said. "Don't... don't... this'll hurt someone."

In one swift motion, he placed the barrel in his mouth. He used his left hand to guide the barrel, upside down, and hold it there while pulling the trigger with his right index finger. The motion was so fluid it was almost as if he had practiced.

"Owwww!" a woman shrieked. "Oh my God!"

Dwyer's body slumped against the wall, blood streaming out of his nose and mouth.

"Don't panic!" Horshock shouted.

"Shit!" a reporter exclaimed.

Someone nearby yelled, "Get an ambulance!" Robert B. Swift wrote in a first-person account for Ottaway News Service. Swift grabbed a phone and dialed 911, asking for a rescue squad to come to the Finance Building. Vathis walked toward Dwyer's body, cursing him for being so dumb.

"At the first sight of the revolver, the initial response of many reporters, myself included, was self-preservation," Swift wrote. "Seated in a swivel chair only feet away from his desk, I looked for a place to dive and hide."

All the subsequent chatter about whether reporters should have stopped Budd Dwyer was nonsense. No one in his right mind would rush a man with a handgun.

The missing page was later given to the press. The final paragraph began:

"I've repeatedly said that I'm not going to resign as state treasurer…I am going to die in office in an effort to see 'if the shameful facts, spread out in all their shame, will not burn through our civic shamelessness and set fire to American pride' (Lincoln Steffens, *The Shame of the Cities*, New York: McClure, Philips & Co., 1904). Please tell my story on every radio and television station and in every newspaper and magazine in the U.S. Please leave immediately if you have a weak stomach or mind since I don't want to cause physical or mental distress. Joanne, Rob, Dee Dee — I love you! Thank you for making my life so happy. Goodbye to you all on the count of three. Please make sure that the sacrifice of my life is not in vain."

John Taylor rushed over to an office across the hall. He said he was with the governor's office, which tended to open doors quickly. He needed a phone. Women were still screaming across the hall. Taylor couldn't get his boss, Bob Grotevant. He got through to William Keisling, the governor's chief of staff, who asked, "What did he do? Did he resign?"

"No, he shot himself," Taylor replied.

Keisling asked in disbelief if Taylor was serious. What struck Keisling at the time was Taylor's professionalism, his matter-of-factness, as though he was dictating a story to the press. Keisling believes that Taylor even provided him with the time Dwyer pulled the trigger.

"Bill, as God is my witness, he pulled a gun out of his briefcase and shot himself."

"Is he dead?"

Taylor replied that he didn't get close enough to see for sure, but most people who stick a gun in their mouth and pull the trigger will die.

Leaving the building, he trudged across the street through about four or five inches of snow, which was piling up fast under a complete white-out sky. He was immediately taken in to brief Casey, Keisling and the governor's chief counsel, Morey Myers, in the governor's office on the second floor of the capitol. Governor Casey, never one for small talk, listened carefully without speaking. There was a protracted silence after Taylor finished telling the story.

Finally, the governor spoke: "Does anyone know if Budd Dwyer was Roman Catholic?" Taylor replied that he didn't know but he didn't think so. It was significant to Casey because suicide is considered a grave sin in Catholicism. But like everyone else in the room, Casey was shaken. His comment wasn't judgmental. Funeral services for Dwyer were held at the First Baptist Church in Meadville.

Budd Dwyer believed he was innocent. A federal jury thought otherwise.

Next: Dwyer's mindset.

6

Denial

Speak with any number of convicts and they will tell you they are innocent, wronged by the "system," something that Budd Dwyer also complained about. If someone has committed a horrific act or participated in one, I believe that it is easy over time to reconstruct his memory to the point that he really believes in his innocence. It's a natural defense mechanism. It's powerful. It's called denial.

Budd Dwyer had convinced himself that he wasn't doing anything illegal before he agreed to take the bribe. In early March 1984, John Torquato met for breakfast at the Marriott hotel outside Harrisburg with William Smith and Budd Dwyer. Torquato later told the FBI that Smith said, "If you give us the contract, I will personally raise $300,000 for your campaign."

Dwyer replied, "No quid pro quo. No quid pro quo. No quid pro quo," Torquato later told the FBI, according to an interview transcript obtained by author William Keisling, son of Casey's former chief of staff. Of course, if one went through with that deal, it was, in fact quid pro quo.

The final offer would come a week or so later. Torquato told Smith that he was willing to pay Dwyer 300 K to get the contract. According to Smith, Torquato was pushing him to do it. Smith suggested that Dwyer take it in "thirds"— $100,000 for himself, $100,000 for his campaign, and $100,000 for the state party. In Smith's account, Dwyer agreed.

The bribery case against him was murky and complex enough for Dwyer to have convinced himself that he did nothing wrong. He was a straight arrow, a country boy from Blooming Valley near Meadville. His co-defendant Bob Asher, a Philly guy, had once called Dwyer that "bumpkin from Meadville." Another reporter who covered Dwyer thought he was naïve and in over his head despite the law degree he earned later in life. The crooked politician's lament was also part of Dwyer's mindset. Others were doing the same thing and only he was singled out.

Torquato was the guy paying the bribe. Asher tried to secure a share for the state Republican Party. Smith, the Dauphin County Republican chairman, was the go-between who stood to make millions of dollars if Computer Technology Associates got the contract. Ironically, no money ever changed hands. A public official can still be convicted for agreeing to be bribed. CTA got the contract. Dwyer signed it. A "Big 8" accounting firm, which had been willing to do the work for a fraction of the cost, was not used.

I am convinced that Dwyer absolutely believed that he was wrongly convicted. His suicide was not only an act to preserve a $1.2 million pension benefit for his family but a way to get the world to look at the facts of his trial and an attempt to convince posterity of his innocence for his family's sake.

One only needed to look at Dwyer's eyes, the expression on his face, the second before he put the gun in his mouth. He was proud. He was defiant. At the very least, he was determined. Yet the moment after Bill Smith left his office in mid-March 1984, after offering the bribe, the former social studies teacher should have called the FBI. But he didn't.

Would an innocent man pull the trigger? Perhaps as former U.S. Attorney David Dart Queen told *The Philadelphia Inquirer* months later, Dwyer killed himself "because he didn't have the b. . . . to go to jail." He had previously expressed concern about U.S. District Court Judge Malcolm Muir's "medieval sentences." The maximum he faced on 11 counts was 55 years.

A retrospective on Dwyer's suicide and his conviction in the CTA scandal by *The Inquirer's* Frederick Cusick, "The Last Dark Days of Budd Dwyer," was published in June 1987. It offered numerous reasons as to why Dwyer might have taken his life. The guilty verdict "was tantamount to a sentence of death," Cusick wrote. "Suddenly all that he had worked so long and hard for was in ruins. [Dwyer] knew that he would lose the state treasurer's job; if he didn't quit, they'd impeach him. He'd have to give up the law license and teaching certificate he'd earned years ago in Crawford County. He would, inevitably, be sentenced to a long prison term, and his family would be impoverished. In addition to legal bills, he might have to pay hundreds of thousands of dollars in fines. They might even find a way to strip him of the pension he had accumulated after 22 years in office." Dwyer had served in the state House and Senate for 16 years.

Budd Dwyer's conviction on bribery charges would have resulted in the revocation of his pension. Bribery and perjury are among the crimes that can trigger revocation. But under Pennsylvania law, a conviction is not final until sentencing.

That was to occur before Judge Muir the very next day, and Dwyer would likely be led away in handcuffs. In other words, he would not lose his pension if he died in office, technically before any conviction had officially occurred. As a member of the pension board, Dwyer certainly understood this. But not many people would kill themselves to preserve a million dollars.

* * *

I did not witness Dwyer's suicide. I was working in Washington, D.C. for Gannett newspapers after spending about two-and-a-half years in Harrisburg. I knew Budd Dwyer and covered the events leading up to his trial. I was stuck in traffic on Capitol Hill in the midst of the blizzard. In Washington, D.C., it was a mega-storm. The metro had shut down. A U.S. House committee hearing adjourned early because of the weather. I walked most of the way to Virginia, where Gannett was headquartered. Eventually, I hailed one of the few available cabs on Constitution Avenue. I had no idea about Dwyer until I got into the office. My phone messages from Pennsylvania were stacked up.

It was a national story. The reporter in me wished I had been there. In a lot of ways, I am glad I wasn't there to witness the life-ending act of a man who clearly began his political career with the best of intentions. At the time, I considered Dwyer to be decent and honest. Except, maybe, for that one apparent moment of weakness, which was revealed in his indictment and trial. He deserved a better last chapter than ending his own life with a powerful handgun.

Could Budd Dwyer have been innocent?

Dwyer's supporters believe that William Smith never offered the bribe. After all, Smith lied at his own trial, saying he did not offer a bribe. He testified at Dwyer's trial that he did so. One of the two times he was lying. Smith admitted he was telling the truth the second time. Dwyer claimed that Smith and John Torquato told federal prosecutors whatever they wanted to hear in an effort to nail a "big pelt"[him]. In his final news conference, Dwyer did admit to meeting with Smith in his office.

Some 23 years after Dwyer's suicide, William Smith was sentenced to one to five years in prison for stealing thousands of dollars from elderly clients. Then 73, Smith pleaded guilty to multiple felonies. His son, William T. Smith II, was in prison in Peru, charged with killing his Peruvian wife.

"The entire CTA case, as it applies to me, hinges on one meeting in March of 1984 with Bill Smith about which he has told two versions, one truthful and the other one in exchange for immunity for his wife and other considerations for himself," Dwyer maintained in his final statement. It seems to me that something untoward occurred, even if Dwyer had convinced himself it was not a bribe. He was in over his head with CTA and saw no way out.

In some ways, Dwyer achieved what he intended — the continued examination of the facts of the case. His suicide, captured on video, aired on some TV stations that day amid considerable controversy. It's been seen by thousands on YouTube.

Dwyer claimed the deck was stacked against him. It was.

The feds historically have about a 95 percent conviction rate, counting guilty pleas. It's so high because it seems the full weight of the federal government is behind a prosecution. The FBI's resources are incredible. Still, it is a very high standard to get a unanimous verdict, the requirement for a conviction. A defense lawyer need only convince one juror to hold out and get a mistrial. The jurors deliberated for four days before delivering a guilty verdict against Dwyer for bribery.

Dwyer never presented a defense during the eight-week trial. I've seen that tack before. It is very risky but sends a strong message to the jury. It indicates that the defendant is confident that the prosecutors did not come close to proving their case. The risk is that the defense may be perceived to have done nothing to counter the government's case except for cross-examining its witnesses.

The reason there is ongoing Internet fascination with Budd Dwyer's case is not only the suicide, but also the conspiracy theory. It goes something like this: Dwyer, a Republican, called out Governor Thornburgh, a fellow Republican and former U. S. Attorney, for charging the state for family members' travel expenses. I remember the reaction of a couple of the older guys in the newsroom when Dwyer went after Thornburgh for his wife Ginny's European travel expenses. "He is toast," one of them said. The newsman meant that Thornburgh would find a political way to stick it to Dwyer. That was my take at the time.

But the conspiracy theory goes much further than political retribution. It holds that Thornburgh got his former Assistant U.S. Attorney, Jim West, who had come to Harrisburg as a prosecutor, to take out Dwyer when Thornburgh got wind of the CTA scandal. It suggests that Thornburgh was indirectly responsible for Dwyer's conviction and suicide.

I do not think it went down that way. I believe that Thornburgh was furious — he said as much concerning Dwyer's assertions about his family — but it's quite a leap from there to the idea that he was meddling in a federal prosecution while no longer a prosecutor.

A conspiracy is the central theme of Dwyer's version of events in the 20-page statement he read and handed out to reporters at his final news conference. It began, he said, with his decision, in February 1984, to refuse payment of a travel voucher for Ginny Thornburgh's trip to Europe with the governor on a trade mission. Then, in March and April of 1984, "chauffeurgate" was brought to Dwyer's attention by Wally Roche of *The Philadelphia Inquirer*. Dwyer criticized the use of state troopers to drive Thornburgh's son to a private school in Massachusetts. Keep in mind that all of this was during the period when Dwyer was being offered money by John Torquato and William Smith.

Why would Dwyer be jacking Dick Thornburgh during this period? Was it a distraction to keep Thornburgh's eye off of Computer Technology Associates? Or was it just Dwyer's reaction to events as they developed? Thornburgh told Bob Asher that he would "get Dwyer," the former treasurer claimed, and supposedly began referring to the 260-pound Dwyer as "The Fat Fuck." In his final written statement, Dwyer was still proper enough not to spell out the F-bomb in print.

"Does that sound like me?" Thornburgh replied when asked about the "fat fuck" reference. "I, as the governor, have the power to influence the U.S. Attorney? Not in a month of Sundays."

Jim West had worked for Thornburgh before in the U.S. Attorney's office and later as a deputy attorney general in 1979. That was a year before the Commonwealth Attorney's Act would establish the first elected attorney general. West went to the U.S. Attorney's office in the Middle District of Pennsylvania in 1982, and later became acting U.S. Attorney.

William Keisling and Richard Kearns espouse the conspiracy theory in their book, *The Sins of Our Fathers*, first published in 1988. The Internet fascination with Dwyer's suicide is evident in the book's heady prices on Amazon. Used copies — in the upper range — are listed from $119 to $730.

Writing about the CTA scandal, Keisling and Kearns wrote, "The real wonder here isn't why Al Benedict called in the FBI. The real mystery is the dizzying speed and selective manner in which the federal prosecutors launched their investigation. The comatose, disinterested FBI office in the state capital is a well-worn joke. A strong case can be made that the FBI and the prosecutor's office spent more time covering up than investigating. Here's a question worth pondering: Why is it that a few days after being called in by Benedict, these sleepy characters in the FBI and U.S. Attorney's office crossed the country to California, stormed John Torquato's house with a warrant, and launched a grand investigation obviously targeted at Budd Dwyer?

"The obvious answer to this, supported by mounting evidence, is that Pennsylvania governor Dick Thornburgh and his staff knew all along that Torquato and his staff were out bribing everyone under the sun. . . . Benedict's call to the FBI was merely probable cause or cover for Thornburgh's people to spring the trap on Dwyer."

Dwyer claimed that Thornburgh had taken control of the U.S. Attorney's office through "his lackey," Jim West.

To me, the idea that Thornburgh controlled the prosecutor's office while governor is convenient but highly questionable in view of how federal prosecutors work. Dwyer said that West refused his request to take a polygraph test and gave unprecedented sweetheart plea deals to Torquato and Smith. Torquato was sentenced to four years, but according to Dwyer, West arranged to have it reduced to 22 months. Smith served three and a half years in federal prison, but his wife, who was also his law partner, was not charged. Dwyer argued that prosecutors had a "house judge" in Malcolm Muir and held the trial in Williamsport to get an "unsophisticated, uneducated jury pool," rather than trying him in Harrisburg.

In the statement he delivered at his final news conference, Dwyer offered no real evidence of a conspiracy. Deals like this are made every day in the criminal justice system in an effort to put away the worst actors or the highest-ranking officials. Like it or not, the system is fueled by plea deals and testimony from co-conspirators. Thornburgh said he never spoke to Jim West about Dwyer or the CTA investigation. West likewise says that they never had a conversation.

"There was no conspiracy and that's it," he insisted.

Thornburgh addressed Budd Dwyer's assertions in his autobiography. He wrote that he had "a couple of run ins" with Dwyer "over his efforts to enhance his own image by embarrassing me and my family." Thornburgh claimed that Dwyer had suggested to the *Inquirer* that Ginny sought to travel at state expense. But a press release issued prior to the trip "expressly stated she would pay her own expenses. Ginny repeatedly asked staff for her share so she could reimburse." When the stories hit the press, "Ginny was mortified and I was furious."

Of all the people I've met who would be least likely to try and slip a European travel expense through the treasury, Ginny Thornburgh would be at or near the top of the list. She is a dear person.

"Dwyer soon added an allegation that we had abused the security detail provided by the state police," Thornburgh wrote. "They had transported our son, Bill, to and from Deerfield Academy in Massachusetts since his enrollment there in the fall of 1981, and once they had driven David to Cambridge, where he was attending Harvard's John F. Kennedy School of Government. Again the explanation was a simple one but unheeded by the press. The security detail provided its services to all members of our household as the officers deemed necessary for our protection. Ginny and I neither asked for nor (as we were to regret) questioned those services, which were no different than those provided to our predecessors."

It was Thornburgh who signed the legislation authorizing the Federal Insurance Contribution Act (FICA) recoveries. The governor has said that when he heard John Torquato was involved, he ordered all discussions to be terminated regarding CTA's efforts to get a state contract. Thornburgh noted that he was wary of the family name because of Torquato's father, John Torquato Sr., a Johnstown political boss convicted in the 1970s when Thornburgh headed the Justice Department's criminal division.

The FICA recovery was done in-house for state employees. "It should be done in-house," Thornburgh insisted. Because the state workers were off-limits, Torquato and Smith tried for the school employees through Dwyer. Torquato named many public officials as bribe targets. Dwyer believed he had been singled out of those identified in Torquato's spreadsheet seized by the FBI.

Attorney General LeRoy Zimmerman then denied claims by Smith that he had offered the chief law enforcement officer $150,000 in campaign money during a telephone call. Smith said it was an off-hand remark, not a bribe. While Smith was seeking a legal opinion from the attorney general on behalf of CTA, Zimmerman charged that Smith had offered $100,000 in campaign money for Zimmerman to the AG's press aide, the late Patrick Boyle. Zimmerman was not charged.

*   *   *

We now come to the troubling question of Robert Asher, whom Dick Thornburgh had supported for state GOP chairman. I would run into Asher at Republican National Conventions. I thought he was a classy guy, and he was helpful to reporters.

The politically astute might question why Asher was included in the indictment. He had been Thornburgh's 1982 campaign chairman. But Dwyer maintained that Asher had "crossed" the governor by not providing Republican State Committee funds for trips to promote Thornburgh's candidacy on the national ticket.

"Asher's involvement was especially troublesome to me," Thornburgh wrote. Asher was one of the state's most effective political operatives, and Thornburgh had supported him for state chairman. "I felt thoroughly betrayed by his involvement in this seedy affair," he added.

Asher was convicted of conspiracy, mail fraud, and perjury. He was sentenced to a year and a day in prison. He is a prime example of how to bounce back from adversity.

A Montgomery County candy company owner, he served his time in federal prison and returned to the political world as a pre-eminent fund-raiser and National Republican Committeeman. In November 2010, at Tom Corbett's election night gubernatorial victory party in Pittsburgh, Corbett addressed the crowd after the results were known. "Where's Bob?" he asked, referring to Asher, who had raised about three million dollars for Corbett and two million for other Republicans in the 2010 election.

"I tell everybody who asks the same thing," Asher, then 73, told the *Tribune-Review* in a December 2010 interview. "I look you in the eye and tell you, I didn't do anything improper. The court did not agree. I paid my dues."

Next, we'll take a close look at another statewide official who was hard to dislike and to this day has denied that he was "corrupt."

7

Ernie the Attorney

June 13, 1995

I'll never forget that day he swaggered into the capitol rotunda. Lackawanna County District Attorney Ernie Preate had *arrived*. Never before, and never since, have I seen a politician as full of self-confidence and as cocksure of his election to the office he sought. He was 48 at the time, physically fit, with a receding hairline and wire-rim glasses. He moved with the grace of an athlete. Dressed to the nines in lawyers' garb — a pin-stripe two-piece suit — Preate had the commanding presence of a military officer. We would shortly learn that he'd been a captain in the Marine Corps during the Vietnam war. He served there in the worst years (1966-69) and received five medals for distinguished service. He volunteered for combat.

As the district attorney in Scranton, Preate had won 20 consecutive drug-dealer trials and 19 homicide cases. He became a force to be reckoned with in the attorney general's race. I would come to respect him enormously after his ultimate trial.

It was as if the office of Attorney General belonged to Ernie Preate and he was here that day in 1988 to claim it. He stood behind a wood lectern, one that had been used by countless legislators, advocates, and candidates of all stripes in the rotunda, with his back to the Grand Staircase, patterned after the one in the Paris Opera House. It's beneath a 272-foot dome that strongly suggests the one on St. Peter's Basilica.

Preate had that trial lawyer's gift of connecting with his audience, in this case, capitol reporters from across the state whose offices are located behind the staircase on the second or "E" floor in the capitol newsroom. He certainly had the academic credentials. His father, Ernest D. Preate Sr., was an attorney, and Ernie Jr. was able to go to Scranton Preparatory School. He then received a B.S. in economics from the Wharton School of Finance and added a J.D. from the University of Pennsylvania Law School. On paper, he had it all: war record, Ivy League academic credentials, and a boffo record as a prosecutor. Little did any of us realize that Preate would leave the office in shame in only seven years.

In 1988, Ernie Preate became the second elected Attorney General of Pennsylvania. He was also the second Republican prosecutor to win the relatively new elective office. Republicans have held it through 2012. Preate succeeded LeRoy Zimmerman, the former Dauphin County DA.

Concerned about public corruption and organized crime, Pennsylvania voters in 1978 decided to switch from an appointed to an elected top prosecutor. The rationale was that an elected prosecutor would be independent of the governor. This was near the end of the Shapp administration, and crime-fighter Dick Thornburgh was on the ballot. The Commonwealth Attorney's Act of 1980 later implemented the voters' decision.

Preate's PR machine was among the best ever on capitol hill, and it cranked out news release after news release about Ernie's accomplishments: from drug busts to cracking down on auto dealers rolling back odometers. Rarely have I seen since such thorough news releases on legal matters. I distinctly remember filing a deadline story for the *Chambersburg Public Opinion,* an afternoon newspaper, on a Preate news release and thinking, what else would I ask? It was all there. Tom Corbett's press releases as attorney general on complex public corruption cases were an even match and technologically advanced.

Preate made such a splash making busts that he was reputable enough for another Scrantonian, Democrat Robert P. Casey, then the state's governor, to team with on an anti-crime tour. Casey was a straight arrow and stringent about the appearances of his staff. He ran a scandal-free administration from 1987 through January 1995. It was an odd pairing, the Republican and Democrat teams from the same hometown.

By late 1994, Preate was the leading Republican candidate for governor. Given Pennsylvanians' proclivity for the "cycle" — switching control of the governor's mansion to the opposing party every eight years — Preate was the favorite to replace Casey in 1994.

But the cloud over his candidacy was the investigation dogging him since about 1990. The FBI and Pennsylvania Crime Commission were investigating allegations that while Lackawanna DA, Preate solicited campaign donations from video poker operators, promising to go easy on them as attorney general.

Preate would go down hard.

* * *

The lust for power drove the crimes of legislative leaders in the early 21st century.

It was no different for Preate, who wanted to win at any cost. In Preate's case, it was incredible risk-taking that would wreck his career as a public official and make him a convicted felon for life. But the goal was the same as other cases to follow: the pursuit of campaign money for elected office. The crime commission dinged him first.

As a reporter with Gannett News Service, I was paying attention, especially by late 1993 when the legislature was moving to eliminate the crime commission, a panel created in 1968 to keep tabs on the mob. The commission had no arrest powers and was merely an intelligence gathering outfit. Law enforcement officials in other states considered it one of the few on-the-record sources about organized crime and a valuable resource. Critics say it smeared ordinary citizens for their "association" with Mafia figures. The commission's chief protagonist was Ernie Preate.

As the commission was closing in on him, Preate turned the heat up on the beleaguered agency. He played the ethnic card, encouraging or condoning angry claims by Italian-American groups that the commission's actions were targeting those of Italian descent. Preate, who is both Italian and Polish, talked about the blatant unfairness of the commission's investigations.

On the day Italian-Americans staged a protest, Preate was making porchetta, a pork dish, with cannolis provided by Senator Vincent Fumo, for the "Fourth Annual Ernie Preate 'Real' Italian-American Caucus Luncheon," as Bob Zausner wrote in *The Inquirer*. Preate branded the commission's investigation a McCarthy-style attack and pretty much left the charge of an ethnic smear to lawmakers of Italian descent.

I still don't quite get it. Mob families traced their lineage to Sicily. People typically couldn't become "made members" unless they were Sicilian. Who else would a crime commission charged with investigating organized crime investigate? The Russians, later. But not in the 1970s and '80s.

I pored through many of those reports, and I wrote a lot of stories based on them. To me, it's a close call whether they did more good than harm. There were detailed reports revealing the mob's tentacles in industries, unions and communities. There were loose associations that appeared to make a person into a crook if he knew any Mafia guys. Growing up in Scranton, Preate understood how sometimes people just knew guys from the neighborhood as friends or acquaintances, even if they had dirty laundry. People were hurt without question, and some of them were honest businessmen.

As a prosecutor, Preate knew the burden the state must meet in the courtroom to prove a case beyond a reasonable doubt. The commission could do an interview or two, toss in some newspaper clips, and draw conclusions. It just happens that in Preate's case they got it right.

It seemed to me that there was a lot lacking in the aftermath of the crime commission. Mob intelligence became the duty of the state police, the attorney general and the FBI. That's great if they've got charges to file. Throughout the late 1990s and the early part of the new century after the commission's demise, I had no idea, nor did most citizens, whether organized crime was still flourishing outside of the Scarfo family dramas in Philly.

I didn't cover the ins and outs of the Preate investigation and instead focused on the political ramifications. I liked Ernie, even the old Ernie. He was always accessible to the press, easy to talk to, great with quotes. Not exactly a wallflower, he played hardball politics.

The reporters out front on the Preate investigation were Peter Shelly and Peter Shellem of the Harrisburg *Patriot-News*. They were way out there by themselves. That's a scary place to be going up against a guy as aggressive and volatile as Ernie Preate.

Preate and his staff were doing everything possible to discredit Shelly and Shellem, both publicly and privately. But John A. Kirkpatrick, publisher of the *Patriot-News*, "never blinked," according to Shelly, now president of Shelly Communications in Harrisburg.

In March 1994, Shelly and Shellem, who is deceased, reported that a federal grand jury probe of Preate's office was widening; at least a dozen subpoenas had been issued, testimony had been taken from two former attorney generals, and the focus was expanded to include Ernie Preate's handling of video poker cases.

Here's how far out they were left hanging, as Preate's spokesman had said just a week before the federal investigation was on the verge of being closed. In response to their inquiry for this story, the reporters were told by the spokesman that there were "loose ends to tie up" before closing the federal case.

The crime commission had one parting shot to take. And the members took it on April 11, 1994. They charged that Preate sought and accepted the backing of video poker operators to expand his political power. The members called for a special prosecutor. Large contributions from operators were made in cash and weren't reported as required by law. In May, the Shelly-Shellem team reported that prosecutor Nels Taber had made a request to grant immunity to video poker operators so they could testify without fear of prosecution, and it was denied by Preate through a top aide. Wounded by the grand jury report and the crime commission's allegations, Preate finished second to Republican Tom Ridge in a four-person Republican primary for governor. Ridge went on to defeat Democrat Mark Singel in November 1994.

The Shelly-Shellem team kept rolling. Five former video poker operators pleaded guilty to "conspiring with an unidentified state law enforcement official" to obstruct state gambling laws in exchange for contributions as part of a federal investigation, they reported in December 1994.

As the investigation neared its end, the *Philadelphia Daily News* featured a cover photo of Preate surrounded by various cards that could be drawn in the electronic game. When an aide showed him the photo, Preate responded, "Wow. Good picture." Never mind his career was in shambles. Ernie's ego was still healthy.

By June, it was over. Preate agreed to plead guilty to one count of mail fraud and resign. At the time, he said he did so to keep the feds from indicting his two brothers, Carlo and Robert. Preate posed for a *Daily News* cover appropriately entitled, "Family Man." What made his conviction far more serious than those of the earlier Auditor General and treasurer is that the Attorney General could send people to jail. An immense power is invested in that office.

Preate's June 13, 1995 resignation letter to Tom Ridge was a statement of faith and an indication that he had accepted his fate: "I shall miss the challenges of this office, but as God closes this door in my leaving, I have faith that He will open another one for me for His greater glory." He added, "I have asked God for his mercy and forgiveness, and I am at peace with Him and with what I am doing. I hold no ill will toward anyone." Within months, it sounded as if he was at peace with no one.

Between his resignation and his sentencing, Preate engaged in an all-out effort to minimize what he had done. He said he could have beaten the charge, painted himself as a fall guy, and called the probe a witch hunt, according to Assistant U.S. Attorney William Behe. What set Preate off was his claim that U.S. Attorney David Barasch violated the plea agreement by filing a document alleging that Preate agreed to lax enforcement in return for campaign money from video operators. What Preate pleaded guilty to was filing false campaign reports — failing to report about $20,000 in cash contributions from video poker operators. When Ernie stuck it in the mail, he committed mail fraud. With the sentencing recommendation, U.S. Attorney David Barasch submitted the factual basis for the mail fraud charge. It was believed that Barasch was as specific as he was because Preate was engaging in revisionist history.

Here's what was going on. Preate could stomach the idea that he failed to report the money. It was a campaign law violation, one might say. Agreeing to go easy on dealers in return for the money took it to an unacceptable level: a quid pro quo. That was never proven, but it was clearly pervasive as an allegation.

To this day, Preate denies any such deal or going easy on anyone. "I wasn't corrupt. I did a stupid thing," he said in an interview. "I violated the state election law. I put it in the mail. It's mail fraud." As for a quid pro quo, "That never happened."

In November 1994, Shelly and Shellem reported that according to a brief filed by prosecutors, if Preate had not agreed to the plea to mail fraud, he would have been charged with racketeering, mail fraud, conspiracy, obstruction of gambling laws and tampering with a witness. Preate scoffed at the notion. "They didn't have any proof along those lines." If prosecutors had it, "they would have made me plead to it."

On December 14, 1995, Preate was sentenced to 14 months in federal prison, a $25,000 fine and two years' probation. By then 55, he was to report to prison on January 15th. With typical bravado, Preate told reporters, "I'm a strong guy. I'm not afraid to do time. I can do federal prison standing on my head." Sixteen years later, he admitted, "I should not have said that."

Preate was sent to a prison in Duluth, Minnesota. Peter Shelly, by now working for *The Pittsburgh Post-Gazette,* traveled there to write a story about his imprisonment. He and Jack Sherzer of the *Patriot-News* were the last faces Ernie saw of the outside world that day, save for his brothers. "He betrayed the trust of the people," William Behe said at the sentencing hearing.

Preate did apologize to his family and the people of Pennsylvania. In Duluth, "it was cold. There was 14 feet of snow on the ground. You wore a winter parka until the Fourth of July. No one can appreciate the impact of imprisonment until it happened. It's the loss of freedom, the little and big things. You can no longer decide when to take a shower, when to watch TV, when to eat."

Ernie's approach was to "be humble" and say little at first. His credo to survive was to "mind your own business." "There was talk" of trouble because he'd been a prosecutor. But Preate's break came when he helped one of his three roommates, a well-known inmate in his fifth or sixth year on a drug charge, with a legal motion. He filed a habeas corpus petition with the federal court in Minneapolis and within 30 days, the guy walked out of prison a free man. The man he sprung was respected and played in the prison band.

"That was one of the things that made me," Ernie remembered. Soon, inmates were "lining up" for legal assistance and for help writing letters.

Preate worked washing dishes, pots and pans in the kitchen. "It was a sweatshop," he recalled. Dishwashers had to wear rubber boots and long rubber gloves so as not to be burned by the steam. It was more than 100 degrees near the dishwashing area. Concerned that pots weren't getting clean enough, he appealed to a supervisor to buy "Tide with bleach alternative." No bleach was allowed inside since it can be used as "a weapon," he noted. It took the prison three weeks to test the soap. Finally, it was okayed. Preate said that within weeks he was able to get most deep stains off the pots. It proved to be his undoing, When Ernie tried to transfer out of the kitchen, he was told there was no way since he did too good a job.

Preate served 11 months. He fondly remembers his last day when about two dozen inmates — white, black and Mexican — showed up at his cell for a going-away party. He still stays in touch with some of those people.

After he served his time, Preate frequently returned to the Harrisburg capitol. I saw him on several occasions. He was indeed more humble. He wore rumpled clothing, not the lawyer's stylish suit. Prison had taken something out of Ernie. He became an advocate, a lobbyist for prison reform and overhauling the criminal justice system. Preate gained a new perspective on life as a result of a near-fatal

1997 motorcycle accident in which he suffered a broken pelvis and fractured his wrist and hand.

In September 1999, Preate addressed the Pennsylvania Press Club and spoke of the lack of compassion in the criminal justice system. "First of all, our programs, policies and laws over the last 20 years have become harsher and mean-spirited with ever increasing mandatory sentences for smaller and smaller amounts of drugs. I admit, I was once a proponent of these laws," he added.

Preate was more than that. He was the poster child for lock'em up, law-and-order prosecutors with no sympathy for drug dealers and other so-called nonviolent offenders.

The bottom line, Preate told the press club, is that we incarcerate too many prisoners in the U.S. and Pennsylvania. He cited then-current U.S. Justice Department statistics that one of every 149 people is behind bars, and the Department of Corrections budget grew from $100 million in 1980 to $1.2 billion in 1999. This from a guy who co-authored "Mandatory Sentencing" in the *Pennsylvania Bar Association Quarterly* in 1987.

The U.S. is incarcerating mostly nonviolent, mentally ill and mentally retarded people, Preate now contended. To compete in the global economy, the U.S. needs to "invest more in pupils than in prisons." "In the name of humanity," he pleaded, "we must do better than warehouse these souls."

Preate's turnaround was remarkable. I spoke with him once or twice during that period and he seemed sincere. "Half of the people don't belong in prison, they really don't," he told me.

Ernie is now a successful attorney in his hometown of Scranton, where he practices criminal, family and divorce law, as well as consumer fraud and car accident claims. He has gone to court for inmates he once would have scorned. He is a *defense attorney*, a segment of the profession he once held in contempt. Preate got his law license back about 12 years ago.

Many believe more public candor about what happened on the video poker investigation, a complete mea culpa, would have been the better course. But you can't argue with the guy they once called "Ernie the Attorney" turning his life around.

He has changed. Asked if a reporter could accompany him on one of his many trips speaking before inmates in prisons, Preate declined because he says it is about the trust of the inmates, not a photo-op. Reminded that he never would have turned down publicity in the 1980s and '90s, Preate replied, "That's the old Ernie."

Ernie is proud of the cases he's won on the defense side of the courtroom, including the acquittal of a truck driver in a Medicaid fraud case in 2011. He beat the attorney general's office in that Susquehanna County trial. God has given him a gift to argue cases before juries, he says.

Now, 71, Preate is remarried and has a 10-year-old daughter he adores in addition to his 40-year-old twin daughters. He marvels at being a soccer dad at his age.

One thing different about the "new Ernie." The swagger is gone.

Next: a potpourri of corruption at the capitol.

8

Potpourri

The 1990s

What former Representative Tom Druce did was worse than any of the stealing that occurred at the capitol. He killed a man. What gets it listed under corruption is the cover-up, and the insurance fraud that Druce engaged in.

He thought he could get away with it.

Druce was a rising star in Republican Party politics. The Bucks County law-maker had been the political director of the state party. Reporters including myself loved him. He was concise and articulate. He would go off the record and tell you what was really going on. He was elected to a House seat in 1992. That was a loss to those of us who counted on him as a state party source.

Tom Druce struck and killed Kenneth Cains, a black Marine Corps veteran, on Cameron Street in Harrisburg in a black Jeep SUV he had leased, courtesy of state taxpayers, on July 27, 1999. (Cameron Street was named after the political boss Simon Cameron.) In that instant, knowing his life would unravel, Druce, 38, kept going. And the lies began.

As I get older, I have often thought of Druce's moment as a defining one in life for all of us. How many of us have a similar moment, even if not as dramatic? At that instant, would most of us show character and act out of conscience? Druce had been drinking, so his judgment was skewed and his conscience was blurred by alcohol.

Would most of us have stopped and called police immediately, knowing it would mean a vehicular homicide or manslaughter charge, a drunk driving charge, a civil lawsuit and the end of a political career? If sober, I like to think that Druce would have done so and that most of us would have as well. Most people I've talked to since then say they would have stopped.

Would you have done that? Is it possible that in a snap-second judgment you would panic and flee the scene? Have you ever driven, when you shouldn't have, after consuming a few drinks?

Even after eventually admitting to the accident, Druce would claim that he thought he hit a sign and didn't know it was a person. That's a Budd Dwyer-style denial. To this day, I am sure he believes that. If Druce had stayed and fessed up that night, he might have faced drunk driving charges, and he might have lost his House seat. It's arguable whether he would have done time.

This was by all appearances an accident. Cains was intoxicated and apparently walked into the path of the Jeep SUV. Was Druce speeding? He did claim he was distracted, some file folders had fallen off the seat, and he had bent over while driving to try to collect them. Or was that part of his cover story? It was a night that began with a few pony bottles of Rolling Rock left over in a cooler from a previous legislative event. Druce began bar hopping with some legislative staffers and a woman with whom he was involved in a relationship. Later that night, Druce and the woman had an argument. She left and he was heading to her residence. He was married with small kids.

Some legislative staffers the next day suspected that Druce's car was involved in the accident because of the vehicle description. An eyewitness tried to get the plate number, but did identify a black SUV. Druce was even asked about it by a staffer for Governor Tom Ridge, with whom he was friendly, according to an October 28, 2000 *Post-Gazette* story.

Dennis Roddy, a *Post-Gazette* reporter who left the newspaper to join Corbett's press office in 2010, invested heavily in the Druce story. Roddy also thought highly of Druce and was fascinated by the tragedy. In Roddy's account, Druce was telling no one, including his former wife, Amy.

In a nutshell, what happened is that Druce's story began to unravel in late 1999. When word got out, it was a time of considerable panic among House Republicans. The late House Speaker Matthew Ryan, normally a genial Irishman who could also be stern, summoned Druce to his office and told him to get the best lawyer he could find. The come-to-Jesus meeting with Ryan occurred in January 2009. Ryan knew the cops were after documents involving Druce's car.

Six months after the accident, acting on an anonymous tip, police questioned Druce. He denied being involved in the accident. Druce had taken his state rental car to be fixed and after the body work was done, he traded it in. He had filed an insurance claim for hitting a construction sign on the Pennsylvania Turnpike. Investigators recovered the car Druce had sold and through forensic evidence established that hair and fiber from Cains' body and clothing were similar to evidence from Druce's SUV.

Druce was charged with eight felonies, including vehicular manslaughter, on January 20, 2000, by Harrisburg police. Druce would plead guilty in September of that year to leaving the scene of a fatal accident, insurance fraud and tampering with evidence. In October, he began serving a two-to-four-year sentence.

Druce was initially taken to the State Correctional Institution at Camp Hill, a "close security" prison in Camp Hill where almost all state prisoners are processed and some remain. His booking photo, a mug shot, showed the pure shock of entering the prison system. I kept that photo as a reminder of how one's life can change dramatically when least expected. Camp Hill is one step down from maximum security. Druce served 56 days in prison before being released pending his appeal of the sentence. During the time Druce was out of prison awaiting the outcome of his appeal, there was a valid criticism surfacing that Druce was getting special treatment because he was a well-liked white legislator.

In September 2004, the Supreme Court upheld Druce's sentence, which his lawyers challenged as unduly harsh. Druce had argued there was an element of bias by a trial court judge who called his claim of hitting a sign "strange." Druce would eventually serve the remainder of his two years at Laurel Highlands, a prison in Somerset County for geriatric and sick prisoners.

There is no excuse for what Tom Druce did. Claiming he hit a sign doesn't cut it. It was indeed strange, as the judge said. But ask yourself, are we any better than he is?

*   *   *

Through 1999, while Druce was still weaving his lies, a good-natured crook was selling his legislative position to line his pockets. Representative Frank Gigliotti, a Pittsburgh Democrat, was known as "Gigs" to other House members. Through the late 1990s, he took bribes for helping to arrange contracts with Alcosan, the Allegheny County Sanitary Authority, where he held a board seat by virtue of his position in the General Assembly. He took at least $17,000 in bribes. Gigs also extorted plane fare and tickets to take his family to DisneyWorld.

In 2000, Gigliotti pleaded guilty to mail fraud, attempted extortion and filing a false tax return. He was sentenced to 46 months in federal prison. A government informant who suggested that Gigliotti give back to the people for a change was told by Gigs, "Fuck the people!"

What set Frank Gigliotti apart was the brazenness of his corruption: a state legislator shaking down contractors, using his official position to extort payoffs. His Democratic colleagues would later suggest that all Gigliotti really did was accept illicit cash so he could take his family to DisneyWorld.

Right.

Gigliotti and Druce were part of a crime wave in the late 1990s of widely assorted flavors. Seven state legislators, including those two, would be convicted of felonies, showing once again the cyclical nature of corruption. There were, however, random acts.

I knew Gigliotti as Mr. Riverboat.

Gigs had this dream of riverboat gambling coming to Pennsylvania. And if he could pull it off, he would be the sponsor. He was the House Democrats' point man on the issue. It was in that capacity that I interviewed him on numerous occasions.

Gigliotti was gruff in speech and rough around the edges. A former ward boss, Gigs looked like he had eaten way too many cannoli. He was a squat, balding man with glasses and a pudgy face. Picture "Paulie," Rocky's brother-in-law in Sylvester Stallone's movie, with grayer hair and glasses.

A former backhoe operator, he landed a job with the city. When Dick Caliguiri ran for mayor against political giant Tom Foerester, Gigs worked his tail off for Caliguiri. Gigliotti's star rose with Caliguiri's victory. He became the city's public works director and in 1982, he unseated Pete Wagner as Democratic chairman of the 22nd Ward. In 1987, he won a House seat.

Gigs could BS with the best of them and was generally well liked in the House. As ward chairman on Pittsburgh's South Side, he knew how to deliver the vote for the Democratic payrollers on Grant Street. He was not the sharpest tool in the shed, but he knew his stuff on riverboat gambling.

I remember stories of Gigliotti, his pockets stuffed with cash, holding court at Scott's, a Harrisburg watering hole for legislators. He had cash and he was throwing it around.

Word travels fast. Gigs crashed in the fast lane.

While he served time in a federal prison, a guy unwaveringly loyal to him was Bill DeWeese. On one occasion when DeWeese went to visit him in prison, Gigs pointed to several hundred inmates lined up for chow. "You see all those guys? They're all guilty and so am I," Gigs told DeWeese. I have to say I was not shocked that Gigliotti was on the take. Maybe it was how he fit the old-school stereotype.

A shocker for me was the case of Senate Majority Leader F. Joseph Loeper, a Delaware County Republican. Loeper was secretly moonlighting as a consultant for a private tax collection firm called MTB from 1993 through 1997. Loeper received more than $330,000 during that period, but he concealed it with falsified documents. He cast votes and sponsored legislation to help the company. He attempted to get state contracts for MTB.

Loeper had decided that his legislative salary, one of the highest in the nation, was not enough. It was pure greed that reached up and grabbed him. In a plea bargain with federal prosecutors, he agreed to plead guilty to obstructing a federal tax investigation. Loeper didn't report the income on his state ethics financial disclosure filing.

I had breakfast with Joe Loeper in 1996 at a McDonald's at the San Diego airport. We were both on our way back from the Republican National Convention in San Diego. A big guy — he had to be pushing 270 pounds — Loeper was scarfing down McDonald's taters and English muffin sandwiches. He was dressed casually in slacks and a sport shirt. As I walked by, bag in hand, he motioned for me to come sit with him. There were no other pols around. Any travelers taking it in would not peg Loeper as the second-highest ranking Republican in one of the largest state legislatures. Nope, just old Joe. He was gracious and humble. Just your ordinary Eagles and Flyers fan on the way back from the left coast.

At the time of the convention, Loeper was several years into accepting income from the head of MTB, *The Inquirer* reported on October 25, 2000. The great lengths he went to conceal that income had to do with the nature of the business he was engaged in. Helping a firm that goes after people for late or underpaid taxes isn't an ideal image for a Republican senator professing support for tax cuts. Loeper was a capable leader, although he was part of the old leadership that squelched dissent and did the people's business in the early morning hours. After Loeper agreed to plead guilty, Tom Ridge called him his friend. Ridge said there was "no one in the General Assembly I respect more." He was, of course, also saddened by the news.

The Philadelphia Inquirer's Ken Dilanian and Thomas Fitzgerald led the way on the Loeper coverage. Their story said Loeper's plea deal structured on the federal obstruction charge was likely to allow him to receive an annual state pension. They were right. In 2012, he was receiving a pension of $43,514, according to state records. He kept the pension because it was a crime technically not related to his state office. Never mind that Loeper blocked legislation that would have hurt MTB's business. He spoke against and twice voted against proposals to amend the business tax to prohibit local governments from collecting the tax outside their borders, wrote the late Pete Shellem of the Harrisburg *Patriot-News*.

The Loeper case became an issue in the attorney general's race in 2000 between Democrat Jim Eisenhower and Republican Attorney General Mike Fisher. The federal prosecution of Loeper showed that Fisher had been "asleep at the switch" on public corruption cases and was too close to Loeper as a former Republican senator. Eisenhower called for a special prosecutor. That never happened and Fisher would go on to run for governor, lose to Ed Rendell in 2002, and eventually land on the Third Circuit Court of Appeals as a federal judge with Rendell's wife, Marjorie Rendell.

Loeper served six months, and he would return to Harrisburg as a lobbyist for the Pennsylvania Trial Lawyers Association. After a one-year prohibition under state law, he was free to lobby his former Senate colleagues. Loeper would later establish his own lobbying firm.

For years, people at the capitol would talk about the Loeper case as different from the rest of the corruption. It was because everyone genuinely liked Joe Loeper. His crime would be summarized by apologists as almost a paperwork mistake, that he didn't report the outside income on his financial disclosure statement.

Maybe there is another reason, a deeper understanding. Legislators who are also attorneys are not required to report their private practice clients. The financial disclosure requirements are weak for everyone. They need only report outside sources of income, such as the name of the law firm or insurance agency. Vincent Fumo, for instance, was "of counsel" for law firms over the years. Other public officials have held that position with firms. It can mean a lot of things, from essentially hanging the politician's well-known name on the firm to being a "rain maker" who brings in big clients.

A lobbyist explained the inside thinking to me on Joe Loeper. What Loeper did was illegal because he was not a lawyer. Lawyer/legislators, whose practice is carefully guarded as the domain of the Supreme Court, do essentially the same thing as Loeper — hide outside income and their clients' identities. They are not required to file disclosure statements with any specificity on their business as an attorney.

A plea bargain also helped another Republican senator in the '90s. Senator Dan Delp of York supplied alcohol to two underage teenage prostitutes and tried to bill the taxpayers. He pleaded guilty to one count of patronizing a prostitute and one count of buying a 19-year-old alcohol. A third charge, based on allegations that he spent $50 of taxpayers' money during this escapade, was dropped.

In typical Pennsylvania pol fashion, even after pleading guilty, Delp made excuses. "I trusted people I shouldn't have trusted," this according to a June 14, 1998 story by the Associated Press' Peter Durantine. Delp reportedly made those remarks after his plea deal. Durantine had the best grasp on the Delp case. He was the former statehouse reporter for *The York Daily Record.*

Barely worth mentioning, except for the fight by Republicans to let him remain in the House until his appeals were exhausted was Representative Frank Serafini. The Moosic lawmaker was convicted of perjury for lying about making an illegal campaign contribution on behalf of a landfill company. He was popular in the Republican caucus, and they didn't want to boot him out. Eventually, "The Fish," as Attorney General, asked a court to remove Serafini and the lawmaker. Seeing the writing on the wall, Frank stepped down.

In Northwestern Pennsylvania, a senator became known as "Senator Sludge" for having dumped raw sewage in a stream while he was a municipal official. Former senator William "Bill" Slocum, a Republican, was indicted by a federal grand jury in 1999 for dumping more than 3.5 million gallons of untreated sewage into Brokenstraw Creek. The Warren County senator had been Youngsville borough

manager. Slocum was indicted on seven felonies. He pleaded guilty to six misdemeanors and was sentenced to one month in prison. He resigned his Senate seat
shortly after he was sentenced.

Perhaps the most bizarre case of the 1990s involved former representative
Tracy Seyfert, an Erie Republican. Seyfert was a psychologist with a Ph.D. from
the University of Pittsburgh. Surrounding the case was the weird talk about witch-
craft. Seyfert at one point actually denied that she was a witch. The allegation was
that she illegally obtained a World War II-era generator intended for firefighters
and then covered it up. The millennium was approaching. World-ending scenarios
were abounding. Was Seyfert in survivalist mode? Some thought so. This was Erie,
and the Northwest was a hotbed for militia activity and government paranoia.
Seyfert told prosecutors she wanted the generator, purchased with a government
grant along with a 500-gallon oil tank, because she had thousands of exotic birds
and incubated their eggs.

As the investigation was heating up, former House Majority Leader John Perzel and his press aide Stephen Drachler traveled to Erie on September 9, 1999 to
help Seyfert with her message. Drachler drove up to her house and saw guys in
blue nylon blazers heading in and out of the house. They had FBI emblazoned on
their jackets. By some accounts, Perzel was there in the car. The house was being
raided! Drachler ever so slowly backed up and took off. By November, Seyfert was
indicted. By May 2000, as part of a plea bargain, she pleaded guilty to theft of
federal property and conspiring to intimidate a witness. Again, the sad story was
that the cover-up was worse than the crime. The conspiracy charge involving witness intimidation was a felony, while the theft charge was a misdemeanor. Seyfert
was sentenced to six months in prison.

After a brief hiatus, Keystone State corruption made its debut in the 21st
century.

9

Hubris

July 7, 2005

I watched in disbelief as six legislative leaders, without comment, rammed through a conference committee report for a massive pay increase for themselves, judges and top state officials. It was after midnight. I was bone-tired from chasing rumors, writing several stories, and reviving myself with half-cold pizza. Or was it Chinese? It was one or the other during these late-night sessions. And it had all become a blur. It was the eighth or ninth straight late night during the past two weeks.

The Pennsylvania legislature was in its final throes before adjourning for the summer. They were going to top it all off by approving H.B. 1521 for executive branch compensation. It was a vote that would change state history.

Copies of the conference report were not available. The bill had been "gutted" and replaced with the pay increase for all three branches. No numbers were provided on the dollar amount or percentage increases. The leaders sat there stone-faced, almost as if they were pretending a dozen or so reporters crammed into the tiny hearing room on the capitol's second floor weren't even there. Save for one, they refused to talk to journalists after the vote. Senate Minority Leader Robert Mellow, a Lackawanna County Democrat, stopped to answer a few questions. I've always admired him for having the guts to do that when no one else would.

The House leaders also bolted from the room: then Majority Leader Sam Smith, a Punxsutawney Republican; David Argall (R–Schuylkill) and Mike Veon, the Beaver Falls Democrat; Senate President Pro Tempore Robert Jubelirer (R–Altoona), who came into the Senate as a reformer, and Senate Majority Leader

David Brightbill (R–Lebanon). In particular, Argall, an academic, looked sheepish. He was working on and would eventually earn a doctoral degree in political science. He knew better. Mellow didn't exactly hold a news conference. He talked to a couple of reporters who followed him and stopped him in a hallway.

I've been to plenty of other legislative hearings where changes in a bill were kept out of the public's hands until after the vote. Here they weren't even releasing what they just voted on. The totality of their action was deplorable. Even in the bad old days there was more disclosure. In 1983, Governor Dick Thornburgh, Senate President Pro Tempore Henry Hager and others held a news conference several hours before a pay raise vote to provide details and to take the heat. Even that was shabby disclosure, with no chance for the public to react. Still, I distinctly remember the pipe-smoking John Scotzin of *The Patriot-News,* dean of the press corps, pointedly challenging the governor and other leaders.

The vote was 119-79 in the House and 27-23 in the Senate.

Cynical as I am, this was the worst demonstration of democracy I'd seen before or since in Harrisburg. Journalists typically keep their emotions out of stories. But this one really fired me up. We had witnessed democracy being trampled.

What took place at 2:00 a.m. on July 7, 2005 was legal but nonetheless an act of corruption. The infamous pay raise vote was hatched in secrecy. The details were kept out of taxpayers' view. There was no public hearing. And legislators approved the pay package without any floor debate. Much later, Representative Tom Tangretti (D–Greensburg), a "no" vote, would apologize to his constituents for not speaking up. As citizen activist Eric Epstein put it years later, "The moral crime was that legislators believed they were above the law."

Russ Diamond, a Lebanon businessman who would become an activist at the epicenter of the discontent, remembered it this way: "For all intents and purposes, they stood right on the capitol steps and flipped us all the bird." So he wrote in *Tip of the Spear,* a book on his experiences in fighting the pay hike: That was the same general notion noted in a July 8, 2007 *Pittsburgh Tribune-Review* editorial: "[*Expletive*] *you* is the clear message from the gang of reprobates who give public service a bad name."

For lawmakers, it was a base 16 percent increase to $81,027, making them the second highest paid legislature in the nation. If they were rank-and-file, committee chairmen or leaders, they received more. Committee chairmen, for instance, got 28 percent increases to $89,1555. Majority and minority leaders were slated for 34 percent increases to $124,788. The top two leaders, speaker and president pro tempore, got a 34 percent boost to $145,553. Judges and top members of Governor Ed Rendell's administration got sizeable boosts.

THE "LAST" PAY RAISE

None of this was supposed to happen. In 1995, Majority Leader John Perzel pushed through what he claimed would be the last pay raise vote. The bill, in addition to a healthy increase in salary, provided an automatic annual cost-of-living increase tied to the Consumer Price Index in the greater Philadelphia area, which is generally more affluent than Pennsyl-tucky and the Pittsburgh region. But 10 years later, it wasn't enough. And Perzel, once again, was a conspirator in jacking lawmakers' pay.

"Perhaps because of Perzel's 1995 declaration, perhaps because they already were so well compensated and knew they would be seen as greedy, lawmakers didn't have the guts to begin a public debate about the question for fear of being unable to win it," said Timothy Potts, co-founder of Democracy Rising PA.

There'd been rumblings for weeks. In late June and early July 2005, I had been actively pursuing a story about a possible legislative pay raise. But security was tight. Then Governor Ed Rendell had invited a pay hike, suggesting he'd consider it if lawmakers approved the higher social spending he sought. I wrote one or two speculative stories about what was under consideration. But the numbers weren't certain. And sources weren't willing to go on the record about it.

The budget was late in 2005, as it was every year under Rendell. He thought the legal requirement for a budget by June 30th was superseded by the need for a good budget. To him, that meant one that spent more.

Former Supreme Court Chief Justice Ralph Cappy had pushed for a pay boost for judges behind the scenes. If that wasn't a sure-fire guarantee that the high court would uphold a raise if they passed one, I don't know what is.

QUID PRO QUO?

But there was more. On June 22, 2005, the Pennsylvania Supreme Court upheld most of the state's new slot machine law, creating the first casinos in the state. Lawmakers like John Perzel , Vince Fumo and Ed Rendell had a political stake in the casino law being upheld in court.

Some would later call it a trade-off for the pay raise. There's no proof, but the timing was questionable. Was it coincidental? It appeared to give powerful leaders what they wanted before they would stick their necks out on the pay hike. Some believe the mere appearance adds up to something.

"The pay raise was a quid pro quo arrangement between all three branches of government to increase compensation in exchange for legislation," said Eric Epstein.

It does seem there was a conspiracy among the branches to raise pay. But there's no evidence to suggest judicial decisions were made in a quid pro quo manner. Two days after the pay bill passed and was signed into law, Rendell remarked, "It's legal and that's all I am going to say about that."

LEGAL?

The bill contained a provision to circumvent the state constitution so lawmakers could get the pay in their current term of office. The constitution prohibited mid-term pay hikes. It holds that lawmakers should have to stand for election before collecting a pay raise they've passed. The bill enabled legislators to take the increase as "unvouchered expenses." That term sounded important, but it only meant they didn't have to account for the money — the difference between the previous salary and the higher one. They had to choose that option if they wanted the cash. It was a backdoor way of getting the raise right away. Legislators, even those who voted against the bill, lined up to claim the higher pay.

Of 253 legislators, 158 took claimed unvouchered expenses. In other words, they took the pay raise early. Among House members, 131 members took the pay while still in office and 27 senators did likewise.

THE REFORM EFFORT IS BORN

The pay raise was a seminal event in Pennsylvania's early 21st-century history. It spawned the first genuine reform movement I've seen in state politics, though it would eventually dwindle to a small core group of activists. It prompted dozens of lawmakers to retire early rather than face the voters' wrath. Other incumbents were mowed down at the polls in 2006. Many survived. In all, about 50 new members would take office in 2007. The pay raise, directly or indirectly, changed the face of legislative leadership. Following the pay raise fiasco, leadership "fell like a house of cards" in the view of polling analyst Christopher Borick, a political science professor at Muhlenberg College in Allentown.

The issue had struck a chord with the public. It was something they innately understood. The pay raise symbolized the "culture of arrogance," particularly among legislative leaders, and the "sense of entitlement" in Harrisburg, said Borick. No one in the private sector, except maybe on Wall Street, got these kinds of increases.

A RECKONING

The pay raise set the tone, just two years later, for Attorney General Tom Corbett to pursue the prosecution of powerful legislative leaders for abuses with under-the-table bonuses.

"The political ash that was secreted from the pay raise volcano created the fertile ground that made Bonusgate possible, if not inevitable," Eric Epstein noted at the time. It was almost a reckoning for virtually every leader who was complicit.

By 2012, only two of the conferees remained: Sam Smith and David Argall. Robert Jubelirer and David Brightbill were defeated in the 2006 primary, Mike Veon lost in the general election to Republican challenger Jim Marshall. Veon would later be charged with using public resources for campaigns. *The Inquirer* reported that Robert Mellow was under federal investigation for having the state pay rent for his district office from a company co-owned by his ex-wife and later himself. He was charged by federal authorities in March 2012 with conspiracy for using Pennsylvania Senate staff and resources for campaigns. Mellow agreed to plead guilty and apparently he lost his $138,959 annual pension, but he chose to appeal that loss.

Among other top leaders at the time, Perzel, facing criminal charges, would lose re-election in 2010; Fumo did not seek re-election in March 2008 while under federal indictment. Bill DeWeese was charged in December 2009 and would retain his seat the following year while facing charges filed by Tom Corbett. Representative Steve Stetler, a York Democrat, was a member of the House leadership who voted for the raise. By 2009, then a member of Ed Rendell's cabinet, he would be charged along with DeWeese for using public resources for campaigns. Former House Appropriations Chairman Brett Feese, a former Lycoming County DA, eventually became one of Perzel's co-defendants for his actions as chief counsel for Republicans. Perzel would testify against him. Feese was convicted of 40 felonies in 2012.

But there was another link between the pay hike and Bonusgate, which would not become apparent until years later. Former Democratic staffers testifying against Bill DeWeese in January 2012 said after the pay raise that DeWeese and Mike Veon were fearful of losing their seats. They increased the pressure on subordinates to campaign for them. Many staffers wanting to be good employees realized the harder they worked on the campaign side, the happier their boss would be. There was also an intrinsic value for the legislative assistant. If the boss lost, the assistant might well be out of work. In Mike Veon's case, there were actual cash bonuses for "volunteering."

This created an absolute mania about winning at all costs. DeWeese, for instance, according to one ex-aide, had seen as many as 100 staffers helping out at various points in Veon's tough primary contest. And Michael Manzo, DeWeese's former chief of staff, said his boss wanted "a Veon-esque effort" for himself in the fall campaign. It was a delicious twist. Just when you'd think leaders would be hurrying up to pass reforms to atone for the pay hike, in reality — though no one on the outside knew it — they were scrambling to survive and in some cases condoning or encouraging illegal activity.

The vitriolic pay-hike reaction was largely based in Central and Western Pennsylvania. In Philadelphia, it was mostly a non-issue, perhaps because so many municipal functionaries are paid more than $81,000, or because people are just so jaded that they expect this type of behavior from their public officials.

"THEY FLIPPED US THE BIRD"

The controversy was stoked by talk radio hosts. And newspapers assumed an adversarial role unlike any that had ever existed. But legislative staffers, quick to dismiss the genuine reaction and blame the media, were out of touch. Most of our stories published online these days include our phone number and email address. My voicemail lit up unlike anything before or since with mostly Western Pennsylvania readers calling to make their views known.

One thing legislators didn't count on was the staying power of guys like Eric Epstein, Timothy Potts, Russ Diamond and Gene Stilp, the real nucleus of reform groups over the next seven years. Changes were initiated around the edges, limiting how bills could be considered and eliminating late sessions. But save for the ban on middle-of-the-night action, there was erosion of other rules as the years passed.

G. Terry Madonna, the political scientist from Franklin and Marshall College who wrote the Preface to this book, is the best polling analyst I've come across in this business: sharp insight, fast and to the point, knowledgeable about everything Harrisburg. He's all of that and more. But Terry was off-base in the first week or so after the pay raise, predicting it would blow over. I had to agree with him, based on the history of pay raises.

We were both wrong. Lawmakers were counting on the issue fading away. They blew out of town on July 7th, and a deathly silence ensued. The unwillingness of legislative leaders — and members — to engage in any debate or defend the pay raise charged the atmosphere even more. But the factor we neglected, and legislative leaders most surely ignored, was the power of the Internet.

The so-called reformers kept the pressure up. These were ordinary guys, though Stilp and Epstein had long histories as anti-nuclear protestors. That experience came in handy in taking on the legislature; they thrived on controversy and confrontation. Potts had inside experience as a former press secretary for the Department of Education and for DeWeese. He knew how things worked. Stilp was trained as a lawyer and was willing to sue anyone who breathed.

Eric Epstein was street-smart and exceedingly bright. He could turn a phrase for a great quote better than the spinmeisters paid by taxpayers (who were saying nothing). Stilp had gimmicks galore and would eventually come up with the symbol of the anti-pay-raise movement: an inflatable, 25-foot-long pink pig. He traveled to lawmakers' districts in a beat-up bus with pig décor. Russ Diamond was a computer-savvy, hard-nosed guy with killer instincts. As he memorably put it, "They flipped us the bird and I was prepared to flip it right back."

Combined, the four activists became the focal point of anger against the Pennsylvania legislature. And believe me, they were truly despised by many lawmakers and staffers.

WEAK "D"

What happened is that in a two-month period, July and August 2007, the pay raise opponents totally controlled the message that went out to the public. There was no defense, or very little of one, save for brief comments by John Perzel to the Associated Press.

At 5:00 a.m. on July 18, 2007, Russ Diamond hit the key and launched a website, PACleanSweep.com. It would become *the* resource for taxpayers angry over the pay raise and the cry for repeal. The intent was also clear: to oust incumbent state lawmakers. The site featured a "Hall of Shame" for legislators who voted for the pay raise

The grousing was considerable from legislative staffers and some lawmakers about this crew of reformers. Some were wannabe lawmakers and indeed Diamond and Stilp had run or would continue to run for state and congressional seats. They loved to see their names in headlines. Privately, staffers were bad-mouthing the reform crew as irresponsible or wrong on the facts here or there. Most of all, they were viewed as grandstanders. This was seen by many as their 15 minutes of fame. I found the reformers to be surprisingly accurate, dedicated and trustworthy.

The other rap on the activists is that (with the exception of Russ Diamond) they were thinly disguised liberal Democrats posing as nonpartisans. Diamond was somewhere between a Republican and an Independent. The criticism never bothered me because the reformers went after both Republicans and Democrats. In the months after the pay raise, whenever legislative leaders would pierce the wall of silence to say something, they did so to their own detriment.

In an effort to show he was tough, like that iron-fisted Democrat of the 1970s and '80s, Jim Manderino, Bill DeWeese, the minority leader, put out word he was stripping 15 Democrats of their seats as subcommittee chairmen because they had voted against the pay raise. The chairmen would lose their $4,050 stipend. How out of touch could you get? This came out in late July, when the public was fuming about the pay raise, and here was DeWeese punishing lawmakers for voting against it.

He got burned badly on that move because John Perzel had apparently agreed to take the same action against Republican chairmen. At least DeWeese thought so. Perhaps sensing the rising tide, Perzel did nothing. The action left Bill DeWeese hanging out in the wind, and left Democrats questioning why DeWeese did it and Perzel didn't.

On August 31st, Perzel was in Harrisburg for the first time since the pay raise. While his members were battered over the pay hike, he had been in China on a trip sponsored by Chinese-American business interests, according to *The Philadelphia Inquirer.* He'd also been planning a gubernatorial bid in 2010.

In hopes of changing the debate, Perzel's office invited reporters to attend the Speaker's Golden Apple Award for Education Innovation. All they wanted to ask about was the pay raise issue he'd been ducking. In response Perzel referred incongruously to U.S. jobs moving to China.

As *The Inquirer* reported in a story by Mario Cattabiani and John Sullivan: "When asked about the pay raise, Perzel again responded with a comment about job flight overseas. 'So you are refusing to talk about the pay raise?' a reporter asked. 'I didn't refuse to talk about the pay raise,' Perzel said. 'There is nothing to talk about. It was passed July 7th.'" Reporters tried to follow him after the event, but Perzel wasn't talking.

THE PINK PIG

In September, the activists, interest groups and talk-radio types sponsored an anti-pay-raise rally. The pink pig presided over the event. Participants chanted, "Repeal, repay, reform or resign." WHP Radio host Bob Durgin, the conservative voice of Central Pennsylvania, riled up the crowd of at least 1,000. Led by Durgin, a smaller contingent demanded to see Perzel and the governor. Aides were sent out to appease the crowds and to talk Durgin down.

David Brightbill ordered his staff to place a wide-angle photo of the crowd on large grid paper (so that people could be counted per grid) in an effort to downplay the crowd's size. The idea that the leadership would go to such lengths in a defensive gesture showed how bad matters had gotten. The photo hangs proudly above my desk.

Then, in October, in an event that almost seemed scripted for fiction, John Perzel faltered badly when he delivered books to Beechwood Elementary School in Pittsburgh. The media was invited to watch the Speaker's educational outreach. A fourth grader asked if Perzel had come in a limo. "I came in a car," he said to the boy within earshot of reporters. His driver was still waiting in a black Lincoln Town Car with limousine plates, the *Tribune-Review*'s Debra Erdley and David Brown reported.

While speaking to the students, Perzel stood against a backdrop of paper cutouts of piggy banks and dollar bills. From a PR perspective, it was stunningly bad. Gene Stilp's pink pig was widely associated with the pay raise. The issue Perzel still refused to address was clearly identified in the photo of him inside the school against a backdrop of piggies. Perzel's staff would later spread the word that he had been "set up" by the *Tribune-Review*. The *Trib*'s reporters and photographer had nothing to do with the piggy motif in the backdrop. Moreover, Perzel chose to stand there. It was just bad mojo from that pay raise.

There was an element of organization to the opposition. Established groups such as the Commonwealth Foundation, Common Cause and the League of Women Voters were pushing for repeal. I attended one umbrella group meeting where they planned the rally and developed strategies. I had to agree that the strategy session was off the record. No other reporters were invited. I didn't participate, but just listened. It was clear they were in for the long haul.

There was no way, I believed, that the pay raise would be repealed. These leaders believed in their own power. But they continued to get beat up over the way it was done. The two and a half months they spent in their own districts made it harder to live with than if they'd been in Harrisburg.

Repeal bills were filed, but leaders made it clear they'd never see the light of day. Senator Jim Ferlo (D–Pittsburgh) was the first legislator to address it on the floor of either chamber. There was a message that some lawmakers wouldn't let it go. Was it possible they'd roll back the pay hike? I still doubted it.

"GOING FOR BLOOD"

In November 2005, I was home, delirious with fever from an infection I acquired in a hospital while there for major surgery. I had to take off work, starting in late October, and I was focused on the surgery. After the operation, I was pretty sick. Two different antibiotics, taken back to back, wouldn't break the infection. I still was carrying my cell phone, but I no longer was a 24-7 news junkie. So I reacted with disbelief when I first heard they were going to repeal the pay raise.

The *Trib* sent Mike Wereschagin to Harrisburg during my illness and recovery. Mike is the superb young reporter who previously worked in Harrisburg as an intern for the Pennsylvania Legislative Correspondents Association. I'd worked with him then and I thought the world of him. When Jim Cuddy was looking to fill a reporter position, he called me about Mike. He wanted to know what I thought of him. I don't remember exactly what I said beyond a strong recommendation to hire him. What I should have said is, "Can you find 10 just like him?" Mike went on to become the *Trib*'s star reporter, at least in my opinion.

In an incredible November 20, 2005 article, Wereschagin told the behind-the-scenes story of the repeal. He wrote that the "end came so suddenly, and from a source so unexpected, none of the leaders could stop it." He told the story of how Robert Jubelirer cajoled the other leaders into repealing the unvouchered expense portion of the raise. He had shepherded the increase through the legislature.

Jubelirer's district was more conservative than those of most of the other leaders. It was also more rural. He became convinced that he could not win re-election with the pay raise intact. He'd seen polling data. But I also believe that he knew it was wrong. Jubelirer had come into the legislature as a reformer in 1975. Other leaders weren't exactly thrilled at his suggestion. It would stir the pot again. And after all, they'd made a deal.

"The fact is we were getting nothing done," Jubelirer told Wereschagin. "It dominated everything. And I felt the time had come to absolutely listen to the public out there."

"I did what I thought was right," Jubelirer told the *Trib*.

After Jubelirer visited Robert Mellow to break the news — he was the highest-ranking Senate Democrat — Mellow called other Democratic leaders. "I never saw it coming," he admitted.

Bill DeWeese was working out at a nearby gym when his chief of staff, Mike Manzo, called him to say, "Jubelirer is getting ready to blow up the train." When DeWeese finally connected with Jubelirer, he asked the senator, "How can you do this unilaterally?"

Well, he couldn't do it unilaterally, but as the highest elected Senate Republican, he could damn well make sure the repeal bill was unleashed. To Jubelirer, repeal at that point meant repealing the unvouchered expenses.

"Jubelirer seemed to be beset by an extravagant case of the jitters," DeWeese remarked.

The problem politically was Jubelirer's half-baked approach. Some of the Senate Democrats, Jim Ferlo in particular, were prepared to amend any bill to repeal unvouchered expenses into a full repeal of the entire raise. "I said, 'I'm going for blood. If they introduce that, I'm going for the full repeal," he declared. You've got to know Ferlo. That's exactly how he talks. Ferlo is stunningly blunt. He pulls no punches. He had voted against the raise.

Former Senator Sean Logan had also voted against the pay hike, but he signed up for unvouchered expenses. He took the first payment. Logan saw just how bad the mood was with the public. He became the first Western Pennsylvania legislator to return the money.

Republicans held back on their partial repeal language to prevent the Democrats from drafting an amendment. Democrats talked to Lieutenant Governor Catherine Baker Knoll, a Democrat who presided over the Senate, urging her to call on Logan first. She did and Logan proposed a full repeal bill.

The legislation would become a state capitol version of ping pong. But it was only a matter of time. Once this force had been unleashed, lawmakers could not go home for the year without passing it. One of the hang-ups, and this would play out later, was a constitutional prohibition on reducing judicial salaries during the judges' term of office. The debate ensued over a repeal for solely legislative and executive branches — or to repeal the raises for all branches. In the end, the entire bill was repealed on November 16, 2005 — almost unanimously. One legislator, Mike Veon no less, voted against it.

But the judges got theirs.

The pay raise for about 1,100 judges would be reinstated by the Pennsylvania Supreme Court in September 2006. That meant that salaries for Common Pleas Court judges jumped from $130,600 a year to about $149,000. Pay for Supreme Court justices shot up from $150,436 a year to $171,800. Salaries for Superior and Commonwealth Court judges were boosted from $145,658 a year to $162,100. Lawmakers who took the unvouchered expenses were not required to pay them back. They would pay a price for keeping the money.

Eric Epstein in particular made his mission in life to track the money and annually expose those who failed to pay it back. Epstein is a holocaust scholar and the co-author (with Philip Rosen) of *Dictionary of the Holocaust*. His painstaking research in compiling not only key words and Yiddish phrases but places and people, from Nazis to victims, was useful in documenting pay grabbers. Epstein focused on pension payouts and how they were "bumped" by unvouchered expenses. He reminds me of an accomplished Israeli Nazi hunter.

In 2012, Rock the Capital was still issuing reports on pay raise-related offenses.

Russ Diamond walked away from the pay-raise episode with a bitter aftertaste.

"The Pennsylvania General Assembly is a world all its own, almost completely removed from reality," Diamond remarked. "The 2005 pay-raise fiasco was merely a symptom of that atmosphere. While it struck a public nerve and goaded the electorate into action against particular members of the legislature, the way business is done under the capitol dome has not changed at all. That's the sad part, because while the pay raise was a major victory for the people — in that we managed to get it reversed — business in Harrisburg is still conducted the same way on much more important matters that have infinitely deeper and more damaging effects on liberty and quality of life for Pennsylvania's citizens."

Next: the defining criminal case from an unlikely suspect.

10

The Dweeb

March 11, 2004

Representative Jeffrey Habay always looked out for the taxpayers unless they happened to work for him. In 1994, at age 28, Habay became the youngest member of the Allegheny County Republican House delegation. Some later would write that he was "a rising star" in the Republican Party, but I didn't see it. A rising star in his own mind, perhaps.

From suburban Pittsburgh in Shaler Township, Habay took office when former Republican governor Tom Ridge was sworn in, and he served without distinction for a decade. He was a back-bencher but for his title of "deputy whip," a bone party leaders threw to him that meant nothing more than a dressed-up letterhead.

A decade after taking office, Habay became big news in Pittsburgh and Harrisburg when, out of the blue, a state Ethics Commission decision surfaced stating that Habay forced his staff to campaign for him. He threatened one employee with loss of health insurance because the employee did not want to attend a fundraiser on the lawmaker's behalf.

According to their testimony, Habay required employees to work on fundraisers, stuff campaign mailings, make fundraising phone calls and post political signs. Before election day, he lined up employees along Route 28 and Route 8 to wave at motorists — the "Habay wave" to show enthusiasm for his candidacy.

Having employees do political work on state time was nothing new. But the notion that employees were forced to do it gave it a menacing edge. The idea that a state agency was going after him for doing so put things in another light.

The Ethics Commission ruling on Jeffrey Habay's case in 2004 and subsequent events changed the legal landscape for state lawmakers. The ruling would indirectly lead to a felony conviction for Habay. But his appeal, decided by the Superior Court and authored by former Allegheny County District Attorney Bob Colville in 2007, would provide state prosecutors with the tool to go after corruption ingrained in Pennsylvania capitol culture.

*   *   *

State political leaders in Pennsylvania by and large weren't getting rich through the use of public resources. But the use of taxpayers' resources to further a politician's career was deemed to be a crime in Colville's decision in the Habay case. He held that there is a personal as well as a political gain.

Habay's legacy became the landmark appellate court decision, which indirectly helped change the face of leadership in the General Assembly. It said that a lawmaker is "not allowed to direct paid state employees under his authority to conduct campaign and or fundraising-related work during state time for his personal benefit." Such work, Colville wrote, amounted to a "private monetary advantage" for the lawmaker, who "obtained the benefit of free campaign work funded by the taxpayers." Colville, who provided the roadmap for future prosecutions, hired Tom Corbett as an assistant district attorney in the 1970s. Taxpayer-funded campaigns helped to re-elect lawmakers, who personally benefited by continuing to collect salaries, state pension contributions, health care and the array of perks paid by taxpayers.

Despite the Habay case, campaign work at taxpayer expense continued among Republicans and Democrats in the Pennsylvania House from 2004 through 2006. The revelation of Habay's campaign abuse charges did nothing to stop the use of tax money for re-election efforts — including the bonus scheme, fundraising at the state capitol, email blasts and sophisticated computer programs that House Republicans purchased.

By the time Colville ruled on Habay's appeal in 2007, Corbett, then state attorney general, had initiated his investigation into the House Democrats' use of bonuses. The ruling, on many levels, was a gift.

Tom Corbett was an aggressive Republican prosecutor who had his eye on becoming governor. He could cite a Superior Court ruling by Bob Colville, the former Democratic DA and his former boss that laid the groundwork for prosecutions of campaign-related abuses. There was evidence that something was severely amiss: $3.62 million in 2005–06 spent on an under-the-table bonus program in all four caucuses. Those bonuses distorted — by underreporting — the public salaries of top legislative staffers. House Democrats topped out at $2.3 million, followed by House Republicans at $919,000 and Senate Republicans at $366,000. The Senate Democrats were the only caucus without substantial bonuses ($41,000). In part that's because Senator Vincent Fumo paid inflated salaries to Democratic staffers doing personal and political work for him. It's not clear how much of the $3.62 million in bonuses overall paid staffers for political work. House Democrats used at least $1.4 million for campaign purposes, prosecutors say. Even without the campaign work, the bonuses were fundamentally wrong because they were a secret salary supplement.

Corbett, the former U.S. Attorney in Pittsburgh who acted more as a prosecutor than a politician, later said when he filed charges against 10 members of his Republican Party in November 2009 that Jeffrey Habay's conviction and sentencing should have put legislators on notice that authorities would not tolerate campaign work on the taxpayers' dime. It was not only wrong but illegal. The appellate court upheld his conviction.

Habay hardly could have known that his ordeal would become the lynchpin of statewide prosecutions of other legislators. A conservative populist steadfastly against higher taxes, Habay also was transparently self-serving. Despite his best efforts to convince people otherwise, he came off as a politician who cared about one thing only: Jeff Habay. He charmed voters with his boyish looks: slightly puffy cheeks, brown hair and a nice smile. He lived, breathed and ate politics. Habay was a devoted conservative, some would say an ideologue. Smart and aggressive, he could sell himself — much like a time-share salesman.

Habay once told me he stayed up past midnight to read *The Tribune-Review* online in stories where he'd been named — postings before the print edition hit the streets. Habay was certainly affable and accessible to reporters. The American University grad had a lot going for him, but there was a character flaw that I missed.

Habay's ego, his drive to succeed, went haywire in his battle with a former staffer and her husband who challenged him. It was as if nothing was going to stop him from his career goals of serving in the state Senate — and beyond that, who knows? His ambition gene had metastasized.

I have to say that I didn't see it at the time. Even after the ethics ruling was handed down, I reserved judgment. I probably would have said that Jeff Habay seemed honest — as much as you can say that about any politician. I did think that he was slightly off-center; odd, maybe even goofy. He was the quintessential dweeb.

A bizarre twist took place by the time of Habay's downfall. In an effort to discredit an antagonist — George Radich, the husband of a former employee — he mailed to himself a packet of white powder. He tried to make it appear as if Radich, an Allegheny County Port Authority worker, threatened him with anthrax. Radich's wife, Rebecca, quit her job with Habay over the dual role of legislative aide and campaigner. He later pleaded no contest to 21 charges in connection with the phony anthrax mailing.

With George Radich, Jeffrey Habay messed with the wrong guy. Radich was a contributor and volunteer for Habay's campaigns when his spouse was in good standing with the lawmaker. Later, he was unrelenting in his pursuit of proving wrongdoing by Habay. He would call reporters to let them know about developments in the case. He represented himself in court along with some others in a civil complaint over Habay's campaign finances, which did not amount to much.

By all appearances, Habay was not by well liked in the House even before his world began to unravel. When the General Assembly was considering a bailout package for the cash-strapped city of Pittsburgh in 2003, three Allegheny County Republican House members came to the capitol newsroom to share their views on the near-final legislation. Habay arrived late. Representative Mike Turzai (R–Bradford Woods) slowly backed away. Two other Republicans did an about-face and walked out.

The Ethics Commission ruling didn't become public until 2004, but Habay knew. He received a copy of the complaint in 2002. He argued that he was targeted and ostracized because he had angered power brokers in the Republican Party by steadfastly opposing public funding for Pittsburgh's baseball and football stadiums. When former state senator Melissa Hart, a McCandless Republican, won election to Congress, the county's party leaders passed on endorsing Habay for her seat. Instead they backed Representative Jane Orie, another McCandless Republican. (In 2010, Orie became a prosecutor's target: charged with corruption by Allegheny County DA Stephen Zappala, a Democrat, for allegedly using her Senate staff to work on the Supreme Court campaign of her sister, Joan Orie Melvin.)

Beneath his populist exterior, Habay was a boss who directed his staff to do more than handle nominating petitions for his campaigns. He asked them to dig up dirt on a Pittsburgh TV reporter, Alan Jennings, whose news reports irritated Habay. Someone tipped off Jennings that Habay and some friends shot up his opponent's campaign signs, and Jennings wound up on Habay's enemies list.

As the ethics case unfolded, there was doubt about the allegations since they came primarily from disgruntled employees. But the Ethics Commission said the weight of all the evidence made it impossible to dismiss the testimony of former employees, whatever their motivation. The commission said Jeff Habay was not a credible witness.

Late one afternoon, I received a call from one of Habay's employees. I didn't know him well, but I knew that he had a solid reputation. He could not go public at that time. But he called to let me know that what happened in Habay's office was out of the norm and far out of bounds.

The story I did with Andrew Conte in *The Tribune-Review,* published on June 18, 2004, when the Ethics Commission released its decision, summarized the context of the allegations against Jeffrey Habay in the backdrop of the tradition of politicking by staffers at the capitol. The Habay decision was made public after the commission dismissed Habay's appeal. Ethics Commission complaints and hearings are secret until a case is final. It was decided on March 11, 2004.

Our story stated that campaign activity in legislative offices was the norm. Yet the magnitude of Habay's abuse seemed unusual. What he was accused of probably was the norm 20 or 30 years ago but not in 2004, said G. Terry Madonna, the famed Pennsylvania pollster. Neither Madonna nor anyone else could have known about the extensive Democratic and GOP schemes under way at that point.

"I have from time to time observed it on a slow Friday or in the summer (of election years) at the capitol," said Barry Kauffman, executive director of Common Cause of Pennsylvania.

We know now that Democrat Mike Veon and Republican John Perzel were ramping up their theft of taxpayers' dollars during this period. What struck me was the compulsory nature of Habay's campaign work, which would surface again later in the case against House Democrats with allegations by a grand jury witness that Veon's chief of staff Jeffrey Foreman struck one woman as "the grim reaper" with his sweeps through the office to get campaigners. Older staffers with kids dreaded those roundups. It was inherent in the boss/employee relationship that if you turned down campaigning often enough, you could lose your job. Jeff Habay's contribution to history was indirectly helping to change the face of leadership in the General Assembly.

In the next chapter, we look at "The Lion of the Legislature." The Habay ruling would be critical to his fate.

Former House Speaker John Perzel, a Northeast Philadelphia Republican, in handcuffs at his arraignment in 2009.
Photo by Joe Appel, *Pittsburgh Tribune-Review.*

The Pennsylvania Capitol is a monument to graft. A scandal related to massive overcharges resulted in the conviction of several officials in the early 20th century.
Photo by Brad Bumsted.

They called him "Big Griz." This monument to crooked political boss Boise Penrose stands near the Capitol.
Photo by Brad Bumsted.

Former U.S. Attorney Dick Thornburgh aggressively pursued political corruption and sent prominent Democrats to jail.
Courtesy of the Dick Thornburgh Papers, University of Pittsburgh.

Reformer Eric Epstein never quit. Seven years after the infamous pay raise, he still tracked lawmakers who kept the money.

Photo by Lindsey Bumsted.

Eugene Stilp exhorts the crowd at an anti-pay-raise rally in September 2005. Citizen anger prompted lawmakers to repeal the pay increase.

Photo by Bruce Shannon, Raintree Multimedia.

Former Representative Jeffrey Habay's conviction for conflict of interest became the foundation of the later Bonusgate prosecutions.

Photo by Justin Merriman, *Pittsburgh Tribune-Review.*

Harrisburg *Patriot-News* reporters Charlie Thompson and Jan Murphy broke the Bonusgate story that sent shockwaves through the political establishment.

Photo by Brad Bumsted.

Former House Democratic Whip Mike Veon faced criminal charges for approving illegal bonuses to legislative staffers for campaigning.
Photo by Jasmine Goldband, *Pittsburgh Tribune-Review.*

Former Senator Vincent Fumo, the premier powerbroker in Pennsylvania politics, was cunning, ruthless and charming.
Photo by Christine Baker, Harrisburg *Patriot-News.*

Former House Speaker Bill DeWeese escaped charges in Bonusgate, but he was later prosecuted by the Pennsylvania Attorney General. His lawyer, William C. Costopoulos, is at right.

Photo by Lindsey Bumsted.

Mike Veon and his staff at a Beaver County fundraiser. Prosecutors said that Veon approved charging state taxpayers for his staffers' expenses. Not all of the former employees shown in this photo were charged or accused of wrongdoing.

Photographer unknown.

11

The Lion of the Legislature

November 7, 2006

Bill DeWeese once told me he considered Mike Veon "The Lion of the Legislature." He believed Veon was one of the best legislators he'd ever seen. Veon was smart, some would say a brilliant strategist. He understood complex issues. But most of all, he was a student of politics. He knew the dynamics of the caucus, the House, the governor, what the Republicans wanted, and how to negotiate.

Mike Veon had this stare. He would use it on staffers who screwed up, or during negotiations with other legislative leaders. He would sit patiently in a meeting, saying nothing, until the time was right. If you spoke first, you lost.

I've seen the stare. When Veon was at the zenith of his power a few years ago, I could not reach him for comment about having the highest expenses of any legislator attending a National Conference of State Legislatures meeting. I staked out a meeting he was attending and finally caught up with him.

"Is that the best you can do? NCSL?" Veon asked mockingly. He tried to stare me down and I ignored it. He had no further comment.

At the time, Veon knew there was far more to uncover; he believed the media would never touch him. To his Democratic colleagues, Mike Veon was more than a leader. He was cool. Take Representative Todd Eachus (D–Luzerne County), a Veon protégé, who would become majority leader in 2009. Eachus "hero-worshipped Veon, as did about half of the House Democrats," Capitolwire Bureau Chief Peter L. DeCoursey wrote. "People forget now, but if the House Democrats were the cast of *Happy Days,* Veon was 'Fonzie,' the coolest of the cool." The same 2006 column called Mike Veon "a charismatic guy who is willing to reward friends and punish his enemies."

In Harrisburg, Veon frequently worked until the early morning hours and often slept on a couch in his office. He would typically go home briefly around 7:00 a.m. to shower and change. Outside of being a clotheshorse and appreciating expensive cigars and Harley-Davidson motorcycles, Veon led a Spartan existence, former staffers and lawmakers say. He didn't put the arm on lobbyists for five-hour, five-course dinners. His one active indulgence was the pickup basketball games he loosely organized on Tuesday nights with other lawmakers and staffers, an occasional reporter or others hanging out by the court. His office picked up the tab for the dinners, and state staffers got the food and set up the post-game meals for lawmakers.

In one of the basketball games at Harrisburg Area Community College, Veon lost a tooth after taking an elbow to the chops. He calmly walked to the edge of the court, placed the tooth on the floor, and returned to the game without saying a word. In the pickup basketball games, Veon, though only five feet 10 inches, played "big." A former participant recalled that he would forget where Mike was on the court, then all of a sudden he'd see him, and he loomed much larger than his size. He'd snare rebounds against much taller opponents.

Veon kept peanut butter, kashi cereal and oatmeal in his office. When he brought in food, it was often fruit and vegetables. Even on the nights of the basketball dinners, he typically shunned the Chinese, Thai, Mexican or Indian carry-out food picked up and arranged by his staff and instead stuck to his simple diet. He'd usually have kashi. There were splurges at taxpayers' expense after some basketball games — salmon imperial, filet mignon and clams casino. Still, Veon stuck to his staples.

Veon was an introvert. He didn't like to socialize. Even though his office would be an after-hours meeting place on Tuesdays for a group of younger lawmakers who idolized him, he would frequently be working on his computer or making calls. Veon envisioned his district office as a congressional service office. He had about 26 staffers in Harrisburg and the district. The districts surrounding his were part of his turf and he would defend them. He created several nonprofits, got them state money and considered them an extension of his district office. Especially in his few final years in the House, he was most comfortable in his bunker — the basement of his district office — smoking cigars and working by himself.

Legislators who heard there was a party on Tuesday nights in Veon's Harrisburg office usually left disappointed after discovering a seminar on all aspects of the Democrats' legislation. Sometimes there was alcohol; more often, cigars. Those who stayed would often get "schooled" on what they never realized went into the preparation for the next day's session. While there was often a side card game of Spades, there was a constant dialogue about legislation, amendments, the Democrats' message, timing, legislative personalities, public perception, polling and national politics. Veon was voted the hardest-working legislator in a 2001 survey by PoliticsPA.com.

Veon's parents had engrained a blue-collar work ethic in their son. He grew up in a home where hard work and public service were valued and unions were held in high esteem. His father, Bob, was a zinc factory worker. Bob and Donna Veon had five children and Mike was the oldest. The Veons had four sons and a daughter.

Veon was a good athlete, but not much of a student. Football was his first love. He had been co-captain of the Beaver Falls High School football team in an area where football is king and in a town that produced New York Jets great Joe Namath. Veon's coach, Larry Bruno, had also been Namath's. He was later a 190-pound guard and center for the Division III Allegheny College Gators, going up against guys 50 to 60 pounds heavier. In his senior year, Veon was elected co-captain. He was a political science major at Allegheny but didn't excel. Frat boy, ballplayer and party guy were more like it. He was president of Phi Gamma Delta fraternity. In March 1977, a fraternity prank went too far. He and six others were arrested for breaking into a half dozen mobile homes in Hadley, Mercer County. They were charged with burglary, theft and criminal conspiracy. They took furniture, a stove and an oil furnace. Dropped to summary charges, Veon and his friends settled the matter with $1,500 in restitution, according to a June 29, 2008 story in *The Pittsburgh Post-Gazette*.

Michael Stevens, who had been Veon's favorite professor, said in a 1992 article by Tim Reeves in *Allegheny: The Allegheny College Magazine* that no one would have predicted his career path for Veon and that he "wasn't one of the strongest" political science majors. At college, he viewed himself as "anti-authority."

Veon went to work in various political jobs in Washington, D.C., tending bar at night, before landing a position with U.S. congressman Joseph Kolter, a Beaver Falls Democrat, in 1982. The following year, he became Kolter's legislative director.

Before 1983 had ended, however, Veon was already looking ahead. In a move that at first saddened his parents, Veon saw an opening and planned to run against Democratic incumbent Barry Alderette. Tim Reeves later became press secretary for Republican governor Tom Ridge, after covering the capitol for *The Morning Call* and *Post-Gazette*. Reeves felt a connection to Veon as a fellow Allegheny grad.

Alderette was vulnerable on at least two fronts, Veon realized. Ironically, Alderette had just accepted a $10,000 pay increase, and Veon, who would later lose his seat over a pay hike, went after the incumbent on that issue. Alderette also had only a 50 percent correct voting record according to the AFL-CIO, and the 14th District was union territory.

Veon visited 6,000 to 7,000 households in that '83 race. He won based on a strategy: he wrote off areas where he had no support and focused on union strongholds in and around Beaver Falls, as Reeves reported. Veon had secured the endorsement of the Beaver County Labor Council.

Bonusgate was about winning and keeping control. Tim Reeves' 1992 article gave a glimpse into the mindset that would prompt Mike Veon to stretch the envelope on Bonusgate. He saw himself as part of a new breed of legislators, daring and willing to take risks. "The members of the new school are entrepreneurs," he told Reeves. "The members of the old school still believe elections can be delivered to them by bosses or county committees. They have relied on that way past the time that could be relied on."

Veon took the biggest risk of all in refusing to back down from the 2005 pay raise. He was already a "member's member," the macho description of a lawmaker who was a standup guy who kept his word and was willing to put himself out on a limb for pension and pay hikes. When Veon became the only legislator to vote against the November 2005 repeal, he rose to legendary status among his colleagues and became an even larger target for the Republicans. Political novice Jim Marshall, a Republican, defeated Veon on November 7, 2006, largely because of the pay raise. Veon's manipulation of the nonprofit he fueled with state tax money, the Beaver Initiative for Growth, didn't help.

After his defeat, Veon founded his own lobbying firm, Mike Veon & Associates, and took on his first client, U.S. Tobacco, which makes snuff and cigars. Former House majority policy chairman Todd Eachus, chairman of the House Democratic Campaign Committee and a Veon protégé, sent Veon's campaign $40,000 to pay off its debt. It was a unilateral decision. Eachus did not check with other committee members, they said. It was, in effect, a political gift from a sitting House member to a lobbyist.

Just around the corner was a revelation that would rock Veon's world.

12

Bonusgate

January 27, 2007

A front-page story in the Harrisburg *Patriot-News* on January 27, 2007 set the stage for a scandal that would unravel over the next four years, hold statehouse politics in its grip and impact the 2010 governor's race. Its origin was a memorandum from "Speaker-designate" Bill DeWeese to certain House Democratic caucus employees dated only "December 2006." The memo said bonuses were being provided to some employees to "recognize people like you who have consistently demonstrated your dedication to the House Democratic Caucus and its goals."

"Since this bonus payment is of an extraordinary nature not widely received by your colleagues, we cannot stress strongly enough the need for you not to discuss this with any other staff person or member," the memo said.

The *Patriot-News* story by Charlie Thompson and Jan Murphy was prescient. As many stories do, it began with a tip. Murphy had a message on her voice mail vaguely describing the bonuses in a letter from DeWeese that they weren't supposed to talk about. They started interviewing House Democratic staffers. One of them called Charlie back and generally confirmed off the record that he'd heard of bonuses for people who worked on campaigns. In a few days, they put it together.

In the story, the reporters hit the key issues that would later develop at hearings and trials. Keep in mind that at that point no one in the media or with the public knew how much was awarded in bonuses or whether other caucuses did the same. The House Democrats sure weren't saying. There was no official confirmation of bonuses for campaigns. That would be denied over the next four years. With 20–20 hindsight, you can almost feel the angst that publication of this memo prompted among House Democratic leaders and top staffers.

The Thompson-Murphy story nailed it: the payments stung employees who didn't get them and "raised questions about whether the payments were tied to work on legislative campaigns." In the November 2006 election, Democrats had recaptured the majority in the state House. Tom Andrews, a spokesman for DeWeese, denied any connection between campaign work and bonuses. He would not disclose how many staffers got bonuses or the total cost to Pennsylvania taxpayers.

Here was the paragraph that shot to the essence of what much later would be dubbed Bonusgate: "Employees contacted by the *Patriot-News* who did not take campaign assignments this fall from former Democratic Whip Mike Veon, D-Beaver, or the House Democratic Campaign Committee, said they did not receive a bonus. They spoke to the newspaper only on condition of anonymity because of the sensitive nature of the issue."

That meant campaign work was the ticket to higher pay. What followed was an avalanche of news about bonuses from newspapers across the state. Events during the next two weeks would see bonus amounts revealed for all four caucuses and serious legal trouble on the horizon.

Two days after the *Patriot-News* story, Gene Stilp, the one-man reform litigation firm and professional protestor, filed suit in Commonwealth Court seeking return of the bonuses to taxpayers. Stilp has a law degree from the George Mason School of Law but is not licensed. It would be wrong to say he doesn't effectively "practice law." Stilp would have acted more quickly except that the Thompson-Murphy story was published on a Saturday and the courts didn't open until Monday, January 29th.

I could see it brewing as a major story for the year primarily because the House Democrats were sitting on the bonus amounts rather than coming clean right away. By their way of thinking, they were awfully good reasons to keep it secret. The furtive language in the DeWeese memo was the giveaway

To see how Republicans might react, I called new Senate President Pro Tempore Joe Scarnati (R–Jefferson County). I saw it as a great opening for several reasons. Scarnati had nothing to do with any Senate bonuses handed out during the previous regime of former President Pro Tempore Robert Jubelirer and Senate Majority Leader David Brightbill of Lebanon County. Scarnati also had new members like Senator John Eichelberger (R–Altoona) and Senator Mike Folmer (R–Lebanon County), who beat Jubelirer and Brightbill, respectively, who ran as reformers and would not tolerate sitting on bonuses.

To his credit, Scarnati didn't hesitate. He told me the bonuses given in their caucus would be disclosed. Surrounded in his office by people who received bonuses, Scarnati said, "I want that [list] out."

Within hours, Scarnati delivered on his promise. Senate Republican leaders paid out $366,000 to Senate staffers during the previous two years. His office emailed me a list with a breakdown of staffers and the bonuses they received. It was, as reformer Eric Epstein remarked, "a live grenade." Reporters are like sharks and there was blood in the water. Am I proud of that? No. But there's nothing reporters like more than controversy, unless it is scandal, and this had the distinct odor of scandal.

Why should the public care about hidden bonuses? It was, like the pay raise, a subversion of democracy. The state payroll is supposed to be the most basic state record available. These numbers meant that the payroll was fraudulent, a lie. And if the bonuses were tied in a systemic way to campaigns, it was illegal.

The Senate's disclosure upped the pressure on House Democrats and Republicans to release figures. The House Republicans were fairly prompt about it, releasing a list of $919,269 in bonuses. But still no word from the House Dems.

On the evening of January 31st, Bill DeWeese, the majority leader, invited reporters to his office. The office was almost dark. DeWeese kept a green exercise ball there that he would sometimes sit on during interviews. DeWeese said he didn't have a final figure, but it appeared that House Democrats spent less than $800,000 on the bonuses for 2005-06.

It was much, much worse.

The House Democrats' two-year total exceeded two million dollars. They spent $435,000 in 2005 and doled out $1.8 million in 2006, the year their all-out effort at the polls won control of the House. It was more than double what DeWeese's records at first indicated.

The tension among the House Dems was transparent. Tom Andrews, their spokesman, was gruff and argumentative. Bill DeWeese seemed frantic. Rank-and-file Democrats were incredulous. Most of them were saying, what bonuses?

"I didn't think anything could be worse than the pay raise. I was wrong," said former Representative Tom Tangretti, a Greensburg Democrat.

My February 11th column gave it a name: "Bonusgate Rocks the Capitol."

DeWeese told me years later that as soon as he saw those higher numbers, he knew it would all hit the fan. That may be self-serving in terms of his knowledge of events. Even if he was surprised by the total, it doesn't mean he was unaware of bonuses being used to reward campaign work. Democratic staffers have told me there's no question that DeWeese knew about the practice, though perhaps not specific dollar amounts.

The Senate Democrats, somehow, weren't in this game. Senator Robert Mellow's office said $38,000 in bonuses was paid out during this period. They'd have trouble down the road of a different sort — from the FBI. All told, $3.6 million in taxpayers' money had been paid under the table.

Many of the same reformers who pounced on the pay raise were demanding an investigation. Gene Stilp and Eric Epstein were calling on Attorney General

Tom Corbett to investigate. A state senator, John Eichelberger, also asked the top state's prosecutor to look into it.

Eichelberger had reason to believe the bonuses might be tied to campaigns. He had seen Senate staffers in the Altoona-Holidaysburg district during his campaign against Robert Jubelirer. Senate Republican political operatives got some of the largest bonuses. In 2006, Jubelirer's chief of staff, Mike Long, the longtime Senate Republican political operative, received a $22,500 bonus, and Andrew Crompton, a GOP lawyer who spent months on the Republican gubernatorial campaign of GOP candidate Lynn Swann, received $19,467 on top of a $101,523 annual salary.

Long's two-year total of $41,402 in bonuses exceeded many state employees' annual salaries, and it was the top bonus amount in the General Assembly. Long was never charged with a crime.

Among House Democrats, Bill DeWeese's chief of staff, Michael Manzo, received a $141,102 salary in 2006 and two-year bonuses of $20,250. Jeffrey Foreman, Veon's chief of staff, was practicing law on the side in addition to his $126,204 state salary and $14,815 in bonuses. His Harrisburg law firm of Foreman & Foreman was also collecting a $4,000-a-month retainer from a nonprofit in Beaver County founded by Veon and funded entirely with tax dollars.

Corbett said through his spokesman, Kevin Harley, on February 12th that he was investigating the bonuses paid by the four legislative caucuses. The reference to an investigation was significant. The previous week, when the scandal broke, Harley had said Corbett was conducting a "review."

In subsequent months, Tracie Mauriello, then of *The Post-Gazette*'s Harrisburg Bureau, did a lot to advance the story. She tied many top bonus recipients to campaigns by matching bonuses with receipts of campaign money for expenses. It showed the bonus recipient was involved in some campaign activity. The broader issue here would come to be using public resources for campaigns. For years, some legislative leaders had political operatives on the payroll. It was understood. Bonuses were only a new twist, albeit an expensive one.

The tradition ran deep.

"I worked for DeWeese and the House Democratic Caucus from July 1990 to October 1997," said Tim Potts of Democracy Rising PA. "Yes, people knew it was illegal. No, they didn't care. Yes, everyone was doing it. There were entire offices of people whose jobs were opposition research, public opinion research, incumbent protection plans and just about everything else you can think of, all at taxpayer expense and all focused on helping candidates win elections. And all four caucuses did it."

As Tim Potts recalled, Bill DeWeese called him "John the Baptist" for refusing to campaign. In 1974, Potts worked at the Department of Public Welfare and was covered by the Hatch Act, which prevented him from doing any campaign work for Milton Shapp. Because his job was federally subsidized, the federal ban on campaigning applied to him. Potts had to take leave without pay to work on the gubernatorial campaign.

There should be a similar Hatch Act at the state level, requiring state workers to leave their jobs to do campaign work, Potts added. He says he did do some political work for members writing speeches or preparing campaign brochures but did it on his home computer on evenings and weekends.

A different view comes from Bill Williams, former director of the House GOP Communications Department (previously the Public Information Department) from 1978 through 1996. Prior to that, he had been the Associated Press bureau chief at the capitol. Previously, Williams had been the day editor for the AP in Philly and a reporter in Reading.

Bill is a substantial guy. You can tell that on first meeting. He's a Navy veteran from the anthracite coal country of Pennsylvania. In retirement, he is a Civil War novelist and has had several books published. Impressive for a guy who flunked out of Penn State in his sixth semester. After serving in the Navy, he had returned to Penn State, but didn't study and had no desire to be there.

"I honestly never heard any caucus leaders, members or staff talk about doing campaign work on the government dime during my 18 years in the House," Williams admitted. "I warned my 28 staffers [which included feature writers, a radio guy, a TV crew and a speechwriter, plus support staff] to avoid campaign work of any type on state time, or any such campaign work after hours in the capitol and other state government buildings, or using state phones, computers, fax machines, etc. for political reasons.

"It may be that such talk never went on around me because everyone knew I had been a journalist in my prior jobs (a spy in the space, so to speak). I can't speak for all of the House GOP leaders or members, but I do recall hearing Matt Ryan [the speaker who preceded John Perzel] talk about the illegality of such work in a private conversation with me. We often had a short discussion (just the two of us in his office) at the end of a workday. Matt Ryan, as GOP leader and then Speaker and Sam Hayes, the number-two man, were very honest and law-abiding guys. They were also very intelligent and cognizant of laws governing political matters. [It's true that Matt Ryan had a great reputation. But he was responsible for one of the worst acts in a democracy. As speaker in June 1995, Ryan struck the vote on school choice when Tom Ridge could not muster enough support in the House. He was protecting his members. He claimed it was a 'malfunction' of the voting machine.]

"Now, were other House members or staffers involved in campaign matters?" Williams asked. "I have no knowledge of that going on. Did I suspect it might be going on in the House D or R caucuses or in the Senate D and R caucuses? Yes, because reelection was a prime consideration of every officeholder, and still is. One would have to be blind to such possibilities to not realize that it was possible. I knew it was illegal and I assume most, if not all, members and staffers knew it too," Williams stated.

It was the way things were done. Bonusgate took it to new levels.

The $1.4 million bonus program institutionalized state-paid campaign work. Under the House Democrats, the mindset resulted in widespread campaign work beneath the green dome that went beyond bonuses. And the pay raise prompted Democratic leaders to be more aggressive. The pay raise "changed the whole map," in the words of Eric Webb, the staffer ranked workers' campaign performance and kept it up to date. Top performers were considered "rock stars."

Many more House seats were in play as a result of the pay hike controversy and more volunteers were needed for everything from opposition research to campaign work in the field, Webb later testified. It was a unique year in 2006 because Bill DeWeese and Mike Veon had serious challenges. That typically didn't happen to most General Assembly leaders.

Here's the way it worked, Michael Manzo, DeWeese's chief of staff, would explain later. On paper, DeWeese was his boss. In reality, Veon was equally his boss because of the "power-sharing" arrangement between Veon and DeWeese. Manzo would get the master list from Eric Webb. Manzo would forward it to Veon, who would add names, and then it would be sent to Scott Brubaker, director of staffing and administration, the recipient of $20,750 in bonuses in 2005-06. Manzo said he sent the lists to Mike Veon; Brett Cott, who was Veon's political guy and researcher; and Jeffrey Foreman for additions or corrections. (Cott was not convicted of bonuses.) The program was "certainly successful" from a political standpoint, Manzo would later say. He added that over a four-year period, the number of volunteers from staff increased tenfold.

Manzo oversaw the campaign-related work for Veon and DeWeese like the "Nader effort." Manzo assigned it and made sure it got done. That's Ralph Nader, of course, and many Democrats in Pennsylvania were intent on knocking him off of the ballot in the 2004 presidential election. There was a frenzied effort by House Democratic staff in August of that year to challenge the nominating petitions of consumer advocate Nader, a third-party candidate. Democrats feared that Massachusetts senator John Kerry would lose the presidential race in Pennsylvania with Nader on the ballot. DeWeese and Veon believed only House Democratic staff had the resources to complete the petition challenge on a very short deadline, Manzo held. In other words, state taxpayers helped subsidize Kerry's victory over George Bush in the Keystone State. Without Nader on the ballot, Kerry carried Pennsylvania. To what extent getting Nader off the ballot helped Kerry is debatable. But top Democrats were clearly worried.

It was part of an overall campaign effort at taxpayers' expense under Veon and DeWeese. One of the categories determining the size of bonuses was participation in petition challenges. While the effort to help Nader with state-paid staffers was secret in terms of how it was conducted, the fact that it was done was not.

"This is a lugubrious and nefarious moment in Ralph Nader's otherwise admirable career of helping American consumers," DeWeese said in a typically pompous press release announcing that the challenge would be launched.

It's ironic that Democrats were looking for fatal flaws, not on nominating petitions of Republicans, but on a candidate whose philosophy tended to dovetail with their own. The "Nader effort" was coordinated in House Democratic leadership offices in Harrisburg and in Mike Veon's district office.

Melissa Lewis, a bright and articulate blonde, was hired by Veon primarily because of her campaign experience in New Mexico and Connecticut. Lewis was involved in the petition challenge in Veon's district office in Beaver Falls. "Everyone in the district office was involved," and it took about a week, she remembered. There were about 12 employees in the district office including a Midland satellite office at that time. Lewis would drive to Pittsburgh each day and pick up petitions. The district staffers utilized a computer program installed on the state-paid PCs to challenge ballot signatures. Veon's Harrisburg staffers would frequently come to the district office to campaign, Lewis recalled. Her testimony indicated that working out of Veon's office under the direction of his aide, Annamarie Perretta-Rosepink, she took part in several local campaigns on her $30,000-a-year state salary. The petition challenge was "massive" and "completely consuming," Lewis admitted.

From 2002 to 2006, no one in the office took leave to work on campaigns, said Richard Pronesti of Veon's Harrisburg office. Campaign work was an expected part of the job, research analyst Karen Steiner later testified.

In Harrisburg, Jeffrey Foreman was trying to build a trail of deniability. He encouraged employees to stay late each day, doing little or nothing, simply to build up "compensatory time" to work on campaigns. Though this was fraudulent, Foreman was at least going through the motions to make it appear legal. In the House Democratic Caucus, most comp time was manufactured. Staffers were expected to stay on the late nights when the legislature was in session. They often had nothing to do. This meant that their entire time-keeping system was bogus.

Then there was Suite 626, on the fifth floor of the state capitol, far from prying eyes. Veon ran a perpetual campaign machine there. It involved graphic design work, editing and preparation of campaign mailers and fundraiser invitations. The invitations, often several pages, needed to be folded, placed in an envelope and mailed. There was a "folding machine" running constantly during regular work hours. Where possible, they were also printed at taxpayers' expense in the capitol office. The operation was brazen enough that some campaign mailings were taken to the House mailroom to be sent out at taxpayers' expense.

The mailers were notorious among Veon's staffers, but unknown to others at the capitol. At one point during that period, I was on a walking and stair-climbing regimen first thing in the morning when I would arrive at work. I'd toss my lunch bag into the newsroom refrigerator, throw my coat over a divider near my desk and head up the stairs a few times. I walked past that room on scores of occasions and had no clue what might have been going on.

There were several key events to follow in 2007:

- The House Democrats went to court and attempted to block subpoenas for documents and requiring staffers to testify, but the effort was rebuffed by the Supreme Court.
- DeWeese brought in former Pennsylvania Inspector General Bill Chadwick to represent the caucus in handling the internal investigation into bonuses and to provide himself with legal cover.
- On or about August 30th, agents of the Attorney General served a search warrant on the House Democratic Office of Legislative Research after that learning documents were being destroyed. The research office had been created to provide a ready army of campaign volunteers.
- In November 2007, DeWeese took the dramatic step of firing seven staffers, including Michael Manzo, after emails Chadwick uncovered linked campaign work to bonuses.

For the time being, Bill DeWeese was on the side of the angels, and the investigation was pointing directly at ex-Representative Mike Veon, who lost his seat in 2006 and was ramping up his lobbying firm in 2007. The rumors built to a crescendo late in the day and evening of July 9, 2008. The Attorney General's press office had gone "dark," meaning that Kevin Harley took himself out of accepting or returning any phone calls. I knew enough to believe that a handful (or more) of Democrats would face charges the next day. It was enough to request assistance from editors in Pittsburgh, who sent Debra Erdley, since she had a stake in this story as well. I wasn't sure enough to write a story to run on July 10th. I also had a few reservations about making the call for team coverage including a photographer. What if I were wrong?

I wasn't.

Grand jury presentments against 12 people with ties to the House Democratic Caucus were made public on July 10, 2008. Tom Corbett held a news conference explaining the charges that would be filed based on the presentments. A presentment is similar to an indictment.

"Let me make this perfectly clear," said Corbett. "This is not the conclusion. This is an ongoing investigation. We are investigating all four caucuses of the General Assembly."

The grand jury presentments followed an 18-month investigation into secret bonuses that legislative staffers received for campaign and other political work on state time, Corbett explained. The arraignment was set for the next day before

District Judge Joseph Solomon. Most of the suspects, including Mike Veon, were "perp-walked" for the media by agents of the Attorney General's office. Michael Manzo didn't have enough cash to make bail. Rachel Manzo got the $10,000 he needed. She did so despite a grand jury presentment saying that he cheated on her with a young woman just identified in the presentment.

Cuffed behind his back, Mike Veon managed some degree of dignity in the dehumanizing event. Against the backdrop of a brilliant blue sky, Veon wore a blue pinstripe shirt with a baby blue tie and slightly darker blue slacks. He face shone like it had been well scrubbed. He had no comment for the press. He managed to look tranquil. A slight tremor in his leg is all that gave him away.

Much as I thought Mike had taken taxpayers for a ride, I hated to see an agent holding the back of his head because it was so difficult to get out of a police car from a sitting position while handcuffed from behind. He was grimacing.

Bonusgate was now in the legal arena.

Running parallel to Bonusgate, for a while, was a federal prosecution of arguably the legislature's most powerful member.

13

The Vince of Darkness

February 6, 2007

No politician in my lifetime amassed the power of Vincent J. Fumo. No one was smarter. No one was, in his own way, more effective in representing his district. Absolutely no one evoked fear among other politicians and those on the fringe of power like Fumo did. He was "The Lord God, King of Influence," said David Taylor, executive director of the Pennsylvania Manufacturer's Association and a capitol observer who closely tracked the Keystone State's corruption cases.

Fumo was generous with those who were loyal. He sought revenge against those who crossed him. He could be "a charmer or a bully," commented James Lee, president of Susquehanna Polling and Research.

"He was an in-your-face, Philly type of guy. A lot of people were afraid of Vince Fumo," Bob Maranto, a political science professor at Villanova University, told the *Tribune-Review*.

Fumo had his people placed in state and city agencies. He got many of them their jobs. People owed him favors. His shadow bureaucracy was built up over decades, the late Al Neri, a friend and journalist, told me in a 2008 interview. With one phone call, he could arguably get things done that governors couldn't do.

"He deliberately amassed power in all corners of the state and in all branches of state government," Neri continued. "He had people planted in the bureaucracy in the city, in the Delaware River Port Authority, the Pennsylvania Turnpike Commission and all branches of state government. He helped elect judges and that gave him sway in the judicial branch. He's the most powerful senator we've seen this generation, and that was with him being in the minority [party] most of the time."

Fumo's success was attributable to "his intelligence and his ability to link things together and see things others did not."

"I acquired power so I could use power in a good way," a tearful Fumo said at his July 2009 sentencing. Earlier he told the court: "I did a lot of good for 11 million people, whether they know it or not."

But federal prosecutors John J. Pease and Robert A. Zausmer argued in a brief: "The government proved at trial beyond all reasonable doubt that, for decades, Fumo engaged in repeated abuse of the power of his office as a leader in the Pennsylvania State Senate and, on literally a daily basis for many years, stole from the taxpayers of Pennsylvania and from two charitable organizations. The corruption exposed in this case was astonishing."

* * *

Fumo justified the use of other people's property and money as part of the most important objective: giving Vincent Fumo more time and more resources to be an even better state senator from — fittingly — Senate District No. 1. The rules were largely an annoyance.

Re-election in this heavily Democratic district typically was not an issue, as it was for most lawmakers. That allowed Fumo to work on expanding his power and increasing his comfort. He had three drivers, a staffer to balance his personal and campaign checkbooks, another to clean his house and a legislative assistant who served as the general contractor on his house. He leased a Cadillac at taxpayers' expense, but later his nonprofit group paid for the van and mini-SUV he used. Fumo effectively had three of his own "IT" guys, paid for by taxpayers, to provide extra layers of Internet and internal computer security.

Or so he thought.

The son of a banker, Fumo was a multi-millionaire with a waterfront Florida home as well as his Green Street mansion in Philadelphia, a gentleman's farm in Halifax, north of Harrisburg, and two properties at the Jersey shore. He was a licensed pilot, electrician, lawyer, banker, senator and farmer. Earlier in his life, he was a teacher. Al Neri, who grew up in South Philadelphia, was one of Fumo's students. Fumo had an MBA from the Wharton School of the University of Pennsylvania as well as a law degree from Temple University. He was all those things. Yet he used what he called "other people's money"(OPM) as his own. His net worth was $9.3 million, even after payment of legal fees, a presentence report revealed. Despite Fumo's membership in Mensa, the organization for people with genius-level IQs, he was not smart enough in the end to outwit the feds. He staged an excellent, almost impenetrable cover-up, having emails erased and hard drives scrubbed. The guy who beat the odds before, getting a 1980 conviction overturned on appeal, couldn't beat the rap a second time. That conviction for putting "ghost" workers on the payroll was tossed out on a technicality. The allegations in the indictment didn't match the allegations at trial stemming from the conspiracy charge in the case. A mummer's band played in the capitol for his grand return after his guilty verdict was overturned in 1982.

Fumo's political patron was Philadelphia City Democratic Chairman Peter Camiel, a co-defendant in the 1980 trial in which the verdict was overturned. There's a rest stop on the Pennsylvania Turnpike named after Camiel.

Fumo replaced Buddy Cianfrani as District 1's senator after Cianfrani went to prison in 1978 following his guilty plea to 110 counts of racketeering, mail fraud, obstruction and income tax evasion. As former mayor Frank Rizzo noted, Cianfrani "went like a man" with no whining about his five-year prison term.

On March 16, 2009, Vince Fumo was convicted of 137 charges brought by the U.S. Attorney's office. Fumo, 65, was convicted of misusing tax money as well as the funds of the Citizens Alliance for Better Neighborhoods that he created and fueled with state grants.

The best "lede" on the verdict story came from *Philadelphia Inquirer* reporters Craig R. McCoy and Emilie Lounsberry, who were out front on the Fumo case with Mario Cattabiani, John Shiffman and others. It was the kind of lede (or lead) that can only be written by people glued to the investigation and trial.

"The FBI pursued him for four years. Its agents interviewed more than 350 people and compiled documents that filled 240 boxes," the *Inquirer* story revealed. "The trial took 22 weeks and 102 witnesses."

"Yesterday, a jury of 10 women and two men wrote the finish. They found Vincent J. Fumo to be a corrupt politician who abused his power to enrich himself," McCoy and Lounsberry wrote on March 17, 2009. Fumo reigned for 30 years as the Prince of South Philadelphia. His every need was met by employees paid by the taxpayers or Citizen Alliance. It may be decades before Pennsylvania has a senator as smart, effective and crooked as Fumo.

The conviction came after four and a half months of testimony. His defense was weak, despite having one of the best criminal defense lawyers in the city in Dennis Cogan along with an appeals specialist, Washington attorney Samuel Buffone. He even had a new judge during jury selection, when the first one became ill.

"Fumo spent close to six days on the witness stand, lying to the jury, hour after hour, on every material issue in the case," according to a sentencing memorandum from prosecutors. Cogan had almost nothing to work with. Based on the trial testimony, Fumo was guilty as sin.

The 139-count indictment issued by the U.S. Attorney's office in Philadelphia on February 6, 2007, just as Bonusgate was unfolding, was a stunning legal document of 264 pages. I've seen dozens of indictments and statewide grand jury presentments against elected officials. None came close in the breadth of alleged criminal activity. The investigation and indictment were overseen by former U.S.

Attorney Patrick Meehan, now a Republican congressman, who had been a prospective GOP candidate for governor in 2010.

Fumo concocted a vast conspiracy to defraud the Senate and Citizens Alliance and a seaport museum of $3.5 million. At the time, he called the indictment "half truths, lies and misrepresentations." Noteworthy is the fact that the first 64 counts of the indictment are based on the Habay case (see Chapter 10). Fumo, of course, could not be charged with state crimes in federal court. But the Habay-like allegations against Fumo were used as the underpinning of the mail and wire fraud charges.

Going to trial against the feds is a monumental task. It's why there are so many pleas and a 95 percent conviction rate. Federal investigators knew that to take out Fumo, the evidence had to be irrefutable. He would have the best lawyers and enormous resources. Before they had a falling out, Fumo was represented by Philly's legendary lawyer, Richard Sprague.

In my view, the issue that would linger for the public was not whether Fumo was guilty, but rather how much time he would, and should, serve. I did not cover the trial in person. God bless *The Inquirer,* though, for its live blog of Fumo events and later providing audio of key events during the trial.

Dennis Cogan told jurors a story about having loved *Alice in Wonderland* as a child and then being ahead of his other law school classmates when, on the first day of his criminal law class, the professor told them to read a segment of Lewis Carroll's book with which he was familiar: "No, no," said the Queen, "Sentence first, verdict afterward." That was what the federal government did in its case against Fumo when it started off with conclusions, Cogan argued.

After the March verdict, on July 14, 2009, U.S. District Judge Ronald Buckwalter sentenced Fumo to 55 months in prison. The sentence sparked outrage across the state. Taxpayers were furious at a perceived slap on the wrist. David Truby, then 71 and a retired journalism professor from Indiana University of Pennsylvania, had this comment: "the small town and rural mood is that if folks had a large gallows and hemp rope, it is certain that chronic liar Fast Eddie, Ronald Buckwalter and Vincent Fumo would figuratively swing in the breeze." He lumped in former governor Ed Rendell, who testified on Fumo's behalf at trial.

It wasn't just a reaction in the countryside. Readers lit up the comment sections of *The Daily News* with email. An *Inquirer* column entitled "Say What?"— by the newspaper's editorial board — had this conclusion: "The judge's logic was both flawed and insulting."

* * *

Two things are important in understanding just how powerful Vincent Fumo was at the peak of his power in the late 1980s and 1990s. For most of that period, Fumo served in the minority party. Those in minority leadership are typically unable to accomplish much. But because Senate confirmation of many gubernatorial appointees required a two-thirds vote, a higher hurdle than a simple majority, Fumo had leverage. Senate Dems could prevent a gubernatorial appointment from going through. Fumo knew how and when to use leverage. It was largely the force of Fumo's personality and political skill, though, that enabled him to be so effective as a minority leader. On an official flowchart of Senate Democratic leadership, Vince Fumo would at best have ranked third. In reality, he was the de facto caucus leader, despite Robert Mellow's designation as Senate minority leader.

Because of the two-thirds hurdle, package deals were typically required for legislation to add county judges, interim judgeship appointments, some cabinet members, confirmation of a turnpike commissioner or an interim statewide officeholder. Fumo could extract a price to obtain more "walking around money" for himself or others. It was also during this period that Fumo controlled some House votes. A handful of House Democrats became known as Fumocrats. At Fumo's behest, they were able to block bills or amendments that he opposed in the other chamber. It was a way to "extort" more project money from other leaders — in effect, to boost state spending. His influence was greatest in shaping budgets and getting extra money for Philadelphia. Fumo helped gain additional power with contributions he made from his political action committee to other lawmakers.

*   *   *

There is no doubt that Vince Fumo delivered for his home city. As he prepared for trial and considered his legacy in 2008, Fumo asked his staff to tally the financial aid he provided to Philadelphia. They came up with a staggering eight billion dollars for the city that he claimed credit for securing, beyond regular state appropriations — money for human services such as welfare, infrastructure and education. Great for Philadelphia, but it confirmed what people in other parts of the state thought about an inordinate amount of state tax money going to the big city.

"To many, Vince Fumo was the poster child for everything wrong with Philadelphia," said public relations consultant Larry Ceisler.

There is no question that he was corrupt on a scale that made other legislative leaders seem like rookie league players. Philadelphia reporters often called him the "Vince of Darkness."

I believe Fumo's corrupt activities expanded over time. In his mind, he was not stealing. He put in endless hours and claimed that he thought of Senate business 24-7. To him it was only fair to use Senate resources, like one would use an expense account (minus legitimate expense reports). Fumo had a gargantuan sense of entitlement. Citizens Alliance wouldn't have existed without his vision to provide services to South Philly residents that city government was largely ignoring. Without his largesse, it wouldn't have had $2.2 million in state grants. Without his lawsuit against the power company, PECO, which resulted in a $17 million settlement payment to Citizens Alliance, the nonprofit wouldn't have been rolling in dough. So if Fumo used Citizens Alliance money for his near-obsession with buying Oreck vacuum cleaners (19 for his residences), power tools, heavy equipment or supplies for his latest "fix-it project," who was worse off?

"If I had taken a bribe, sold my office, I would have quit my office in shame," Fumo told reporters in 2008 following his "swan song" speech in the Senate. "But that didn't happen."

Funny, that was the same view of Fumo's crimes taken by Judge Buckwalter. No one was harmed. There were no bribes. His employees still got paid. This idea of the taxpayers being cheated just didn't seem to resonate with the judge.

* * *

High-dollar investments by Citizens Alliance attracted the FBI's attention in 2003, which led them to the PECO settlement, and that led to everything else. Vincent Fumo, however, did a lot more than buy Oreck vacuum cleaners.

"During his three decades as a state senator, Fumo frequently directed his publicly paid Senate employees to attend to his personal needs and political interests during their working hours, as well as at night and on weekends," wrote Judge Julio M. Fuentes of the Third Circuit Court of Appeals. "Fumo's Philadelphia district office was staffed by 10 such employees, whose duties included providing constituent services to the residents of Fumo's district. However, the staffers often also provided Fumo with campaign and personal assistance: organizing political fundraisers and mailings, processing bills for business accounts, and handling various aspects of Fumo's personal finances.

"Various aides also acted as his housekeeper, drove him from place to place, managed the refurbishment of his 33-room house, ran personal errands, and even drove his daughter to school," Fuentes wrote. "During Fumo's annual trip to Martha's Vineyard, Massachusetts, his Senate aides would drive two vehicles from Philadelphia and back, filled with the luggage of Fumo and his guests. Staffers also used their time to assist a Philadelphia city councilman who was Fumo's ally and, for two months, to advance the campaign of an ultimately unsuccessful Pennsylvania Democratic gubernatorial candidate [now Senator Robert P. Casey Jr.]. Moreover, Fumo misused his Senate staff in Harrisburg — several of them assisted the development of a farm he had purchased in 2003 as a residential and business enterprise. In exchange, Fumo arranged salaries for his employees that were substantially greater than those designated by the State Senate for comparable Senate employees."

Fuentes continued: "Fumo also provided non-staffers, such as contractors, family members and girlfriends, with access to Senate resources, including laptops and computer assistance. Further, he used Senate funds to hire contractors for non-legislative tasks. For instance, Fumo obtained a $40,000 state contract for a private investigator who, in addition to his legitimate activities, conducted surveil-lance on Fumo's former wife, girlfriends, ex-girlfriends, boyfriends and, at times, political rivals. He obtained an $80,000 state contract for a consultant who spent much of his time assisting Fumo with political races, and a $45,000 salary for an individual who spent most of his time assisting with Fumo's farm. Mitchell Rubin, the boyfriend and later husband of [co-defendant] Ruth Arnao, was paid $30,000 per year for five years, without doing much, if any [Senate] work at all." Rubin had been chairman of the Pennsylvania Turnpike Commission. Arnao, a former Fumo staff member, was convicted on 45 counts of fraud, tax evasion and obstruction of justice. Buckwalter had sentenced Arnao to one year and one day in prison.

Prosecutors would later argue that Senate business was not as pervasive in Fumo's world as he made out. He spent about four months a year on vacation. From looking at the overview of his habits, the Senate was only one of numerous interests he devoted time to. Farming, shopping, yachting, vacations and legal work also competed for Fumo's attention.

John Contino, former executive director of the Pennsylvania Ethics Commis-sion, was asked on the witness stand about the notion that a case involving theft of state services by incumbents — using public resources for campaigns — isn't of the same magnitude as bribery.

"Well, with all due respect, I don't agree with that. As I said before, I think the continued and systematic manipulation or attempt at manipulation of the electoral process is an offense to the fundamental foundation of the democratic process," Contino testified. "[It] far outweighs individual, isolated attempts to obtain per-sonal gain through a corruption of your office…I don't know how else to say it. Democracy is a victim here."

Fumo's conviction, Patrick Meehan noted, "underscores the importance of the message that no one is above the law and there is a duty of public officials to live by the oaths of office they take and to serve the public and not themselves."

*   *   *

Two major laws in recent years can be attributed largely to Fumo and his staff. Legislation allowing 14 casinos in Pennsylvania was crafted in Fumo's office in 2004. A former lawyer on Fumo's staff, Christopher Craig, wrote the bill. Many lawmakers offered input, but Fumo's office was command central for expanded gaming. It took about 18 months for support on the slots bill to jell. The Senate Republican Caucus, which runs the chamber, was largely opposed to slots. A Republican senator who favored slots, Tommy Tomlinson of Bucks County, insist-ed to GOP leaders that he had to have a vote on it because slots were crucial to Philadelphia Park, a horseracing track in his district.

For months, Fumo held up gaming, infuriating Ed Rendell. Fumo insisted that one or two of the licenses go for "Indian gaming." Unlike Western states,

Pennsylvania is not home to many Native Americans. In the original 13 colonies, the Native Americans for the most part were long gone. Fumo was accused of holding up "property tax reform" that would supposedly come with gaming revenues. Fumo eventually dropped this gambit. I am not sure what he got out of it. I suspect he won control of crafting the bill. Native American interests were quickly forgotten.

Former Senate majority leader David "Chip" Brightbill of Lebanon, a Republican who personally opposed slots, allowed Tommy Tomlinson to have a Senate vote. A few Republican senators from the Southeast backed the bill, but it was clear that Democrats would have to carry the weight for passage. Repeated closed-door sessions in Fumo's office produced a bill.

Because the Senate was supposedly the tough sell on slots, the House had little choice but to accept Fumo's version. John Perzel was crucial to House passage. Rendell was the chief cheerleader, saying proceeds would reduce property taxes. The authorization of up to 61,000 slot machines — a total second only to Nevada's — occurred in the early morning hours of July 4, 2004. At the time, Fumo compared the action to the early 1970s, when Pennsylvania instituted a state lottery to provide help for senior citizens, and first levied a personal income tax to pay for other state programs.

"In the past 30 years, I don't believe we have done anything that will change Pennsylvania economically and culturally as much as the process we have set in motion here," Fumo stated after passage of the slots bill. The law created the Pennsylvania Gaming Control Commission, which was beset by problems in its early years.

In July 2007, another complex proposal began in Fumo's Senate office: a long-term plan to fund transportation and transit needs through borrowing, higher turnpike tolls and levying tolls on Interstate 80. The federal government had rejected I-80 tolling. The law, Act 44, has provided almost a billion dollars for Pennsylvania roads and bridges and has helped stabilize mass transit with more than $600 million, according to figures from the House Appropriations Committee and testimony before that panel.

"Fumo was able to turn two seemingly innocuous proposals — money for property tax relief and funding for roads and bridges — into two of the most corrupt, special interest-driven pieces of legislation," said Matthew Brouillette, president of the Commonwealth Foundation, a Harrisburg-based policy group. He uses "corrupt" in a general, not criminal, sense.

"And both pieces of legislation were largely crafted behind closed doors, with little discussion and without public input or knowledge," he added. Through the years, however, Fumo's mission appeared to be "to make sure Philadelphia got its share, if not more, of the pie," said author and former Senate aide Vincent Carocci.

*   *   *

Ronald Buckwalter, a former Lancaster County district attorney, evidently no longer saw things from a law enforcement point of view. His reasoning was twisted beyond any standard of logic and common sense. Many people asked privately whether the fix was in. There was absolutely no evidence of that, and watching Buckwalter, I didn't think that at all. But it was talk on the street. How could a powerful politician, who wouldn't consider a plea and forced the government's expense of a lengthy trial, and who effectively stole millions from taxpayers, be sent to prison for four years and seven months?

Former House Democratic whip Mike Veon, sentenced in Dauphin County Court for engineering a $1.4 million bonus scam, was sentenced to six to 14 years in state prison. In Philadelphia, former city treasurer Corey Kemp, who accepted gifts in return for steering contracts, received a 10-year prison term. Former city councilman Richard Mariano, convicted of bribery, fraud and filing a false tax return, was sentenced to 78 months in prison.

The real irony is that with his personal wealth, Vincent Fumo could have paid for all of it, from the taxpayers' money he used for a private detective to spy on political enemies and a former girlfriend to the use of the Independence Seaport Museum's yacht. The U.S. Attorney's office appealed Fumo's sentence to the Third Circuit Court of Appeals and on August 23, 2011, the court issued its ruling. Fumo must be resentenced.

Next: Frank LaGrotta, a small fry compared to Fumo, was the first legislator in Attorney General Tom Corbett's sights.

14

The Appetizer

November 14, 2007

Reporters and photographers spotted him as soon as he turned his white Hyundai Elantra into the parking lot. "There he is," someone shouted as if they'd sighted a 12-point buck while jacklighting. Former legislator Frank LaGrotta was on his way to his first criminal arraignment. He was scared to death.

LaGrotta, his sister and niece left Ellwood City in Lawrence County at 2:30 a.m., in order to make it to Harrisburg District Judge Joseph Solomon's office by 8:30. On the final leg, he made the familiar drive on Front Street along the Susquehanna River.

Frank LaGrotta's arraignment this fall morning attracted far more media attention than a rank-and-file member from Western Pennsylvania normally would warrant because he was the first person charged in Corbett's investigation of the legislature. He faced criminal charges for putting his sister and niece — also defendants — on the state payroll in "ghost jobs." No-work jobs were part of Pennsylvania's heritage in state payroll abuse. Political patrons got you the job. You got full pay. The nice part was you didn't need to show up.

Driving on the Pennsylvania Turnpike that morning, LaGrotta recalled that he'd "never been more afraid in my entire life." The darkness added to the gloom. The sun didn't come up, he said, until they were 17 miles outside of Harrisburg.

"When we arrived, the hoard of media was gathered around the [justice's] office," LaGrotta would write in his still-unfinished memoir, which he shared with me. For his court appearance, he wore a black leather jacket and jeans.

A "swarm of bees with cameras and notepads" closed in on him, LaGrotta wrote. His sister was hit by a TV camera.

"Frank, how do you feel?" someone shouted.

"Did you do it?" another reporter asked loudly.

"Are you going to apologize?"

"Did you testify against anyone in Bonusgate?"

"No comment," he remembers saying.

Scenes like this made me ashamed to be part of the "media." I understand that TV crews need their shots for the evening news. Newspapers need photos for the front page, and perp walks are included in this book. But from a print reporter's perspective, these events are worthless. Nine times out of 10, the defendant says nothing. You have to be there in case the defendant or his lawyer wants to talk.

Inside the judge's office, the arraignments are cut and dried. The charges against LaGrotta were read. "We were photographed, fingerprinted and that was it," he recalled. From LaGrotta's perspective, the hunt was still under way when he left the office. "Outside, the vultures were still hovering," he recalled.

"Do you think you owe your constituents an apology?"

"Are you sorry you got your family into this mess?"

I watched this unfold and just tried to stay close to him in case he said something.

Frank LaGrotta was arraigned in Harrisburg on November 14, 2007, just 13 days before his 48th birthday. There was never much doubt what would happen next. With his relatives charged, he would do anything to save them. LaGrotta's guilty plea and sentencing would be held in February 2008 in Dauphin County Court.

Dauphin County President Judge Richard Lewis would prove accommodating to the media at LaGrotta's sentencing. As it turned out, he was not first on the docket. The judge told reporters there for the start of court that he had other matters to hear. He suggested they return in about an hour for LaGrotta.

From LaGrotta's perspective, sitting there in the court, Lewis was "ingratiating" himself with the media, sucking up as if it might someday help him land a Supreme Court position.

I said hello to Frank in the courtroom, and he gave me a nod and a "hey." I'd known him a long time, though not well. I had quoted him in stories over the years. He pleaded guilty to two counts of conflict of interest. He was sentenced to six months of house arrest, fined $10,000, and ordered to pay $27,000 in restitution. After the plea, he told reporters, "I want to apologize to the people of Pennsylvania."

As a result of the plea deal, LaGrotta's crimes didn't fall among the 22 requiring pension forfeiture, such as theft, perjury and obstruction of justice. He would receive an annual pension of about $36,000, and was entitled to a $103,000 lump sum from the pension system at age 50. He agreed to cooperate with prosecutors. It was a great deal, but one that privately upset LaGrotta. He later claimed that he did not do what prosecutors charged him with, that they bullied him into the plea and gave him no choice by using his sister and niece as a wedge against him.

Voters retired Frank LaGrotta, an Ellwood City Democrat, in the 2006 Democratic primary. He brought this on himself by voting for the 2005 pay grab and then vigorously speaking out about it over the summer. The voters' anger had swelled by August 2005. Defending it was insane. Even Ed Rendell had begun to back off. A top aide in Rendell's office told me in late July 2005 that they had assessed a voter rebellion under way.

LaGrotta said he made up his mind by 2005 that this would be his last race and final term after 20 years in the legislature. Frank was on radio talk shows defending the pay raise. He told the story of how a woman at a supermarket had called him a crook. I could never figure out why a state legislator would repeat that. People might believe it. In this case, the woman was right, based on LaGrotta's guilty plea.

Frank, in those days, had a big mouth. Mike Veon got him a job as a Democratic Caucus staffer. He was on the road to deal with "district office issues." LaGrotta provided the information used here from his memoir, and emailed answers to questions and phone interviews. The quotes from media before and after his arraignment are from his memoir. They are substantially as I remember them.

In the prosecution's version of events, LaGrotta lost the primary and believed he was entitled to more. After all, he voted for the pay raise that the leadership called for, and he had loyally defended it. A little something more meant cushy state jobs for his relatives. Both important to the story, LaGrotta's sister, Ann Bartolomeo, and his niece, Alissa Lemmon, were charged with false swearing. They eventually would plead no contest.

From 1998 through 2007, Ann Bartolomeo was a full-time schoolteacher in the Ellwood City School District. Her employment agreement with the House stated that she would be paid $1,932 based on a 37.5-hour work week. Her agreement was backdated to February 1, 2006 in a document she signed with Frank LaGrotta and Bill DeWeese. She applied for the position as legislative assistant on June 5, 2006.

In a face-to-face meeting, Mike Veon approved the employment of his sister, LaGrotta would say later. An "Employee Payroll Information" document obtained by the grand jury authorized her to receive $19,329 on June 20th and to revert to a bi-weekly salary of $1,932. This was supposed to be her "back pay" under the antedated contract.

Ann Bartolomeo told the grand jury that she actually worked 451 hours — an average of 20.5 hours per week — an hourly wage of $46.29, the Attorney

General's office reported. Alissa Lemmon, who joined the Pittsburgh Convention and Visitors Bureau by January 2006, was paid $6,216 by the state House in 2006 for work she didn't do, the grand jury stated.

To this day, Frank LaGrotta insists that he did nothing wrong. His sister and niece did do the work he requested, sorting through boxes of archives. A disgruntled employee told a false story that burned him, LaGrotta contends.

LaGrotta is like a lot of convicted pols who try until the last minute to rationalize their behavior. At his sentencing, he at first called what happened a "bookkeeping error." In the next breath, he accepted "full responsibility."

Never mind the nepotism.

These were not no-show jobs, though the women later would have to admit to exaggerating their hours to "purify" themselves with Senior Deputy Attorney General Anthony Krastek and the grand jury, or so LaGrotta claimed. They were specifically called "ghost jobs" by the Attorney General. The truth is probably in between: the relatives did some work, but cheated the Commonwealth on their hours.

LaGrotta contends that this was all about Tom Corbett getting a notch in his belt by taking his first Democrat scalp.

Democratic House Leader Bill DeWeese and his "Republican prosecutor" Bill Chadwick, the former acting DA of Philadelphia and a former state inspector general, turned an incriminating email over to the Attorney General's office. Chadwick was paid $1.7 million by House Democrats over two years.

LaGrotta maintains he was joking in the email to his niece. But he said his attorney told him it was problematic. Here's what it said, according to the memoir LaGrotta is still compiling:

> Following is the verbatim exchange that took place from 9:49 a.m. to 11:20 a.m. on January 18, 2006:
>
> *LaGrotta:* Hi.
>
> *Lemmon:* Hi. Did you ever figure out the paycheck thing?
>
> *LaGrotta:* They kept you on benefits through January 31st and mistakenly kept you on payroll. Just keep it. They don't want it back.
>
> *Lemmon:* Well, isn't that nice of them.
>
> *LaGrotta:* You may get one more, too! How's your dog? How's your life?
>
> *Lemmon:* Isn't that illegal? Not that I'm complaining! The runaway is fine — he looked longingly at the door this morning! Life is fine — busy but fine!
>
> *LaGrotta:* Not illegal. Mistake. You can pay it back if you choose, but no one here is asking that. Besides it is like your severance pay.
>
> *Lemmon:* Eh, works for me!
>
> *LaGrotta:* You can give it all to me! I am broke.
>
> *Lemmon:* Hell no!

This one email out of thousands in LaGrotta's hard drive had been discovered by the team Bill Chadwick had combing through emails in the House Democrats' system.

Chadwick was a caucus attorney, DeWeese had explained, working for all Democratic members. But DeWeese's chief of staff, Mike Manzo, later testified that he didn't trust Chadwick because he was clearly DeWeese's lawyer. Chadwick had bona fides with state prosecutors since he was the former acting DA in Philadelphia. LaGrotta called DeWeese "a frightened man driven by self-preservation at any cost." DeWeese would later use his effort to clean up corruption in the caucus through Chadwick as a major part of his own defense in a 2012 trial.

Frank LaGrotta cooperated with investigators, but it appears that he didn't have much to give them. He never appeared as a witness in the subsequent Bonusgate case. He did explain it was not DeWeese, the minority leader who ran the caucus, but really Veon and Manzo who masterminded the scheme. He informed investigators about Kevin Sidella, DeWeese's state-paid fundraiser.

LaGrotta at first insisted that to consider a plea, his sister and niece had to walk. But the Attorney General's office turned that down through LaGrotta's attorney, Stephen Colafella, the son of former representative Nick Colafella. The ARD (Accelerated Rehabilitative Disposition) program was not an option in public corruption cases, he was told.

Ann Bartolomeo and Alissa Lemmon pleaded no contest to charges that they lied to a grand jury. Bartolomeo was fined $3,000 and was placed on probation for a year. Lemmon was fined $3,000 and sentenced to 18 months' probation. Bartolomeo would eventually lose her job as a kindergarten teacher as a result of the plea.

About $27,000 total in phony benefits is small stuff in the vast stream of patronage and nepotism abuse over the years. But the LaGrotta case must be viewed in the prism of Tom Corbett's corruption investigation. Frank LaGrotta clearly was a small fish: a stretching exercise for Anthony Krastek, who later would handle the first Bonusgate-related trial. His case warmed up Corbett's press secretary, Kevin Harley, in issuing corruption-related news releases. It was an appetizer for the statewide media closely watching Corbett's vow to investigate "all four caucuses"— the House and Senate Democrats and Republicans — after the bonus revelations earlier in 2007.

From Frank LaGrotta's perspective, it was all about Corbett — he thinks of him as "Tom Terrific," the cartoon character — racking up headlines through the bonus investigation that fell into his lap.

LaGrotta believes the entire mess stemmed from his decision to make this his last term. That's what prompted the archiving. So he offered the work to his sister and niece.

It's unclear how much LaGrotta helped Corbett's investigators. His story about Scranton businessman Louis DeNaples giving legislators "blank checks" didn't pan out. At the time, DeNaples was a casino owner facing perjury charges. The perjury charge was dropped as part of a deal to turn the Poconos casino over to his daughter.

Back in Ellwood City, living on his state pension, LaGrotta made himself a target once again by writing a daily blog highly critical of Corbett, the man who prosecuted him.

I felt sorry for him despite the fact that he brought this on himself. We emailed each other a lot around the time he launched his blog, "Politics as (Not) Usual." He was a hell of a good writer. He had a B.A. and M.A. from Notre Dame. From 1981 to 1983, he had been a sportswriter with Gannett newspapers covering the NFL. He'd been a hotshot sports columnist at South Bend's famed university.

I considered LaGrotta a valuable background source. For the most part, he didn't have specific information. Though very critical of DeWeese, his rants had to be taken with a grain of salt. He had been an insider in the House Democratic Caucus, which the Attorney General's office was actively investigating in 2008. He helped me understand the thinking.

I struggled with this chapter more than any other. I have strived to present a fair, objective view of Frank LaGrotta. On the other hand, I am closer to him than any of the other subjects as a result of the length of time I've known him and our email relationship. He was both a subject and a source for this book. I am indebted to Frank for his cooperation. Because I consider him a friend, this was a hard piece to write.

LaGrotta and DeWeese shared a common bond as criminal defendants: their intense disdain for Tom Corbett, the state's next governor. LaGrotta was also writing a book about the legislature. Or maybe that was part of the memoir. He sent me a sample chapter about DeWeese, and it read well. But his writing was so packed with vitriol against Corbett and DeWeese that it was hard to take seriously.

Though a Roman Catholic, LaGrotta considered himself a born-again Christian. He told me he prayed regularly. He took part in helping with church plays. I thought things were looking up for Frank.

During this period, however, he became addicted to Xanax. He falsified prescriptions to obtain larger quantities of the anti-anxiety medication. Here's the crazy part. Frank had legitimate prescriptions, but he changed the numbers so that 120 became 180 pills and two times a day became three. I had no clue about his addiction. We communicated mainly through email.

LaGrotta appeared in court in Western Pennsylvania on June 13, 2011 for his sentencing on the drug count — the charge of acquiring a controlled substance through misrepresentation. He knew that jail time was coming. LaGrotta collapsed and had to be carried out of the Lawrence County Courthouse on a stretcher before the judge could finish the sentence. He was hospitalized but returned to the court two days later, so visiting judge Eugene Fike could wrap it up. Frank was sentenced to three to 12 months in jail and two years of probation.

That part about collapsing saddened me. I can only imagine how Frank felt. Now, after all he'd been through, he was going to jail. Going to jail is bad enough, but he'd been tortured with the threat. Frank probably deserved to go to jail in the first instance, but he caught a break. In the second incident he needed help. He spent 15 days in drug treatment and requested that the time be taken off his sentence. Fike denied the request and the troubled ex-legislator was finally taken to jail.

LaGrotta was incarcerated at the Lawrence County jail from June 13th to September 13th. "I was very afraid of going to jail," he wrote to me in an email. "In fact I had prayed incessantly for a year before I was sentenced that God would spare me from jail. However, for whatever his reason, I was sentenced to three to 12 months. The first two days I spent in the booking area — a single cell with 24-hour fluorescent lights, a metal toilet and sink combination and a narrow steel bed. I was very uneasy. I spent those 48 hours praying and just being afraid." LaGrotta later was housed in a dormitory-style cellblock. There were no cells per se, just a large room with steel beds. "For the next 90 days I did very little besides pray and sleep," he told me in an email.

LaGrotta was never hassled by another inmate, but was given a "hard time" by one or two guards who did everything they could to make him miserable. When I asked him about the food, he said that he lost 23 pounds in 93 days. The unsanitary conditions and lack of proper medical treatment for inmates, which LaGrotta claimed he'd seen, sounded appalling. His faith, he says, got him through it. In the end, jail was not as bad as he thought it would be. LaGrotta believes Tom Corbett's deputies were responsible for getting him locked up because of his blog, which was heavily critical of Corbett. But Anthony Krastek, the prosecutor, was not the guy shoving Xanax down LaGrotta's throat or falsifying prescriptions. It was the treatment of his sister and niece that he is most bitter about. We all have periods of our lives when we don't live the way we know we should.

It was ironic that Frank LaGrotta went to jail and some conspirators in the bonus case who cooperated with prosecutors did not. Specifically, what got him through the legal hurdles, and finally jail, was a Bible verse, Job 5:18: "God injures, but he bandages."

LaGrotta decided against going to trial, but one of the Bonusgate defendants, in a broad sense, would be the first to test the Attorney General's muscle in court.

15

Vindicated

December 10, 2009

The tall boy with sandy-brown hair stood shyly in the background of a photo with former President George H.W. Bush and a large group of kids. Sean Ramaley was then a high school student, one of two Pennsylvania boys selected to serve at the American Legion's "Boys Nation" state government council in Washington, D.C.

A native of Economy Borough in Beaver County, Ramaley (pronounced RaMAILee) was president of his class at Quigley Catholic School in Baden — three times. A member of the National Honor Society, he played soccer and clarinet in the school band. According to his mother, Christine Ramaley, "Sean was never one to do anything he shouldn't do."

At Allegheny College, Sean received the Ethical Leader of the Year Award in 1997. In 2002, he received his J.D. from the University of Pittsburgh Law School. He wrote opinions in the U.S. Department of Labor for the Office of Administrative Law Judges. As an adult, he assisted with worship at his parish.

Seven years after getting his law degree and four years after proudly taking the oath of office as a member of the state House of Representatives, Ramaley sat in a Dauphin County courtroom in 2009, waiting for a jury to announce a verdict on six felony counts against him.

It just didn't fit. The all-American boy on trial before a jury of six men and six women? How had his passion for politics come to this?

Prosecutors say Ramaley agreed to take a no-show job in Representative Mike Veon's Beaver Falls office so he would have income while running for the House in 2008. A statewide grand jury asserted that Ramaley used the state-paid position to campaign for office.

A journalist from another era once referred to a segment of the state's lawmakers as "Pennsylvania crude." Ramaley was anything but that. He was a tall, clean-cut man of 34 years when he went to trial. Nothing about him looked sleazy. He sat ramrod straight at the defense table, stoically showing no reaction — or emotion — as a prosecutor expounded a theme that Ramaley stole from the taxpayers. His wife, Stephie-Anna, was an assistant district attorney in Allegheny County. She sat on one of the courtroom's oak benches with Ramaley's parents, able to do little from a legal standpoint.

Prosecutors said Sean Ramaley held a $2,500-per-month position that was really a "ghost job" — a claim that testimony contradicted or muddied. Commonwealth witnesses said Ramaley's state-paid "job" amounted to making fundraising calls and knocking on doors as a candidate. The issue was whether he did any work. If so, it was hard to call his a no-show job. After a five-day trial, jurors acquitted Ramaley on all counts on December 10, 2009.

"Vindicated!" he said in a booming voice as he exited the courtroom, facing a few reporters. Ramaley's reaction was surprising, given his reserved demeanor. He did not testify. I was surprised by the power of his voice, which seemed to express five weeks of pent-up frustration and a year and a half of angst.

I met Sean Ramaley briefly before, in January 2005, on swearing-in day for legislators. It was his first day in office. I sought him out as one of the new members in hopes of somehow getting a story. He was circumspect, introverted and a bit stiff. He didn't smile much. There is nothing wrong with that, but it is uncharacteristic of politicians, most of whom are over-the-top extroverts, full of themselves.

Ramaley's case was of larger significance for two reasons: it was the first to go to trial in the Attorney General's public corruption investigation — the first test for the office in the Bonusgate and Computergate grand jury presentments. Second, when indicted, he was the Democratic nominee for an open Senate seat previously held by former Democratic senator Gerald LaValle.

Party leaders pressured Ramaley to bow out of the race following his indictment in July 2008. (LaValle's entanglement with Mike Veon would indirectly result in legal troubles for LaValle's wife, Darla. Gerald LaValle was not charged and offered testimony for the Commonwealth in a case dealing with Veon's alleged misuse of a nonprofit, which he and Veon co-directed.)

Philip Ignelzi, a Pittsburgh defense lawyer, arguably won the case for Sean Ramaley in August 2009 when he convinced Dauphin County Judge Richard Lewis to sever Ramaley's case from those of Veon and 10 other co-defendants. He did so because no one alleged that Ramaley was involved in the bonus program. It turned out that Veon and only three co-defendants would actually go to trial in 2010; the others cut deals with prosecutors.

Ramaley would stand alone and not alongside Veon and his former aides Brett Cott, Annamarie Perretta Rosepink and Steve Keefer. Prosecutors could not paint Ramaley as part of a criminal enterprise that used tax money to improve the chance of winning campaigns. Jurors acquitted former Veon aide Keefer, a peripheral figure at best, so there's a chance that the Veon jury would have kicked the charges against Ramaley. Still, as experienced trial lawyers say, one rolls the dice with juries. Unlike Keefer, Ramaley had been a legislator. That hurt more than it helped. It could have made him an unconscious target in jurors' minds.

Ignelzi, elected to the Allegheny County Court of Common Pleas and preparing to take the bench in January 2010, was quick on his feet, sharp, and at times shrill. He would raise his voice in theatrical outrage. He was tenacious, and his Pittsburghese — almost a midwestern twang — was thicker than that of senior deputy AG Anthony Krastek, considered one of the Attorney General's top trial lawyers. Ignelzi told me this was his "swan's song," the last case he would try before donning a black robe.

Krastek was more laid back, in some ways more polished than Ignelzi. But he showed little fire or flare. And the Commonwealth's case was thin. Ramaley held a "sham job," Krastek argued to the jury.

Five former Veon aides trooped through the courtroom to say that Ramaley didn't really do any work. He was marginally there some mornings and was out knocking on doors during afternoons and evenings to talk to voters, they contended. Four defense witnesses said he did work.

According to the records, there's no question that Ramaley held a part-time job with Veon from July through November 2004. But Krastek contended that Ramaley, when there, was "dialing for dollars" — raising money for his campaign.

To me, the troubling part was that the Commonwealth never presented phone records of Sean Ramaley's calls, nor did it bring in donors or potential donors to verify approximately when Ramaley supposedly contacted them. Ignelzi hammered this point home to the jury. It became clear through testimony that Ramaley did some work in Veon's office; how much we may never know. The defense suggested that he provided legal advice. He certainly campaigned.

Ramaley never testified. Instead, Philip Ignelzi brought in his mom to talk about her son's virtues. That probably was more effective than hearing from Sean Ramaley. His mother choked back tears at times. She described him as studious and ethical. When he went away to college, he was disheartened to see the binge-drinking and wild parties, she claimed. He would return home, driving icy roads most weekends, to get away from the campus mayhem. Krastek gently cross-examined her so as not to make the jury dislike him. He could have grilled Sean Ramaley, but not his mom.

Both extremes are laid out in such a trial — on one hand, it was a "ghost job"; on the other, Ramaley met all his responsibilities. There seemed to be no doubt that Veon provided the job as a favor to give Ramaley some income while he ran for the House.

Based on the testimony, it's fair to conclude that he worked and campaigned. Maybe his work schedule was curtailed. Who knows? But this wasn't like the "ghost jobs" prevalent in the 1970s in Pennsylvania, when "ghosts" would be on the payroll, but never needed to show up.

I was told that Sean Ramaley's acquittal reverberated through the Attorney General's office. It would prompt a series of phone calls from Tom Corbett to prosecutors over the Christmas season. Corbett was running for governor, and he could not afford to lose the Veon case.

A new legal team, led by the Philly guys and a top deputy, Frank Fina, was brought in for the Veon trial to start in February. It was easy to see how Anthony Krastek may have been a scapegoat. But he sure didn't have much to work with.

Ramaley, his wife and his parents hugged each other after the verdict. "First, I've got God to thank," Ramaley told reporters. "He's gotten me through this, without a doubt. ... Faith, family and friends carried me through this."

Krastek told reporters he had "no apologies for this prosecution." I liked Krastek. He was one of the most experienced trial guys for the Attorney General. But he had to know, as a matter of perception, that this loss would hurt his standing. My view is that the AG's office took this case too lightly.

According to Krastek, the case against Ramaley was only "a little sliver" of the larger case against Mike Veon. Another jury would hear new evidence, so no one should draw a conclusion about the Ramaley verdict. He was right about that. Prosecutors Patrick Blessington, Marc Constanza and Frank Fina were probably better off at the Veon trial not having the former "Boys Nation" selection sitting at the defense table with Mike Veon. It would have diluted the picture.

By Christmas 2009, Tom Corbett was actively running for governor after posting convincing numbers in the 2008 Attorney General's race. He had managed to win resoundingly in a Democratic year. He announced his candidacy three months before the Ramaley trial.

In the end, the Ramaley verdict had no impact on the Veon trial or the Perzel case. But at the time, some people — especially Corbett's critics — viewed it as a chink in the armor, a harbinger of a legal train wreck. Buoyed by the Ramaley verdict, Veon's lawyers knew this prosecutorial team could be defeated.

16

Mixed Martial Arts
in the Octagon

February 1, 2010

When Patrick Blessington rose from the prosecution table to address the jury in *Commonwealth of Pennsylvania v. Mike Veon, Annamarie Perretta-Rosepink, Brett Cott and Steve Keefer*, I was, at first, thoroughly unimpressed. A lean, angular man with a gray, Wyatt Earp mustache and a thick Philly accent was the best the Attorney General's office could offer? The best in the state to handle a case that people from Pittsburgh to Philly were watching closely? It was a case of more than casual interest to Attorney General Thomas W. Corbett, a Republican candidate for governor. In fact, Corbett could not afford to lose. His persona as a tough crime fighter was integrally linked to this case against Veon, the former number-two House Democratic leader.

Blessington was going up against experienced defense attorneys, two of them the size of defensive tackles. Veon's lawyers, Dan Raynak and Joel Sansone, were hungry and they were looking for an upset win. It appeared that they were invested heavily in the notion that Veon was being persecuted by Corbett for partisan gain. Bryan Walk and William Fetterhoff, representing two of Veon's co-defendants, were seasoned pros. Raynak, in particular, made it clear from day one that he was the alpha dog and he was laying claim to the courtroom.

Blessington seemed a bit rough around the edges in front of the Dauphin County jury. He didn't have the smooth delivery and commanding presence of top-flight defense attorneys like William Costopoulos, Brian McMonagle or

Dennis Cogan, Vincent Fumo's Philly lawyer. Insiders called Blessington the "Steve Carlton" of the Attorney General's office. It was a comparison to the former Phillies ace who delivered on the mound but who wouldn't talk to reporters, period.

Blessington was a plodder. His style was choppy. His opening argument was very good, but there was not much sizzle. Only over time would I learn what an amazing prosecutor he is. Whether the defense lawyers knew it or not, they were up against a prosecutor from Northeast Philadelphia who has devoted his life to taking down bad guys. He has practiced and studied his art on a level comparable to a martial arts master. It's what he does and who he is. Those who have worked closely with him say he does virtually nothing else. He studies his cases on evenings and weekends. He knows every nuance.

It's the blue-collar work ethic: he will not be outworked.

I had no idea at the time but would later learn that as a state prosecutor, Blessington had won death penalty murder convictions in three different counties: a father who murdered his two sons, a toddler and an infant, in Columbia County; the 2004 murder of two deputy sheriffs in Bradford County; and the robbery murders of three elderly women in Lackawanna County. He also convicted a doctor for the 25-year-old Susquehanna County murder of a lawyer, with whose wife the physician was having an affair. As a senior deputy Attorney General on Corbett's public corruption unit, Blessington was a street-smart guy from the row houses of Northeast Philadelphia, whose past generations produced many of the city's cops and firefighters. He was at times loud and argumentative, particularly when provoked by Dan Raynak.

Walter Cohen, former acting Attorney General, won a jury trial as a defense attorney in a separate public corruption case against Patrick Blessington. You can't outshout him, Cohen maintained. The trick is to play beneath his rage and let the jury see that your argument is rational and sensible, he added.

Still, Blessington got results. He was apparently the best trial lawyer the Attorney General's office could offer. He does not "wow" you. Very gradually, he grows on you, and I suspect it might have been the same for jurors.

DARKENED COURTROOM

For nearly two months in 2010, prosecutors and defense attorneys for Mike Veon and his co-defendants squared off in Courtroom 1 on the fifth floor of the Dauphin County Courthouse before Judge Richard Lewis and in the hallway outside the courtroom.

My memories of the trial are colored by some of the highlights, but also by the depressing atmosphere. By late afternoon in February, this courtroom held several shades of darkness. The hallway outside the courtroom, where some of the combat took place, was even darker. I've never been to a trial where both sides were on edge to this degree.

The Bonusgate trial was bitterly fought. Veon got what he would call a "fierce and ferocious" defense from Dan Raynak and Joel Sansone. It's what he wanted. Normally, there's some collegiality among attorneys outside the courtroom. That was not true in this case. In court and in the hallway, there was constant tension and backbiting. Head games — almost a form of Psy-ops — were employed by defense lawyers to try and throw the prosecution off its game. Raynak and Sansone would complain about the earlier intimidation of witnesses by prosecutors and agents, and the large presence of the Attorney General's personnel in the courtroom each day, ranging from a handful to more than a dozen.

I had no doubt that this group of prosecutors was an intimidating bunch in f-bomb-laced tag-team interviews of potential witnesses. Of course, they were tough interrogations. They never denied the in-your-face proffer sessions to determine who would get immunity. Attending a proffer is voluntary.

These sides just did not like each other. In a pretrial hearing, Bryan Walk, attorney for co-defendant Brett Cott, delivered some heated words to Patrick Blessington after the judge was out of the courtroom. Blessington stood still, saying nothing. It was tense. Most of it was out of earshot of reporters attending the hearing. It foreshadowed the enmity that would play out at trial.

Being from a rough Philly neighborhood, Blessington did not shy away from conflict. Again, he was underwhelming to look at, but he was an experienced street fighter in his youth.

DAN RAYNAK: A POLITICAL TRIAL

It was personal to Dan Raynak and Joel Sansone. Raynak played football with Mike Veon at Allegheny College. Sansone was Raynak's boyhood friend from Newcastle. They were representing a leading Pennsylvania Democrat. The stakes were enormous. Veon's life was on the line. Tom Corbett could not afford to lose back-to-back corruption cases after Sean Ramaley's acquittal.

To Veon and his lawyers, this was a political trial. Raynak and Sansone did everything within their power to make it about prosecutorial misconduct, selective prosecution and the 2010 governor's race. They lost a pretrial motion on those grounds, so they were limited in how far they could go during the trial. What they couldn't get in during court sessions, they offered to the media during courtroom breaks. At this point, 10 Republicans, including John Perzel, had been charged, but that didn't stop Raynak from painting Bonusgate as a Corbett-led GOP jihad against Democrats. Prosecutors viewed it as a large-scale criminal enterprise they had dismantled. Taking a step back, here was a prosecution of former top Democrats by the Republican Attorney General who was running for governor. It was unprecedented in Pennsylvania.

SHAKE-UP

Over the 2009 Christmas season, after Sean Ramaley walked, there were high-level talks in the AG's office about who was going to handle the Veon case. Eventually, a team would emerge: Patrick Blessington as lead trial attorney; Chief Deputy Attorney General Frank Fina, a New York native and former federal prosecutor, whose soft courtroom voice belied his toughness; E. Marc Costanzo, a flamboyant Philly guy and smooth operator who would emerge as the team's spokesman and was nicknamed "The Fonz"; James Reeder, a former York County prosecutor, and chief deputy Chris Carusone, perhaps the most cerebral of the bunch from the Attorney General's appeals section. That crew, plus at least three agents, had Dan Raynak constantly complaining about the army of prosecutors and what it was costing the taxpayers. Bonusgate was after all about costs to taxpayers.

Frank Fina provided the core strength. A Bonusgate witness who was not charged later told me about his interview with Fina. He cited his almost telepathic ability to know whether someone did anything wrong. Fina knew. And he knew how to get at it. If you did something wrong, the last guy you wanted on the case was Frank Fina.

Fina had worked in the U.S. Justice Department as a prosecutor for the Inspector General in the U.S. Attorney's office in the District of Columbia, and as an assistant DA in Union County. He is one of the quickest lawyers on his feet I've ever seen.

Blessington and Costanzo were guys, formerly with the Philly DA's office, who had each handled hundreds of trials. Anthony Krastek, who lost the Ramaley case, was out. The Attorney General's office prosecutors seem to have had a Messianic complex about doing their job, a defense attorney told me. People involved in a case become witnesses for them — or defendants. Like most prosecutors, their world is black and white, truth and lies, perps and victims.

IGNORING THE SANDUSKY CASE?

Dan Raynak's rants about wasted resources on Bonusgate would later be raised by Bill DeWeese in 2012, suggesting that Tom Corbett shortchanged the sex abuse investigation of Jerry Sandusky, which took almost three years. According to the *Patriot-News*, which won the Pulitzer Prize for Sara Ganim's coverage, there was only one state police investigator assigned to Sandusky in 2010. In 2012, DeWeese was bellowing about it to anyone who would listen, saying there had been 14 agents and prosecutors at various times on his case and just one for a suspected serial child abuser.

Corbett would later claim it was "absolutely false." There were two Bureau of Narcotics investigators on the Sandusky case, he said. Trial testimony identified four agents overall who worked on the case, according to Nils Frederiksen, spokes-man for the Attorney General's office.

In secret grand jury investigations it is usually impossible on the outside to tell who is doing what. But one investigator in the Sandusky case became a "fact" due to lack of any evidence to the contrary at first and by the repeated assertion by numerous media outlets.

Nils Fredericksen would say the critics of the investigation were of three kinds: politicians, defendants and defense attorneys.

"A BRILLIANT SCHEME"

Most of the defendants charged with Mike Veon in Bonusgate had agreed to plea bargains with prosecutors by the time of trial in February 2010. Two former key aides were slated as witnesses. One was Michael Manzo, former chief of staff to Bill DeWeese, but also the de facto chief of staff for Veon, and Jeffrey Foreman, who held the formal title of Veon's chief of staff. They were prepared to testify that Veon approved the bonus scheme in which $1.4 million in tax money was paid to staffers who worked on campaigns.

On February 1, 2010, the marathon trial began.

In his opening statement, Patrick Blessington told jurors that the bonus sys-tem was a "brilliant scheme that worked like a charm." Veon and Manzo knew, since the scheme was illegal, that they couldn't advertise bonuses for campaign work. Staffers needed to hear about it and discover it for the scheme to work, the prosecutor suggested. By the spring of 2006, the word was clearly out. By the fifth year, Blessington noted, "a veritable army of people were volunteering."

"They knew a check was coming. These bonuses were absolutely, positively, and illegally linked to campaign work," Blessington was quoted as saying by *The Phila-delphia Inquirer.* "What this comes down to is very simple. All of these charges involve these defendants using taxpayers' money, taxpayer-paid resources for cam-paign work," he added.

It is against the law to use taxpayers' money to win elections, the prosecutor pointed out. It was "a classic example of organized institutional, criminal behavior," Blessington told the jury. He was passionate about the Commonwealth's case, but still hadn't sold me. He became emotional on objections and in doing battle with Dan Raynak.

Raynak was forceful in his opening. He is a hulking man with a goatee and gray hair combed straight back. He eschewed the "uniform" of dark, pinstripe suits favored by prosecutors. He dressed more causally in a sport coat and slacks. He was very quick on his feet, personable at times with jurors, but frequently loud and angry about the perceived injustice to his friend. His manners just got in the way.

At times, Raynak could be obnoxious. But when he spoke, due to his great size, he commanded the attention of virtually everyone in court. I found myself frequently wondering what he would do next. As a court-appointed attorney, Raynak represented a lot of homicide defendants in Arizona. If your life was on the line in Arizona, you might want him on your side. In a political corruption trial in Pennsylvania, Raynak was playing in a different league. He was also emotionally invested, but lawyers shouldn't represent their friends at trial.

DEWEESE DID IT

Mike Veon's defense was simple. As Mario Cattibiani wrote for his "lede" in *The Inquirer* on February 2, 2010: "It was all Bill DeWeese's fault." DeWeese controlled the purse strings. He was "the head guy, the top of the food chain," Dan Raynak commented. "That's the guy who was in charge."

DeWeese was an "unindicted co-conspirator" in the bonus case. Raynak said he would call DeWeese to the witness stand. And that would be a confrontation. (Over a month later, in the defense phase of the trial, after he was subpoenaed by Veon's lawyer, DeWeese came to the courthouse and took the Fifth Amendment in Judge Lewis' office, a story I reported on March 9th while filing from the courtroom. He slipped into the courthouse early and reporters were backtracking to put together what happened. Raynak would say nothing. And Blessington? He was like Steve Carlton, who wouldn't talk after a no-hitter. So it required some intricate sourcing.)

As the trial opened, Raynak told the court: "There was a conspiracy all right but it had nothing to do with Mike Veon."

Eight of the 12 people charged admitted their guilt and most of them testified at Veon's trial. It's hard to get a half-dozen people to lie. Raynak and Sansone went after them, accusing them of cutting deals to save their skins. Raynak was tough on cross-examination, but his approach was often over the top. Still, Veon's lawyers only needed to convince one juror of reasonable doubt. If that happened and the jury was hung, there'd be a mistrial. The Commonwealth would have to decide whether to go to trial again. They would do so and it would be a black eye for the Attorney General's office.

TWITTER TIME

The Veon trial was the Grand Twitter Experiment. Judge Richard Lewis allowed reporters to use their laptops and phones to transmit stories and tweet from the courtroom. It was unusual in a state that does not allow televised trials. Lewis, a former DA, thought outside the box of the courtroom. He knew the importance of this case to the public. Twitter was a new medium, and Lewis wasn't about to close the door on it automatically. There would be an unsuccessful motion to prevent it from Annamarie Perretta-Rosepink's attorney, Michael Palermo. The rap against Twitter was that because of the instantaneous nature of the reports, jurors and witnesses would be able to see what other witnesses said or what attorneys were arguing without the jury in the room. That's conceivable, but they are not supposed to be looking at their phones or iPads anyway. They could read all sorts of things they shouldn't.

Before the trial, I was barely aware of Twitter. I was signed up and used it to post my stories each day. I still was of a firm belief that any breaking news should be on the newspaper's web site first, not on Twitter. I thought it was a fad until I started looking at the exponential growth of my own page.

I tried tweeting during the Veon trial, but found it to be a distraction. By the time I posted something, a witness would say something else, something better, and I might miss some of it. I found it hard to concentrate on what the witness meant and the nuances. I was supposed to be doing web page updates primarily and writing an a.m. story. At that time, my editors were not requiring me to tweet as part of my job. But it would be a good place to experiment. I was comfortable tweeting about the next witness up, a major event with the jury breaking for the day. It wasn't until the Penn State cover-up case almost two years later when my editors wanted wall-to-wall tweeting. They were smart enough to send a second reporter, Deb Erdley, to help with it.

By 2012, there was a formal proposal before the Supreme Court to ban tweeting and electronic transmissions from courtrooms. That was absurd given that the court seemed proud of the fact that it had its first televised session. TV is OK but news blurbs aren't?

To some extent I suppose it's a function of age.

My younger competitor, Tracie Mauriello of the *Post-Gazette,* was the Queen of Twitter. Hundreds of people at the capitol, including Tom Corbett, followed the trial through her posts and periodic tweets from the rest of us. At the time, I didn't care what she tweeted. I thought it was more important to break stories.

> Here are some of Tracie's tweets as pgPoliTweets:
> *Raynak:* Employees called Manzo "the chief." He was in charge. #bonusgate
> Raynak is quite animated and loud now, even for him. #bonusgate
> Raynak is recapping six weeks of testimony in two hours. Not by filtering anything, but by speaking at warp speed. #bonusgate
> *Blessington:* "Every tax dollar is paid for with the sweat of taxpayers. . . . This is all about taxpayer resources."
> *Raynak:* Mike Veon is not Ted Stevens or Rod Blogo. #bonusgate
> *Blessington:* Don't believe one word of the attorneys that represent Mike Veon. #bonusgate

Blessington says defense has been treating this trial as a political campaign. "It's all about spin." #bonusgate

Defense has said prosecutors want to use this case to grab headlines that will launch boss Tom Corbett into guv's office. #bonusgate

Blessington: Veon staff institutionalized the criminal use of state resources. #bonusgate

Blessington: There is a direct correlation between amount of time staffers volunteered & amount of bonuses they got. #bonusgate

Throughout the trial, Dan Raynak was constantly pushing Judge Lewis for every inch he could get in the courtroom. Lewis is one of the most patient men I've ever seen. Some say he lost control of the courtroom to the flamboyant Raynak. Several weeks into the trial, by March 14th, Lewis finally hit his breaking point. After the jury left for the day, the judge told Raynak he could be charged with contempt. He cited Raynak's defiant behavior and his shouting. Lewis criticized him for talking at "breakneck speed." Raynak could be fined or jailed if the behavior didn't stop, the judge added. He put up with far more than most judges would tolerate.

In my view, Lewis realized that if there were a conviction, he needed a bullet-proof appeal. The last thing a judge wants is a verdict that is overturned because he muzzled the defense attorney, especially a Republican judge who was a former DA shutting down the attorney of a prominent Democrat in an allegedly political trial. Lewis warned Raynak that if he kept acting out, he should bring a checkbook and a toothbrush.

"SHOCKING TO THE CONSCIENCE"

The licks Dan Raynak couldn't get in during court, he'd reserve for the court of public opinion. During the defense phase of the trial, he complained about defense witnesses having been bullied by attorneys and agents during the investigation. Nancy Thompson, a former Veon aide, testified that she had been screamed at and berated by James Reeder during an interview.

"It's just out-of-control, inexcusable behavior, as far as I am concerned. That's not how you get at the truth," Raynak told reporters. "It's really almost shocking to the conscience what they've done with this case…We have witnesses who said they called them liars, swore at them and tried to put words in their mouth," he added. "It's not what you'd expect in the great state of Pennsylvania. It's certainly not what you'd expect in the United States. This is something you might hear about in a country far away where they don't have any justice."

The prosecutors weren't trying to coerce confessions. They were testing people to see if they were lying, if they told the whole truth, and how well they would hold up on the stand.

THE NEW JURY

It was very tense on March 19, 2010 when, on the sixth day of jury deliberations, a juror was released due to illness and "personal reasons," according to Judge Lewis. That decision followed a lengthy consultation with the defense lawyers and prosecutors. The recently constituted jury would begin anew. Two days earlier, when the jury reported back to the courtroom at the end of the day, the juror who was dismissed and two others were crying. The woman who was eventually dismissed said then that deliberations were "hard on everybody" and that jurors were turning against each other. Lewis told reporters in the courtroom that the woman's departure had nothing to do with the case or her position on the charges. Members of the new jury were smiling and upbeat by the end of the day on the 19th when they returned to the courtroom before going home for the day.

Dan Raynak and Joel Sansone were not happy campers. Their request for a mistrial, along with attorneys for two co-defendants, Bryan Walk and Michael Palermo, was denied. In his first major trial, Palermo, who was Annamarie Perretta-Rosepink's attorney, said it was improper to replace the juror who complained of migraines, mental illness and nausea in the middle of deliberations. The lawyers for Corbett's office argued that Lewis was following procedure. The judge agreed with them. A verdict would come quickly with the new jury.

THE VERDICT

"That's it? That's the best he [Corbett] can do?" Brett Cott said on March 22, 2010. A guilty verdict is like a death of a loved one. You may be expecting it like when an elderly parent or relative faces a terminal illness. When it happens it is still a shock. Even when expected, death still stings. Like death, a guilty verdict causes pain, separation and dysfunction among those close to the person convicted. Until it happens, there is still a belief that the outcome could be changed. In Mike Veon's case, a guilty verdict seemed likely to me. But on how many counts? He faced 59 charges. Many of them could be reduced to misdemeanors if the jury felt the crimes were less than $2,000. If he were only nicked on, say, one charge, the sentence would be relatively light and the defense would be vindicated in its condemnation of the Attorney General's investigation and prosecution. It was a Monday, and only the second day since the new juror was on board.

Overall, it was the seventh day of deliberations and followed six weeks of testimony. Just that day, Judge Lewis had turned down a motion for a mistrial from the defense, claiming the jury was deadlocked. It was believed to be the longest criminal trial in Dauphin County history. Word came in early in the evening of March 22nd that a verdict had been reached. It was after 8:30 p.m. before all the verdicts had been read. With spin sessions by both sides in the hallway, it was close to 9:00 p.m. by the time the outside world reacted. Facebook lit up at 9:04 with a series of messages, starting with "about time."

The courtroom was dark, unusually so. It lent a surreal atmosphere to the reading of the verdicts. All eyes were on Mike Veon. He showed no emotion. Steve Keefer walked. He was acquitted of 16 charges. Keefer was a casualty of the Attorney General's investigation. The former IT supervisor for House Democrats, Keefer was clearly a Veon guy. But I could not recall any incriminating evidence against him from the trial. It's not clear why he was charged. William Fetterhoff said he never should have been charged. Keefer says it is simply because he would not tell the Attorney General's office what they wanted to hear.

Keefer had called me after the charges were filed. I had never met him before that. We agreed to meet at the Hilton. He made a plea that I look into his innocence. He swore he'd done nothing wrong, but that he just wouldn't lie about the other defendants.

It's what I'd do if I faced a similar situation: go to someone, anyone, who could help. I'm sorry I didn't do anything. The particulars of Keefer, from Lebanon County, as the low man on the totem pole were really not news in Pittsburgh. He looked more like a bouncer than a state staffer. He was husky and muscular with a shaved head and a goatee. I didn't know at the time about Keefer's artistic side: he was also professional photographer.

The prosecutors went 0 for 16. It was a resounding victory for Keefer and for Fetterhoff, who delivered a three-hour closing argument on behalf of his client. Keefer burst into tears. He immediately tweeted the news.

For Brett Cott, the verdict was mixed. He was guilty of three of 42 counts — none on bonuses. Annamarie Perretta-Rosepink went down on five of 22 charges. Mike Veon was convicted of 14 of 59 charges — 13 felonies and one misdemeanor.

"They [the jurors] did a good job of sorting it out," Bryan Walk remarked. "Let's be honest. The Commonwealth brought 140 charges. They put these people's faces up at a press conference...22 charges of 140 is what they get?"

But Frank Fina called it a "good day for the people of Pennsylvania. We hope it sends a strong signal to the rest of our elected officials...to stop using the people's money for their own benefit."

Raynak would later boast on his web site that "in one of the largest political corruption cases in Pennsylvania history" he won acquittals "on the vast majority of charges." That is true, as is Walk's statement. The defense lawyers deserve credit for reducing the potential prison time for their clients. But the bottom line was that Veon was going to prison, as were Cott and, probably, Perretta-Rosepink.

"Another time, another day," Veon said upon leaving the courtroom. His wife, Stephanie, wearing black, was escorted from the courtroom by a phalanx of three women and two men, who cut a path through reporters. "Tom Corbett, corrupt!" a woman could be heard saying. "Tom Corbett, all for political gain. Perzel, you are next."

Veon's problem was that he faced another round of felonies filed by the Attorney General's office in 2009 for alleged misuse of a nonprofit he founded and funded with state grants. The Beaver Initiative for Growth (BIG) case was still hanging out there.

Brett Cott, standing a few feet from prosecutor Marc Costanzo, called him a "douche bag." I could not believe the guy's cajones. A conviction is supposed to humble you. By this point, I'd be looking to impress the court with my remorse. Not Cott. "That's it? That's the best he [Corbett] can do? I hope this helps him get elected governor," Cott said in the hallway. "Good for him."

For Mike Veon, the acquittals included billing taxpayers for food after basketball games and using public resources to get Ralph Nader off the ballot. What stuck was the bonuses. The jury found Veon guilty of approving $1.4 million in bonuses for political work.

In May, Cott was sentenced to 21 months to five years for stealing taxpayer resources for campaigns. Bryan Walk noted that there are drug dealers prosecuted by the Attorney General who receive less time. The sentence "sends a loud, clear message this kind of activity will not be tolerated," Costanzo remarked.

Patrick Blessington said Brett Cott showed no remorse. According to prosecutors, Cott was paid $262,561 in salary and bonuses by taxpayers from 2004 to 2006, and during that period he illegally worked on 20 campaigns at the state and local level including judicial races of interest to Veon. Cott was not convicted on bonuses. His crimes were a "violation of the public's right to a fair electoral process," Judge Lewis noted.

Cott served less than 21 months and was out by the time Bill DeWeese was on trial.

Veon was sentenced on June 18, 2010 to six to 14 years in prison, plus a $37,000 fine and $100,000 in restitution. Lewis called his crimes "a flagrant abuse of power." At sentencing, Veon still refused to accept responsibility for what amounted to the theft overall of $1.9 million in public resources, including bonuses and other activity, Blessington noted.

"I have made mistakes in my life and career," Veon admitted. "I am sorry for those mistakes." That's as close as Mike Veon would get to an apology.

He was cuffed after the sentencing and was transported to Dauphin County Prison, a holding area for state inmates before they go to Camp Hill State Correctional Institution for processing. It's not clear to me why Veon was handcuffed and taken immediately. Other Republican and Democratic defendants were given reporting dates. Lawyers have told me there is no rule or logical explanation.

Annamarie Perretta-Rosepink seemed sincere, or her attorney put the fear of God in her. "I apologize to this court and I am sorry for what led me here today." She admitted directing people to work on campaigns. She received a three- to six-month term in jail, which meant a county rather than a state facility. But down the road she also had to face the BIG nonprofit charges with Veon.

Annamarie Perretta-Rosepink and Brett Cott lost their appeals in Superior Court. Veon's is still pending.

After the Bonusgate verdict, Patrick Blessington moved to the Philadelphia DA's office and won the first-ever case against a priest supervisor charged with covering up abuse of children by priests. In June 2012, a jury found Monsignor William J. Lynn guilty of child endangerment. Frank Fina went on to sit second chair with "Hollywood" Joe McGinnis on the successful prosecution of Jerry Sandusky in Centre County. McGinnis came back to the AG's office to help fill the void left by Blessington's departure.

There would be a lull in the corruption cases until Vincent Fumo got another day in court.

17

The Resentencing:
"Mumbo-Jumbo Justification"

November 10, 2011

The public wasn't alone in thinking Judge Ronald Buckwalter erred in sentencing Senate Democratic powerbroker Vincent J. Fumo to 55 months in prison. The Third Circuit Court of Appeals, in August 2011, ordered Fumo to be resentenced after a new sentencing hearing. It looked like the judge's number was finally up. People across the state were watching. But the remedy, by law, required Buckwalter to sentence Fumo again. Surely he could not give Fumo another pass. The judge wasn't obligated to change the sentence.

How Fumo got away with the outlandish charges he made to the Senate of Pennsylvania to begin with is a scathing indictment of the Senate's lack of oversight of senators' spending. How could it go undetected?

The week before the new hearing, prosecutors filed documents with the court revealing 12,068 pages of email Fumo had sent from his prison in Ashland, Kentucky. Like other inmates, Fumo had been given full warning that his email was monitored by the Department of Corrections. Even his email to his lawyers was not privileged.

Fumo compared himself to Christ, denouncing the "dumb" jury, and his "so-called crimes." "There were no victims," he wrote.

Fumo kept an enemies list, many of them reporters. Almost no one — from former lawyers, former friends and the prosecutors — escaped his wrath. "I will repay all these fuckers one day," Fumo promised. Only Judge Buckwalter was exempt. Fumo knew the sentence he was serving was a good deal. "I do feel Christ-like in the injustices I have suffered throughout this whole nightmare," he stated.

Fumo had big plans upon his release. He planned to write a book, "Vince Fumo, the most effective legislator in America." He planned to return to the capitol as a lobbyist, buy an antique tractor for his farm in Halifax, and acquire a Key West property.

Again with the victim complex, Fumo wrote: "I feel like Caesar and Christ all tied into one with Brutus and Judas both stabbing me in the back." He compared himself to Jews in concentration camps, prisoners at Guantanamo and the Mubarak family in Egypt. Not only did the emails show an unrepentant Fumo, prosecutors said, they showed an inmate intent on seeking revenge.

Judge Buckwalter was having none of it. He made it seem like the prosecutors had gone too far, prying into the man's personal life. The victim shtick seemed to work. Sporting a white beard and long, silver-streaked hair in court, Fumo looked nothing like the affluent powerbroker he once was when he returned to Buckwalter's courtroom in November 2011 to be resentenced. He wore an olive prison jumpsuit. He was handcuffed behind his back and wore slip-on sneakers, courtesy of the federal prison in Ashland. Prosecutors were seeking a 15-year prison term.

More than 50 friends and supporters of Fumo's, including state Senator Michael Stack (D–Philadelphia), packed the courtroom, four rows deep. Fumo broke into a big grin when he stood for the lunch break and turned to see about 20 well-wishers waving to him from the courtroom. Many were relatives and friends. I talked to some of them and they absolutely loved Vince Fumo.

Fumo was 68 at the time of the resentencing hearing. He has heart disease, diabetes, and suffers from depression and anxiety disorders, his lawyers told the court. But he had gained 10 pounds since entering the prison system in 2009, and his medical tests have improved in key areas, a federal prison official stated. I thought he looked relatively healthy despite the jailhouse pallor. He also had a pronounced facial tic that I had never noticed before.

The new sentence was delivered by Judge Buckwalter in open court at the end of the second day of the hearing on November 10, 2011. Buckwalter said that after the first sentence some believed he was in awe of Fumo. He insisted that was not true.

It seemed like it to me.

Buckwalter, a semi-retired senior judge who was 74 at the time, was sympathetic to Fumo's physical ailments. He seemed to buy into the senator's patter. They even exchanged information about a book on the penal system.

"I have a copy right here," Fumo said, as if he were going to lend his personal copy to Buckwalter. Ronnie and Vince's book club.

So there it was at last, the sentence. Fumo would spend six more months in prison, the judge decided. Six months? That meant a total of 60 months on the 137 counts. I wasn't sure I heard it right.

Fumo was also ordered to repay $1.1 million in restitution on top of the $2.8 million he'd already paid. He'd fleeced the taxpayers, the nonprofit and the seaport museum for his personal and political needs.

If cameras were permitted in the courtroom, a picture of the faces of feds sitting in the first and second rows on the prosecution's side would have been priceless. Of course, they couldn't say anything. But the long looks of disappointment said it all. I couldn't tell how many were attorneys or agents. But they included FBI agent Vicki Humphreys and former agent Kathleen McAfee, the lead investigators in the Fumo case.

Buckwalter's explanation for the resentencing was that he believed the government had overcharged Fumo in connection with four events. The best commentary on the resentencing hearing was given by Pulitzer Prize winner Buzz Bissinger in a *Philadelphia Daily News* column on November 15, 2011:

> "The upshot: A corrupt politician who should have gotten at least 10 years on top of the original 55-month sentence, got an additional six months.
>
> "Buckwalter obscenely kissed Fumo's ass last week by joking with him. Just like in the original trial in 2009, he apparently decided resentencing based on some mumbo-jumbo justification that only he believes is right. In doing so, the judge let a man of evil, vindictiveness, arrogance, nastiness, not to mention serious criminal behavior in which he showed no remorse, look like a persecuted public servant who had a few teensy-weensy mistakes."

If Vince Fumo was the king of deal-making, the prince with a similar sense of entitlement presided in the House of Representatives.

18

Prince of the House

February 6, 2012

Imagine being locked in a room for two and a half days with a full-blown narcissist, teetering on the edge of megalomania. Naturally, he dominates the conservation. He lectures. Virtually a politician on steroids, he's supercharged, on edge and surging with unbridled emotion. There's no escape.

That's what it was like spending several hours on Thursday, February 2nd, Friday, February 3rd and Monday morning, February 6, 2012 with former House Speaker Bill DeWeese as he awaited the verdict of a Dauphin County jury. The jury was deliberating on six felony counts against DeWeese brought by a statewide grand jury in December 2009 under the direction of former Republican Attorney General Tom Corbett, who was now Pennsylvania's governor.

DeWeese had a captive audience — off and on — of Angela Couloumbis of *The Philadelphia Inquirer*'s Harrisburg Bureau; Mark Shade of Reuters; James Roxbury of Roxbury News; Kendra Nichols of ABC Channel 27; Peter Jackson, the Associated Press Harrisburg Bureau Chief; Rock the Capital's Eric Epstein and me. The wait was nerve-racking. So God only knows how it was tearing him up waiting. . . and waiting. After a long rant, DeWeese would head back to the defense table where he'd sit by himself, sometimes talking on a cell phone, maybe dictating.

There was no one else in the courtroom save for a deputy sheriff or two. On occasions, Matt Miller, the *Patriot-News'* court reporter, sat near the back. On the day of the verdict, DeWeese sat with reporters at a table in a hallway because there was some type of closed-door meeting involving parental rights in the courtroom.

The reporters were waiting outside the fiefdom of Dauphin County President Judge Todd A. Hoover. He had it made it clear that he didn't give a hoot about the needs of statewide reporters camped out in his courtroom. No tweeting, he said. No jury list available to reporters. No explanation given. We couldn't take a chance we'd get a call or email from the judge's office on time to make it from the capitol, a brisk 15-minute walk away.

So here we were with DeWeese, who loves to hear himself talk as much as anything in the world. For his entire career, he has studied and absorbed polysyllabic words to impress people. Yet he is somehow different, transmogrified as he would say, from the arrogant legislative leader I've known since 1983. That was a word he actually used on February 6th, and I had no clue what it meant. Merriam-Webster defines transmogrify as "to change or alter greatly and often with grotesque or humorous effect."

Facing six felony counts and possible prison time humbles you, as one lobbyist reminded me. There's a dash of the superciliousness we've long known, but more of the Greene County boy born to J. Victor ("Vic") and Louise ("Dotty") DeWeese, the son of a garage/auto dealer owner and a beautician, who grew up in small-town America and became a career Democratic legislator and leader. Dotty is the person who clipped the "word of the day" from a local newspaper and sent it to her son every day while he was in the service.

Or was this kinder, gentler Bill DeWeese a calculated move, an act to win the media over on the issue of his innocence, knowing the battle he faced? During the year before his trial, DeWeese made numerous visits to the capitol newsroom, at times bellowing and ranting about Corbett, during the year before his trial. He was cunning and looking for every edge.

On February 1st, DeWeese was standing behind the railing that separates the courtroom participants from the spectators. His small audience of reporters sat in the near-empty courtroom. He talked and talked: about his case, his unequivocal innocence, his attorney, William C. Costopoulos, whom he seemed to idolize, and most of all about his nemesis, Tom Corbett, whom DeWeese believed was out to get him. He talked "on background," meaning reporters could use it — he wanted us to use it — but not quote him by name on specific phrases or quotations. DeWeese was an expert with 35 years of media experience in flipping back and forth between "on the record" and "off the record." He said he'd never been burned.

So I won't quote him from those courthouse sessions — except for one word. And the source of that word, "transmogrified," could only have been H. William DeWeese. Besides, DeWeese being DeWeese, he'd already said most of this on the record on other occasions.

Bill DeWeese's big problem with Tom Corbett boiled down to this: while majority leader in 2007 and 2008, DeWeese turned evidence over to Corbett that helped the prosecutor win convictions in Bonusgate. With his contract lawyer, former Inspector General Bill Chadwick, DeWeese turned in Frank LaGrotta and the prince's top aides later convicted in Bonusgate, including his chief of staff Michael Manzo. DeWeese called Chadwick his "Republican prosecutor." He had stature with the state prosecutors. He was the former acting District Attorney of Philadelphia.

Bill Chadwick had to find the incriminating emails. His security firm searched the House Democratic Caucus computer system for key words and phrases. He hired dozens of lawyers in Washington, D.C., for the temporary job of going through tens of thousands of emails. He then turned the emails over to Corbett; they played a vital role in convicting Veon, Manzo, and Veon's former aides.

Chadwick's firm was eventually paid $1.7 million by Pennsylvania taxpayers — more than the Democratic caucus bonuses. In all taxpayers would shell out more than 10 times the $1.4 million in illegal bonuses paid by House Democrats for private law firms to represent the House and Senate on the overall legislative investigation, including the Republicans' Computergate. In the bigger picture, taxpayers paid at least $13.9 million in legal fees for all four caucuses from 2007 to 2012 to defend against corruption charges. (Once someone is charged, the state no longer pays lawyers.) The $13.9 million doesn't count fees by Senator Robert Mellow (D–Lackawanna County). Disclosure of Mellow's fees was in litigation.

It's never come out as a fact, but I believe that Chadwick secured informal immunity for DeWeese that he would not be prosecuted on bonuses in return for his cooperation. More likely it was a gentleman's agreement rather than anything formal. Prosecutors honored that and charged him with something else. DeWeese would say it's because he was innocent on the bonuses. There actually was evidence against him in Bonusgate: a 2004 email from research analyst Karen Steiner to DeWeese thanking him for the bonus "for campaigning." He responded, "U R Welcome." DeWeese was at an evening event, saw the email, and responded on his Blackberry, he claims, without reading far enough. On another occasion, an excuse was offered that it was not him but a staffer who responded in his stead. At Mike Veon's trial in 2010, DeWeese took the Fifth Amendment in Judge Lewis' chambers. The bottom line: he presided over the caucus where Bonusgate occurred. For several years at least, Bill Chadwick secured his freedom.

Michael Manzo had testified that DeWeese knew about the illegal bonus scheme, but a Bonusgate case against him would have been thin. After all, DeWeese was described by numerous witnesses as detached from the day-to-day operations of the caucus. Veon and Manzo ran it, according to Manzo's testimony. DeWeese liked the pomp and ceremony, the travel and dining out at someone else's expense (usually lobbyists or taxpayers). You don't attack a king (or a prince) and wound him — it must be a killing shot. Furthermore, clearing DeWeese from the field as a Bonusgate target allowed prosecutors to focus on Veon.

After sitting through both of their trials, I believe that Michael Manzo, more than anyone, conceived of the bonus-for-campaign-work scam and saw that it was carried out. Both Veon and DeWeese were told about it. Those who knew Manzo say he didn't operate without the bosses' approval. It just so happened he had two bosses, one of them paying little attention. Through his deputies, Corbett did not promise DeWeese that he would never be charged on anything.

Bonusgate was a blow from which Bill DeWeese never recovered. His power evaporated with the prospect of being charged. By 2009, he was demoted to caucus whip. I remember DeWeese's analogy that it was like a third baseman being moved to second because his rifle-arm was gone. He had given up those who had been close and most loyal to him, and would eventually turn on Veon. He did whatever he thought he had to do to survive. DeWeese was still a sitting representative when he was charged and at trial in 2012.

Despite all the legal troubles, he was still winning re-election in his district.

After helping to pass the 2005 pay raise, DeWeese was re-elected the following year by a slim margin over an enthusiastic opponent, Republican Greg Hopkins, a former star arena football player. In the 50th District, including Greene and pieces of Fayette and Washington Counties, DeWeese won in 2008 despite the indictment of 12 people with ties to his caucus in Bonusgate. In 2010, while under indictment himself, he was re-elected. Many in the prince's district loved him for bringing home the bacon, including a maximum security state prison with good-paying jobs and benefits.

To save himself, DeWeese made a last-ditch effort in December 2009, voluntarily agreeing to testify before the grand jury investigating him. Virtually every former prosecutor and defense lawyer I've spoken with says it is something one just doesn't do. The deck is stacked against people being investigated in the grand jury process. They can be arrested on the spot for admitting a crime. Perjury is a very real possibility. Politicians try it because they are confident in their ability to persuade. It's what they do.

DeWeese's hubris resulted in a voluntary meeting with agents and appearing as a witness before the grand jury. He was proud of the fact that he was never charged with perjury and equated that with telling the truth. But this decision, no doubt made over the objections of attorney Walter Cohen, a former top state prosecutor representing him at that time, would come back to haunt the prince.

In December 2009, DeWeese was charged by Tom Corbett for using his district office and Harrisburg staff as his campaign apparatus and for keeping a taxpayer-paid fund-raiser on staff. Kevin Sidella, in fact, did campaign fund-raising at the capitol right outside DeWeese's door. Sidella got immunity to testify against his boss. Five felonies were lodged against him: four counts of theft and one count each of conflict of interest and conspiracy. Longtime district aide Sharon Rodavich, who directed DeWeese's campaigns in the district, was also charged.

DeWeese felt used and abused by Corbett. His anger against the white-haired prosecutor, now become governor, had grown in 2011 until he was in full-throttle rage by the time of his trial. From his perspective, he had done everything possible to cooperate with the Attorney General's office.

DeWeese promised a fight. In the final months before trial, he took to the House floor on several occasions to talk about the cost of Corbett's investigation, the refusal of the Attorney General's office to provide information, and what he considered to be selective prosecution and hypocrisy by Governor Corbett. I thought it was unseemly for state lawmakers like Bill DeWeese and Senator Jane Orie to use their positions that way on the floor in the General Assembly. Save it for the courtroom. But DeWeese was saying to Corbett: bring it on.

*   *   *

"All I want is a chunk of bread and a bowl of soup," DeWeese said as he got on an elevator after his first morning at trial as a criminal defendant. "A forbearer of things to come," he said jokingly, meaning that it sounded like the menu in state prison.

"They serve a lot of mac and cheese," I told him.

"Just what I need for my expanding girth," he replied.

He would remain in amazingly good humor through seven days of trial in late January through February 1, 2012. He called it "gallows humor." DeWeese really thought he was going to win. He told me he didn't even think about the possibility of losing until the judge charged the jury on the seventh day.

DeWeese was heading out for some soup. Just a few years before, he could have commanded a legislative staffer to make a run for a "small salad in a large bowl," "a small coffee in a large cup," or even a specific number of M&Ms. Staffers balanced his checkbook, picked up dry cleaning, got his groceries and bought him condoms. DeWeese would tear up pieces of paper into small strips and hand them to someone to throw in the garbage, whether there was a trash can nearby or not, witnesses told a grand jury. "I know members who asked their staff to run out to their houses when they were in Harrisburg to shovel a sidewalk when it snows and make sure my grass got cut over the weekend, stuff like that, but Bill took that to a whole different level," Michael Manzo testified.

Bill DeWeese was the "Prince of the House," with all his needs taken care of by taxpayers. He had a taxpayer-paid driver in a taxpayer-paid car. He regularly used the state plane for trips and in a little more than a year, he ran up $24,000 in bills. Taxpayers paid for his Blackberry and most of his meals. Taxpayer-paid staff set up his dinners, when he put the arm on lobbyists to pick up the tab, or invited history professors to dine with him and discuss his topic of the year — African-American history one year, Jewish history another, the Civil War, the labor movement — DeWeese made a command and it was fulfilled. A former aide described how there once was trouble in getting a professor for a dinner. DeWeese left an angry message on the answering machine: "Get it done."

"Bill's staff was there to serve his personal needs as much as his political needs and his policy needs," Manzo noted.

When he was picked up in his car, DeWeese expected that it was freshly waxed and his driver had all the implements in the trunk organized in a certain way and itemized on a card.

"Bill spent a lot of time focusing on making Bill happy," Manzo would say.

DeWeese later insisted that he always paid the person who ran errands. He had defended the frequency of his flights on a state plane, saying that he represented a rural area without the easy access to metro airports that other leaders enjoyed. Even so, all his needs and whims were met when he served as a top legislative leader: House speaker as well as majority and minority leader.

If DeWeese beat the rap, he had a $119,000 annual state pension awaiting and lifetime health care, according to a pension estimate prepared by Eric Epstein of Rock the Capital. That's a very conservative figure.

* * *

From 1988 through 2008, Bill DeWeese was in the upper echelons of Democratic leadership in the House of Representatives. In 1993 and 1994, he was speaker of the House. He was a "character out of political casting," reformer Eric Epstein remarked. In the old days, he was prone to bow ties, part of the effort to distinguish himself. Those days when I was "trapped" with him at the courthouse, awaiting the verdict, exemplified the conflict I had over such rogue politicians. It angered me when I thought about taxpayers being abused over the years by guys like DeWeese. He had a huge sense of entitlement. On the other hand, Bill was very likeable. At times, he could sound quite literate. But with reporters, he'd go off the record and swear like the Marine he once was. I think he liked to try and shock people with his profanity. But like so many others, DeWeese began in 1976 as a reformer. He was, by all accounts, a very good legislator in the 1980s. He was the first non-lawyer appointed to chair the House Judiciary Committee.

People either loved or hated Bill DeWeese. I tangled with him on countless occasions through the '90s, dinging him on stories about "walking around money" (often called WAMs) or using the heavy hand of leadership. I covered a number of reform-minded legislators from Pittsburgh's suburbs like former Representative Pat Carone, a Democrat-turned-Republican from Cranberry, and Democratic Representative David Mayernik of Ross Township, another North Hills area lawmaker and would-be reformer who got his share of WAMs, but battled the leadership on occasion. It was during that era that DeWeese, in an interview, referred to WAMs as a "cudgel" used by the leadership. I used it often to describe how at least one leader looked at it: if you don't vote our way — no WAMs. Even at his trial he would good-naturedly joke in the hallway about the "cudgel" quote.

I liked the guy despite our at-times stormy relationship and his eccentric tendencies.

I mean, how can you not like someone who, while Speaker of the House, came to the newsroom to lament the deal Democrat Tom Stish of Luzerne County had made to throw control of the state House to Republicans just as former Republican governor Tom Ridge was taking office in 1995. Stish switched his registration to Republican. There was no excoriating phrase DeWeese overlooked in bad-mouthing Stish

On a Friday afternoon, DeWeese was in a corner of the newsroom talking to Robert Swift, then of Ottaway News Service, and me. He graphically demonstrated for us what we'd later call his "Stish dance." With mirthful glee, DeWeese cupped both hands behind his backside and worked them in and out as if he were being reamed in the butt. He was demonstrating what Stish had done to the Democrats.

In 2012, when DeWeese stood trial, we were both 61. He was a fitness fanatic and could easily have passed for a man in his early 50s. He once crushed my fingers in a handshake during one of the periods he was aggravated with me. Whether it was ever diagnosed or not, Bill was compulsive about organization and had a touch of "germaphobia." I saw him at a Gridiron Dinner using a napkin to pick up pieces of celery and carrots from a buffet table. At his preliminary hearing, I unexpectedly bumped into him in the men's room where he had used a handkerchief to hold the handle while opening and closing the door.

* * *

Bill DeWeese was first and foremost a political animal. Another reporter would say, DeWeese thinks like a dog: always in the present for a bone or a walk, but without thoughts of the past or future. DeWeese had an animal's instinct for survival. He became Speaker in 1992 with a coup that unseated former Speaker Robert O'Donnell, a Philadelphia Democrat. He did it in an alliance with Representative Dwight Evans (D–Philadelphia) as his appropriations chairman. It kept Philly's power where it needed to be — in the money.

In 2007, DeWeese hung onto power, but he had to yield the speakership. Democrats held a one-seat majority in the House, but the prince did not have the votes to become Speaker. The previous Speaker, John Perzel, thought he could win with a few Democrat votes. In a surprise move, DeWeese put together a coalition with Republican Representative Dennis "Denny" O'Brien, of Philadelphia. Dennis was a true RINO (Republican in name only). This enabled DeWeese to block a stunned Perzel from presiding again. A key player was Representative Josh Shapiro (D–Montgomery), whom DeWeese would anoint as "Deputy Speaker," even though there is no such title, and co-chair a Speaker's Reform Commission. It appeared that Ed Rendell had his hand in all this. A year later, Shapiro would be one of the lawmakers who would publicly call for DeWeese's resignation as leader.

* * *

On the first day of trial, Bill DeWeese was dealt a severe blow. His longtime aide and campaign coordinator, Sharon Rodavich, pled guilty over the lunch hour. The defense knew it was coming after Rodavich failed to appear the previous year at a preliminary hearing. But at the start of trial, she was officially still DeWeese's co-defendant. Now Rodavich would be testifying against her former boss, along with Michael Manzo and Kevin Sidella. Those were the big three for the prosecution. She was close to the DeWeese family, celebrating Serbian Christmas with them in January. When Rodavich, 56, did take the stand as a Commonwealth witness, it was clear that she felt bad about it, but she had no choice.

Prosecutors said DeWeese stole at least $125,000 from taxpayers by having key staffers campaign for him.

Michael Manzo told the jury of seven women and five men that DeWeese wouldn't have won re-election in 2006 without his legislative staff as the nucleus of his campaign. Manzo recalled DeWeese saying he wanted a "Veon-esque" effort like the 80 to 100 staffers who had worked on Mike Veon's primary campaign. Kevin Sidella testified that he did extensive campaigning for DeWeese on state time and was essentially his campaign manager in 2006.

Sharon Rodavich confirmed accounts by other witnesses that at a meeting of top staffers and aides, DeWeese threatened to fire anyone who refused to do campaign work. No one was fired, she said, but the pressure to do campaign work came from the top. The defense contended that DeWeese always asked his staff to use "leave time" they had accumulated, through comp time and unused vacation days, when they hit the campaign trail.

William Costopoulos, the premier criminal defense attorney in Central Pennsylvania and one of the best statewide, established that there was a large corps of volunteers working on Bill DeWeese's campaigns. DeWeese's own witnesses spoke of his repeated sermons to state aides that they had to have "leave slips." Costopoulos effectively gave the jury an option that there was reasonable doubt about the district campaigning.

* * *

The highlight of the trial was when DeWeese took the witness stand, which he had long vowed to do. One school of thought among defense attorneys is that the best a defendant can do is break even, said former federal prosecutor Bruce Antkowiak. Smiling and jocular before court, DeWeese became serious when taking the oath as a witness. "I swear to God," he said loudly in a strong voice.

Wearing a navy blue suit, white shirt and blue-and-white striped tie, DeWeese described how he left Wake Forest College upon graduation, joined the Marine Corps and served a year in Okinawa. He was 26 when first elected to the House in 1976. When Deputy Attorney General Kenneth Brown pressed him on the fact that several of his staffers testified that campaign work was required, DeWeese fired back: "after you [prosecutors] came to the district and dropped the F-bomb 400 times and beat them with a proverbial rubber hose." People were scared about not cooperating with the Attorney General's office, DeWeese maintained. But Brown was a plodder. Methodical, totally unexciting and steady.

Costopoulos had some flash when needed, but most of all, he had gravitas after 40 years in courtrooms. Trust me, you don't ever want to be cross-examined by him.

Bill DeWeese more than held his own under cross-examination by Kenneth Brown. It was his decision to testify before the grand jury, not the trial court, that sealed his fate. Brown's cross-examination was sub-par, but his closing was a grand slam. He reminded jurors that DeWeese had been asked whether he would change any of his grand jury testimony. "*Not one word,*" Brown repeated with the heavy emphasis that DeWeese had used on the witness stand. Brown then flashed DeWeese's grand jury testimony on a large video screen with his admission that he had a taxpayer-paid fund-raiser on his legislative staff. DeWeese had also said that everyone at the capitol was doing it. That's virtually an admission that he was doing it himself. It's an excuse, not a defense.

Chief Deputy Attorney General Frank Fina had asked DeWeese questions before the grand jury. At trial, he read his questions while agent Robert Gift took the witness stand and read DeWeese's answers. Garnering the admission was skillful questioning. The way the charges were structured with overlapping theft charges and conflict of interest and conspiracy linked to each theft charge, the jury could convict on the Kevin Sidella episode alone and find DeWeese guilty of six counts.

* * *

After the first day of jury deliberations, Bill DeWeese, in clipped sentences, told reporters after court, "We're heading to our nightly bivouac. I respect the tribunals [the court and the jurors]. I am in the sixth year of this travail. I am looking forward to going back to being a state legislator."

DeWeese hugged his mother, 91-year-old Louise "Dotty" DeWeese, in a long embrace after the jury began deliberations at 10:20 a.m. on that day, February 1st. She sobbed loudly as Judge Todd Hoover instructed the jury, and at one point she was led from the courtroom and briefly slumped to the floor in the hallway. After two days of deliberations, there was no verdict. The jurors didn't meet over the weekend and on Monday, February 6th, they resumed deliberations.

The first hint that a verdict had been reached came as a rumor — that jurors told sheriff's deputies that they would not need lunch. By mid-morning, it was official; the jury had reached a verdict. Matt Miller, the court reporter for *The Patriot-News*, got the word first. About 11 a.m., the prosecutors; William Costopoulos; his assistant, Jayme King; the defendant and the media were back in court for the bailiff to read the verdict. The first count — guilty, cut through the courtroom. DeWeese's girlfriend, Stephanie Lupacchini, cried out in shock and sorrow.

Bill DeWeese showed no emotion at the defense table after the jury convicted him on five of the six counts. They found him not guilty on one theft charge, which made no real sense other than perhaps jurors were throwing him a bone. Afterward, DeWeese insisted he "did nothing wrong" and vowed to run for re-election despite the conviction. It struck me as denial of the first order.

Under Pennsylvania law, as evidenced in the Budd Dwyer episode, a conviction isn't final until sentencing. DeWeese said he would remain in the House until he was sentenced. The prince failed in what he pledged would be his motto as House Speaker when he took the oath of office on January 5, 1993: "Politics has to be secondary to policy."

Bill DeWeese became the third sitting or former House Speaker convicted in the past 35 years. Former Speaker Herbert Fineman, a Philadelphia Democrat, resigned in 1977, two days after his conviction on two counts of obstruction. Taxpayer-paid portraits of Fineman, Perzel and DeWeese adorn a capitol hallway along with another speaker, Benjamin Franklin.

Now we look at Mike Veon's Beaver County venture that was like Citizens Alliance West.

19

Mr. BIG

February 20, 2012

John Gallo stood alone in an alcove outside the judge's office in Dauphin County Court. He had already been on the witness stand in Mike Veon's second corruption trial and would return after the break. To calm himself and regain his focus, while waiting in the hallway, or in court while the attorneys were arguing at sidebar, the Geneva College professor would repeat the first two words of Psalm 46:10: "Be still." It brought him peace in the face of an unrelenting onslaught by Veon's attorney during cross-examination.

Gallo, the former executive director of the Beaver Initiative for Growth (BIG), was the first prosecution witness against Veon. On direct examination, he testified that he saw questionable check writing during a month-long absence from BIG in 2002, due to the birth of his child amid medical complications — his baby was born with Down's syndrome. Annamarie Perretta-Rosepink, Veon's confidante, district office chief and a BIG employee, took over the check writing in Gallo's absence. While he was gone, checks had been written to numerous people who had no connection to the nonprofit. One, for instance, was a $5,000 check to a former Democratic legislator who did no work for BIG and had no ties to the organization. Gallo remembers thinking at the time, after seeing the expenditures, that this would land before a grand jury some day. Little did he know how far it would progress in the legal system and that he would be at the center of a raging storm. He kept copies of the questionable checks.

Veon was accused by a grand jury in 2009 of misusing BIG funds for his own political and personal agenda. Perretta-Rosepink was charged with him. BIG was a nonprofit, but all of its money came from the state taxpayers. As a powerful leader, Veon secured $10 million in grants over a decade to fuel BIG.

Already a state convict, Mike Veon was presented to the jury by his lawyers as a "retired politician." He was serving a six- to 14-year sentence on the Bonusgate charges when the BIG trial took place in 2012. At risk for him was, in effect, an extension of his sentence. Most cases like this after a first verdict would be settled with a plea bargain and the prospect of a concurrent sentence. But not for Veon and his lawyers. They wanted another shot at defeating the Attorney General's office. Even if Veon won, he was heading back to prison.

On the stand, Gallo was cross-examined by Veon's attorney, Joel Sansone, for almost eight hours over two days. It was as brutal as any cross-examination I've ever seen.

Sansone accused Gallo of being a thief. He hammered that point home again and again with innuendo suggesting that it was Gallo, not Veon, who was responsible for any improprieties at the nonprofit.

It turned my stomach. Anyone could see Gallo was a straight arrow. The Attorney General's investigation didn't find a hint of wrongdoing by Gallo. Sansone didn't have a shred of proof. Deputy Attorney General Laurel Brandstetter told the jury that the cross-examination of John Gallo was a "travesty of justice." Sansone was trying to shift the jury's attention from Veon and his co-defendant, Annamarie Perretta-Rosepink. As defense attorneys sometimes do, Sansone was creating a "straw man" — someone to blame for the irregularities other than the defendant in hopes of establishing "reasonable doubt" in at least one juror's mind. Judge Bruce Bratton warned Sansone at the outset that he needed something solid to back up this line of inquiry. He didn't have it, and Bratton never held Sansone accountable. He did at least block the defense from dragging Gallo's wife, Christine, into the case. Defense lawyers had subpoenaed her as well as the couple's personal financial records. John had to hire a Harrisburg lawyer to quash Christine's subpoena. That at least prevented a second character assassination.

Sansone brought up more than $7,000 in checks with no note on the memo indicating the purpose of the expenditure and almost $24,000 in computer-related purchases from 2000 through early 2003. They came from a Quickbook account recreated after John Gallo left the organization. Gallo's not even sure most of the documents he was questioned about were checks he actually wrote. Moreover, the category was "computers and equipment," and included filing cabinets, desks, chairs and cubicle partitions for the start-up organization. Sansone was trying to suggest that Gallo was squandering BIG's money on computer games and that he used the money to make three of his mortgage payments.

Earlier, Sansone had flashed Gallo's Geneva College web page listing on a giant screen. He pointed out that one of Gallo's hobbies was computers. That was the supposed justification even though, in actuality, his specific hobby is Apple computers, which operate in a different universe than the PCs he was buying for BIG.

Sansone walked Gallo through individual expenditures. Many expenses were "round numbers," Sansone pointed put, such as "$250 or $400." Gallo testified that he never used BIG money on anything other than legitimate expenses for the organization, but after 12 years, most of the actual receipts were no longer available. Gallo's faith helped him get through the grilling. During the lunch hour, he got his iPad back from Agent Greg Policare. He would read the Bible verses his students sent him to cope with the ordeal.

Why would a judge allow a defense lawyer to go after an innocent witness to this extent? The defense is allowed broad range on cross-examination to impeach prosecution witnesses. There's no way Judge Bratton wanted this case overturned on appeal because he would not let Veon's lawyers pursue a "theory" that Gallo was really the bad guy. Everyone knew it was a crock. In the real world, it's absurd to think an innocent man like this could be attacked with no proof. In a courtroom, a place that is supposed to bring about justice, it is perfectly acceptable. Gallo's testimony was just one slice of the evidence in a trial that would last 11 days.

In the end, Sansone's gambit may have backfired. Mike Veon, 55, and Annamarie Perretta-Rosepink, 48, were convicted by a Dauphin County jury on March 5, 2012. Veon was convicted on 10 counts and Perretta-Rosepink on six. Veon was convicted on six counts of theft and one each of conspiracy and conflict of interest along with two misdemeanor counts of misapplication of entrusted property. He was acquitted of five charges. The jury of six men and six women found Perretta-Rosepink guilty of three counts of theft and one count each of conspiracy, conflict of interest and misapplication of property. BIG was like a mask a bank robber would wear robbing a bank, Laurel Brandstetter told the jury. Veon used it as cover for the diversion of taxpayers' money for his own agenda, she said.

THE WISDOM OF SOLOMON

Dan Raynak was especially bitter about this case because on May 21, 2009, he and Sansone had managed to get the charges thrown out by a district judge. Judge Joseph Solomon — with ties to some of the Democrats involved — appeared to rule inappropriately by claiming that the Commonwealth would not be able to prove the case beyond a reasonable doubt to a jury. Anthony Krastek, the prosecutor, was furious. The standard for a preliminary hearing is a prima facie case. He and Solomon had words afterward. Solomon recused himself, he told the Associated Press, because of what Krastek said to him after a day-long hearing. He didn't say what that was.

"District Judge Solomon," wrote the anonymous "Battlescar" in response to *The Patriot*'s story on Pennlive.com, "Who is this clown? Who screwed up at the

AG's office…? Now we need more investigations to see what happened with this case. Our court system is so screwed up!"

The Attorney General's office refiled a majority of the charges. The new district judge for the case selected by Richard Lewis couldn't have been more pro-law enforcement.

Veon and Perretta-Rosepink were held for trial at a preliminary hearing before Judge William Wenner on September 4, 2009. He was a former Susquehanna Township police officer and a detective for the Dauphin County District Attorney's office. While DA, Lewis had hired Wenner as an investigator. He administered the oath of office to Wenner as a district judge in 2003.

"MRV"

There were essentially three incidents that the charges concerned: BIG's paying for a satellite legislative office for Mike Veon in Midland, which had been included in his district in the previous redistricting, and for an office above a cigar store on Pittsburgh's South Side, way outside the small Beaver Falls nonprofit's sphere of operations. In reality, the South Side office was used for a powerful Democratic staffer, Mike Manzo, to hide his mistress, whom he'd placed on the caucus payroll. The second incident was BIG's paying a $5,000-a-month retainer to a Harrisburg law firm whose partner, Jeffrey Foreman, was Veon's chief of staff. Foreman said the retainer was a reward from Veon. Another incident based on Foreman's testimony was Veon's intervening to get a $160,000 salary for his brother, Mark, from Delta Development Company, a consultant that received two million dollars from the House Democratic Caucus and BIG from 2004 to 2006.

Dan Raynak told the jurors they would hear from Leroy Kline, Delta's president, and Mark Veon, who would say that what Jeffrey Foreman described didn't happen. They never heard from Mark Veon, but it didn't matter. It was Foreman's word against Kline's. They didn't believe Foreman. It didn't help that he had eight felony convictions from Bonusgate.

The convictions came primarily on the office rent. Personally, I thought that was the weakest of the three incidents. But it was in black and white. In the exhibits the jury reviewed, the rent figures didn't lie.

The prosecution's theory on the Midland rent made sense to me. I wondered whether the jury would get it. As a leader, Mike Veon could get just about as many district offices as he needed. But the money had to come from the Democrats' $12.5 million Special Leadership Account, a slush fund that Bill DeWeese controlled. The fund was a matter of public record, Mike Manzo testified, and reporters would periodically do stories about the expenditures. Veon would not want other members to know he was taking money for another office when many of them complained about insufficient staff or facilities. BIG's renting a South Side Pittsburgh office was outrageous on its face.

The rest of the case was "he said—he said." On the retainer, it was Jeffrey Foreman's word against his twin brother and law partner, Bruce Foreman. Bruce testified that the fee was not excessive. What was clear through the testimony was that Veon used BIG for the betterment of Mike Veon and that his legislative district office and BIG were co-mingled. Apparently, there were some good projects. I'm surprised that we didn't hear about them from the defense.

When John Gallo was nearing the end of his tenure at BIG, he requested a meeting with Mike Veon. They met in the "smoking room," Veon's basement office in a converted back building. It was where he would work and smoke cigars — his bunker.

Gallo had been dissatisfied with the direction of BIG, and he was worried about expenditures, such as when a man showed up one day and asked for a $10,000 check to fund an orchestra concert. Gallo knew nothing about it, and he said no. The man was no sooner out on the sidewalk with his cell phone when the office phone rang. It was Veon. Cut him the check, Gallo was told. It was all part of economic development, Veon contended. It had the feel of using BIG to dispense WAMs.

In the smoking room, Mike told Gallo to sit down. Veon took a piece of paper and drew a circle. He drew spokes around the center of the circle, with a spoke signifying his district office, another in Harrisburg, one for his campaign committee, a spoke for BIG, and two other nonprofits he controlled. At the center of the circle, Veon wrote "MRV," his initials, and explained to Gallo that all these entities existed for one reason: to re-elect Mike Veon.

John Gallo left the organization shortly afterward. Laurel Brandstetter told the jury in her closing that the center of the circle should have been Pennsylvania taxpayers, not MRV.

Her heartfelt closing nailed the guilty verdict. I really felt that it could have gone either way.

I also believed that the AG's office could have presented a much stronger case if they had dug a little deeper. Mike Veon and Annamarie Perretta-Rosepink have appeals pending in the BIG case.

A CLEAN SHAVE

Mike Veon was handcuffed and the cuffs were linked to a chain around his waist. He came to court in manacles and left that way. The cuffs and chain were removed before the jury arrived. Veon appeared in the courtroom each day in a tailored suit. He sported a conservative look for his trial, abandoning his trademark broad pinstripes for solid blue, gray and black suits, subtle patterned ties, crisp white shirts and a white handkerchief folded neatly in his breast pocket. His goatee was neatly trimmed. The manacles seemed a bit much for a nonviolent criminal, but I was told it was standard policy for handling a state inmate.

This was a getaway of sorts for Veon: two weeks away from Laurel Highlands State Correctional Institution. He had a cell reserved at Dauphin County jail during the trial. That was far from an actual vacation, though. The Dauphin County jail is a very rough place, some say far worse than being in a state facility. After 17 months in state prison, Veon was thinner. His hair was whiter, his skin was pale, but he looked fit. He'd been working out hard and pumping iron, Joel Sansone reported. He still carried himself with dignity. But he appeared a decade older than his 55 years.

One morning, Mike Veon evidently couldn't get a clean enough shave at the Dauphin County Prison. Dan Raynak, his other attorney, used an electric razor in the courtroom to trim any residual whiskers off Veon's face before the jury or judge appeared. Raynak was his former Allegheny College football teammate who had a criminal defense practice in Phoenix.

After the Bonusgate trial, Veon no longer had the money to pay Raynak and Sansone. As Dan ran the razor over Mike's face, I was touched by the depth of loyalty of an old college buddy. Raynak would also bring Veon a paper-bag lunch almost every day from the deli on Market Street. "What do you want today?" he said before one lunch hour. "No more chicken. How about some roast beef?" Handing him a lunch bag on another day, Raynak told Veon to "eat the cookie." It seemed clear that Veon was sticking to his health-conscious eating despite Raynak's best efforts to bulk him up a little.

"Mike is the strongest man, emotionally, physically and mentally, that I know," Sansone remarked before the trial. He called Veon a "political prisoner" and compared him to Nelson Mandela. Veon was still being persecuted by Tom Corbett, the former Attorney General and now Republican governor who had filed the charges, Sansone added. Never mind that Mandela spent 27 years in prison or that he was protesting apartheid.

When the verdict came in, Sansone was still blaming Corbett. He warned that, as his grandfather used to say, "what goes around comes around," suggesting that the governor may someday find the tables turned against him.

ORIGINS

John Gallo deserves credit for helping investigators crack BIG. Moreover, he had the courage to get on the witness stand and subject himself to false accusations. But Gallo didn't go to the Attorney General's agents. They came to him, and when they did, he cooperated fully. As important as Gallo in a criminal case moving forward was my *Tribune-Review* partner, Debra Erdley, and her local contact, Gerald Hodge, senior regional manager of the National Association of Manufacturers. My paper's interest in BIG began with a story Deb and I worked on in the aftermath of the pay raise.

As a powerful legislator, Mike Veon normally didn't need to give re-election a second thought. But this was only a few weeks since he had been the lone vote against repealing the 16 to 54 percent legislative pay raise lawmakers awarded themselves in the middle of the night in July 2005. Anti-pay groups and reformers were at full throttle. If Veon survived, his reputation would become legendary.

Deb was curious about BIG. Curious enough to drive to Beaver Falls on an overcast, freezing, typical Western Pennsylvania day in November 2005. She sized up the BIG office and asked for the group's federal tax statements. Driving back to the paper's office at the Clark Building on the North Side, she thought the story was starting to fit together. Driving back gave her time to think and look at the big picture. Reflecting on what she had just seen at the BIG office, Deb thought, Wow! Holy crap! What have we tapped into?

Debra had obtained 990 forms from BIG and saw that some members of Veon's staff were paid by the group. She also saw firsthand that BIG shared office space with Veon's district office. It seemed to be an unhealthy co-mingling. She learned about Mike Veon's involvement in the Beaver Initiative for Growth almost by accident.

*   *   *

In the days following the 2005 legislative pay raise, I had gathered spending records from the House leadership. One of the bills — $450,000 for a group called Delta Development — stuck out among the larger tabs. But it wasn't until a source told Debra Erdley that Delta had just opened a Western Pennsylvania office and Mike Veon's brother Mark was running it that the pieces began to fall into place. Armed with the Delta tip, she called Delta president Leroy Kline. He confirmed to her that he had indeed hired Mark Veon at Delta. He said that Mark was a great hire in the early spring of 2004. Several weeks later, he said Mike approached him about doing some work for the caucus, and the $450,000 contract was set. Mike Veon consistently referred reporters to his state "spokesman" and dodged interviews. He blew off a scheduled interview with Erdley early in the fall, which only heightened her interest.

After we ran the Delta story, Deb got a call about another man who had been asking questions about Veon's dealings in Beaver County. Gerald Hodge, who had worked with Veon years earlier when the two were aides to former congressman Joe Kolter, had been pressing questions publicly for months about the inner workings of BIG. Hodge just wasn't getting answers. He wrote letters to the editor of the *Beaver County Times*. Hodge kept pushing.

After a simple Google search, Erdley was stunned: Veon and Senator Gerald LaValle were actually funding the organization with state money and had installed themselves as co-chairs. There was nothing secret about it. BIG had a newsletter that boasted of the lawmakers' clout. Their activities had been covered in the *Beaver County Times*, apparently without question.

The hiring of Mark Veon by a House contractor had been a good story. But I was not sold at first about digging into a nonprofit. There was still so much unexplored material about leadership expenses that BIG, for me, didn't rise to the top. But Erdley persisted. And she convinced me.

Shortly before Thanksgiving, Debra made the trip to meet with the day-to-day staff of BIG and get their 990s. She learned that Annamarie Perretta-Rosepink had been on the BIG payroll at the same time she was on the state payroll. There were other staff overlaps as well. And all of it was being funded with state grants for which Mike Veon and Gerald LaValle took credit. Delta Development was also a major contractor with BIG.

But there was more. Erdley discovered that Veon had formed two other nonprofits in the 1990s: BRIDGE, the Beaver Race Initiative Development Group Effort, and the Lend-A-Hand Network. Both of them also had received small state grants and, like BIG, were housed in Veon's district office. He was building a little empire.

Through it all, Mike Veon agreed to only one interview with us — a conference call in which he and LaValle defended BIG and insisted that they never profited personally from it. Veon insisted that Delta had hired Mark only because of his qualifications. Mark Veon was never accused of any wrongdoing.

Gerald LaValle was not charged. He would testify as a prosecution witness at the preliminary hearing and at trial. But like Veon, he stumbled over the use of state grants. In 2007, authorities began investigating the small nonprofit, Voluntary Action Center of Beaver County. The *Tribune-Review* disclosed in late 2007 that the agency that came to rely on state grants for income was paying LaValle's wife, Darla, 40 percent of its revenues. At its peak in 2006, LaValle's salary at the tiny nonprofit was $122,000. He retired from the Senate at the end of 2008. Darla LaValle ultimately would plead guilty to four counts of inflating her salary and failing to pay benefits to employees and was placed on four years probation in 2010.

* * *

The footnote to the BIG saga is that the state apparently never determined what happened to the $10 million in tax money. The Attorney General's investigation never resolved it. It never came out at any public hearings or trials.

A federal tax form filed on November 3, 2009 showed that BIG had a little more than one million dollars as of December 31, 2008. That year, the tax form states, the organization doled out $452,960 in state money, including expenditures for riverfront improvements, blight reduction and downtown upgrades. There were some good projects, but there was no overall accounting.

In 2012, after Veon was convicted in the BIG trial, I filed a Right-to-Know Law request with the Department of Community and Economic Development, asking for any reports or email addressing what happened overall to the $10 million. This agency was the one used by lawmakers as a warehouse for WAMs. (The state was unable to produce any such overall accounting. I received a form called "Agency Attestation of Non-Existence of Record" on April 10, 2012, which essentially said that they could not find such documents.) There were piecemeal records of accounting on individual grants, but no one seemed to be able to say what happened overall to the $10 million.

* * *

On June 19, 2012, Mike Veon was sentenced to one to four years on top of the six to 14 he was serving in Bonusgate.

"Mike's [first] sentence was harsh and we miss him terribly," his mother, Donna, told the court. "In five years in two trials, Mike was never accused of putting a dime in his own pockets."

"There is a siren's call in the hallways of the state capitol that seems to alter the way of the career path of public service," Judge Bruce Bratton remarked. "It is a sad commentary on a public life that ends in this venue and these circumstances," he added.

Next: the Republican Kingfish.

John Perzel's portrait hangs in a Capitol hallway along with two other speakers convicted of felonies. The portraits cost taxpayers as much as $7,000 each.

Photo of portrait by Brad Bumsted.

Former Attorney General Tom Corbett, a Republican, outlines criminal charges against GOP officials, including Perzel.

Photo by Joe Appel, *Pittsburgh Tribune-Review.*

Mike Manzo was the right-hand man to both Democratic leaders Bill DeWeese and Mike Veon. A judge remarked that Bonusgate appeared to be his brainchild.

Photo by Jasmine Goldband, *Pittsburgh Tribune-Review.*

Rachel Manzo, the wife of Mike Manzo, also faced felonies, but she would plead guilty to a misdemeanor.

Photo by Jasmine Goldband, *Pittsburgh Tribune-Review.*

Bill DeWeese, an ex-Marine and former House Speaker, faces his day of reckoning.
Photo by Dan Gleiter, Harrisburg *Patriot-News*.

John R. Zimmerman, charged in Computergate, played in the U.S. Marine Band, the "President's Own."

Photo on loan from John R. Zimmerman.

Charges were dropped against Zimmerman by the Attorney General's office.
Photo by Shari Zimmerman.

Janine Orie (left) and Jane Orie, who both faced trial, discover the media was waiting for them.
Photo by Andy Russell, *Pittsburgh Tribune-Review.*

Supreme Court Justice Joan Orie Melvin backstage before her induction
ceremony in 2010.

Photo by Barry Reeger, *Pittsburgh Tribune-Review.*

Angry voices at an anti-pay-raise rally in 2005. The since-repealed pay hike
should be a constant reminder for elected officials not to cross the voters.

Photo by Bruce Shannon, Raintree Multimedia.

20

The Kingfish

March 21, 2012

It was for power, not money. John Perzel's own words on the witness stand, recorded on October 18, 2011, confirmed this central tenet of the criminal case against him and most of the other legislative defendants since 2009.

"You don't govern if you don't win," Perzel testified on this memorable day, the climax of the two-year case against him. As a result of his plea deal in August, the former House Speaker was owned lock, stock and barrel by the Commonwealth of Pennsylvania. It was quite a shocker that Perzel, who would have been the number-one defendant, was testifying for the Attorney General's office against his former lieutenant and ex-Republican caucus lawyer, Brett Feese, and Feese's aide Jill Seaman, the only two of nine remaining Republican defendants still standing. One could argue that his plea was the climax, but there was little explanation on that day and, of course, no cross-examination. So there was no full explanation in his own words until he took the stand.

John Perzel was a pretty good witness, a subdued version of the arrogant, testy leader who could be in your face pretty quickly if you were a Democrat or a reporter. Dressed in a trademark blue business suit with a somewhat lighter blue tie, Perzel did the job, though I could see resentment beneath the surface. He fessed up, but not as completely as he would at his sentencing the following year. As Perzel had told reporters after the preliminary hearing in 2010, when asked what he'd learned from seven days of testimony, it was "that being a politician is now illegal, that's what I've learned."

There was anger smoldering beneath the surface. Perzel believed that he'd been tagged for doing what everyone else had been doing. That was especially unfair since he spent a ton of campaign money on staff, including reimbursements to state workers for campaign work they did.

* * *

I reached John at his home when doing a story in the spring of 2011 on the cost of legislative staff. I didn't call him to talk about his case. He eventually took it there. Someone else answered the phone, possibly his wife, Sheryl. I explained who I was and for whom I worked. "John?" the woman called. I could hear some clatter before he got on the phone and I said again, "This is Brad Bumsted of *The Pittsburgh Tribune-Review.*"

"I know who you are," Perzel answered. "You think I lost my mind when they indicted me?" After a routine interview about how lawmakers shared a secretary for office duties when he started and how it was important to have policy and technical staff to be on an even plane with the governor, the talk turned to the charges against him. Perzel said he was at home going through mountains of documents obtained in discovery. He spent each day poring through documents. He talked about how his campaign spent $17 million in four campaigns. With that kind of money, John said he didn't need to "steal from the taxpayers." It was more than anger — he was incredulous that he now faced 82 criminal charges. Perzel talked about perhaps letting me view the discovery documents, but said he'd have to check with his attorney. That, of course, never came about. He also claimed that no one at his preliminary hearing testified that they did campaign work on state time. "That's not true," I said. "Who?" Perzel shot back. I was thinking of Daphne Uliana. She testified that House Republican staffers were told not to do campaign work on state time, but it was not enforced. Uliana testified that it became blurred during workdays and it was hard to distinguish the two. But like many other staffers, she was reimbursed by Friends of John Perzel in addition to receiving a state salary.

That is what grated Perzel, I believe. Unlike the Democratic caucus, he had pretty much followed the rules on separating state and campaign work done by employees. He tried to make the distinction. Perzel explained in his October 18, 2011 testimony that it took time to come to grips with his guilt. "I know now I committed a crime," he testified.

Back to his statement about his motivation, what drove the lust for data and the latest technology, prosecutor Pat Blessington asked. "Win what?"

"The elections," Perzel replied. "If it's 102 to 101, you might as well have zero if you are at 101" in the 203-member House."

"Explain that to the members of the jury, why is it so important to have the majority?" Blessington asked.

"Well," Perzel explained, "if it's 102 to 101, which it was for the number of years that I was majority leader, the 102 gets the chairmanships. They decide the calendar, the flow of legislation. In the minority, you don't decide anything. You don't decide what bills come up. You do not have a proportional share of what's going on. You have zero.

"So the agenda of your party is what is pushed if you win the majority. If you win the minority, you don't push anything. And so it's *winner take all*."

Those three words more than anything, I thought, hit the essence of why legislative leaders were willing to take great risks to be in control. What Perzel pleaded guilty to essentially was cheating in a colossal way to keep the power that went with holding the majority. The Speaker, the highest elected House member, was almost always from the majority party. Members of both parties voted for Speaker. Serving as the top elected member of the minority party meant serving a step down as minority leader, someone out of power. Perzel had done both and knew the difference.

In a cruder and more blatant way, Democrats were doing the same thing: cheating to get the all-important 102nd vote in the 203-member House. The Dems did it with shoe leather and taxpayer-financed bonuses. The Republicans relied on millions of dollars worth of technology and old-fashioned door knocking. The Democrats prevailed in 2006.

To think that it was bonuses over technology would be shortsighted. That is only one of a myriad of factors. The overall mood of an election is determined by national politics and by 2006, though not a presidential year, there was clearly "George W. Bush fatigue" in the country. It was a Democratic year and Democrats captured the U.S. House and Senate.

It's true that Perzel and two aides dabbled in a private business venture to sell the data taxpayers had paid for. But that business really never got off the ground. Their effort to get rich off a taxpayer-financed program was part of the criminal case, and it would have been difficult to beat. Despite the fledgling company they formed, there's no question that Perzel's illegal effort centered on power.

* * *

If Perzel had gone to trial, it seemed that his defense would be an extension of the expression used by his attorney, Brian McMonagle, in the preliminary hearing: "No harm, no foul." Data purchased by House Republicans, courtesy of Pennsylvania taxpayers, in theory had dual uses. It could be compiled, along with some data mining, into useful constituent profiles. So if data intended for state uses was eventually used for campaigns, where's the harm? The problem is that most of the purchases from the very beginning were intended for campaigns, as Perzel himself later testified.

Perzel had a vision whereby his campaign and the House Republican campaign committee would know virtually everything about all prospective voters. Their likes and dislikes. Which issues they cared about. Marketing data was bought showing which magazines and other subscriptions they purchased. When blended with census data and voter data, this would provide a complete picture of each voter. For example, taxes are your top issue and hunting and fishing your top pursuits. You vote in every primary and general election. You're a Republican and own a $150,000 home. You are computer literate and once contacted your Republican state representative about the Pennsylvania Game Commission's deer management policy. Email and campaign brochures and letters could be tailored and targeted for all those who fit that profile.

There was also an election day program whereby Perzel's workers with handheld computers at the polls kept track of who voted and fed that back to the mother ship to determine who hadn't voted, and if any were likely Perzel voters. Then they called or visited in an effort to bring that person to the polls.

John Perzel's vision can be traced back to a computer show he attended in Princeton in 1980. The vision was that computer technology would be the edge one needed to succeed in politics. Computers were primitive in those days, but the thought stayed with him. Perzel was not a techie; he was an idea guy. If he had been in business instead of politics, he'd have been a CEO.

Then, in 1987, he met Billy Tomaselli. They met when Tomaselli was running a city council campaign in Philly. Perzel started attending the weekly meetings for Republican Kevin Pasquay, and he and Billy became friends. Unlike Perzel, Tomaselli understood how the technology worked. He'd been a hands-on guy since about 1980 when his mother gave him a Radio Shack TRS-80 that he loved to fiddle with. Finally, Perzel had found his personal IT guru. At age 59, Billy shared the same vision, understood politics and knew the streets of Philadelphia.

Tomaselli had a Philly accent so thick he made Perzel sound like a Midwesterner. When he was in Harrisburg — living with Perzel, Brian Preski and former representative Tom Gannon in a house on State Street, two blocks from the capitol — Tomaselli stood out as a character. He dressed casually, shunning professional attire, and name-dropped Perzel at every turn. Whether he spoke for Perzel or not, people thought he did. They couldn't afford to think otherwise. Bureaucrats and staffers used to dealing with polite and courteous officials got a screwball thrown their way with Tomaselli, who would be in their face in an instant.

The problem was that the technology just didn't match their ideas: getting voters to the polls, targeting voters, mining data, marketing political campaigns via the Internet. It wasn't until the late 1990s that they could really put their ideas into action. Even then it all depended on the data. The data had to be good, and that was a constant search. Still rising in the ranks, Perzel attended a computer show nearly every year in Las Vegas. In the lower rungs of leadership, he didn't have the cash to buy a lot of the technology.

When he became majority leader in 1995, Perzel suddenly had money — more money than he ever imagined, to buy the hardware, the software and most importantly the data. He controlled an IT department with a $10 million budget and a special leadership account that ranged to $12.5 million. His always-flush campaign fund — he'd spend about four million dollars in a given year — wasn't used for the big technology expenditures. Eventually, he would use the entire state-paid IT Department within the House Republican Caucus as an adjunct of his campaign.

The Vegas show fueled Perzel's imagination. He charged the Friends of John Perzel for the trips. It would become a couples event for Perzel, his wife Sheryl, and Brian and Kelli Preski. Brian was his $160,000-a-year chief of staff, who also received a $56,000 salary in 2005 to run John's campaign. In 2004 and 2005, he was reimbursed $264,000 by "Friends" for expenses ranging from bottled water to Super Bowl trips.

Pennsylvania's vague law on campaign spending requires only that the expenditures be made to influence the outcome of an election. The computer shows and gatherings of political leaders in Vegas were "either to review election-specific technology for use in my re-election campaign or to meet with experts and colleagues regarding my re-election campaign," Perzel said in a 2006 statement to the *Tribune-Review*. As campaign expense records show, it would have been a good thing to be near Brian Preski, or at least be in the same bar. Preski paid for 41 glasses of beer and mixed drinks in 29 minutes at Casino Royale in Las Vegas, from 10:47 to 11:16 p.m. As usual, the Friends of John Perzel were picking up the tab.

I spent three days with my colleague Deb Erdley in 2006, crammed into a tiny room in Perzel's accountant's office in Merchantville, New Jersey, reviewing boxes of campaign receipts. Under state law, Perzel was required to show us the receipts. But the law didn't specify where he made them available, so he chose not to do it in Harrisburg. They showered us in a blizzard of paper. The accountant, Gordon R. Johnston III, was Sheryl Perzel's nephew.

As outlandish as Perzel's campaign expenses were, even providing takeout for the Preskis' babysitters so Brian and his wife could attend campaign events, it did appear that he was making a healthy effort to pay state staffers for campaign work. And the expenses — such as $1,349 for drinks at Davio's in Philadelphia for members of the Supreme Court Rules Committee; $41,109 for meals in Philly, where John and Brian lived; and $9,000 for airfare, meals and lodging in Jacksonville and Houston for two Super Bowls — were legal under the state's Swiss cheese campaign finance law. Little did we know that all the computer shows over the years would, indirectly, cost the taxpayers millions.

* * *

Panic struck the Perzel campaign in 2000 after he won his election by a few dozen votes, and this was only after the absentee ballots were counted, Tomaselli told the grand jury. Perzel put everyone on notice: this would never happen again. His interest in technology now became a priority. It wasn't just Vegas. He was traveling to computer shows around the country. As time went by, campaign work became so pervasive that it was "institutionalized," to use Tomaselli's term.

A permanent campaign office was established in Northeast Philadelphia. Then came the litany of computer programs that Republicans would buy and use at taxpayers' expense for assisting campaigns. Perzel also made sure that the new district in reapportionment would make it virtually impossible for him to lose: "I reapportioned the districts so I wouldn't have that problem again."

The 2000 near-loss was a seminal event for John Perzel as was his meeting in New Orleans with Greg Rigamer of GCR & Associates in 2002. That's when Rigamer talked about providing customized political software under the contract it held with the House Republican Caucus. Perzel said later that he did not tell Rigamer "to make sure that everything was kept separate. That was my mistake. That was my error. I've admitted my mistake." He said he should have specified that political services get billed to the campaign and legislative services to the state: "I did not make that distinction. . . ."

"Then can we assume that when you said you made a mistake, what you meant to say was you had formed an intention to use state money for your personal purposes?" defense attorney Joshua Lock, representing Brett Feese, asked Perzel.

"I didn't say that," Perzel shot back.

"I know you didn't say that," Lock replied. "That's what you mean. Isn't it true?"

Perzel: "I am not going to speculate as to what I meant."

Lock: "Are you telling us you don't know what you meant?"

Perzel: "I am telling you I knew I wanted to use the data politically, yes."

Lock: "You knew that the data that you were acquiring to use for campaign purposes was being paid for exclusively with state funds; isn't that right?"

Perzel: "The data we are collecting here at this point in time?"

Lock: "Yeah, GCR, that's right."

Perzel: "Yeah, I knew they had a state contract."

Lock later asked, "Did you know, February 1, 2002, that what you were doing was not a mistake. It was a crime, yes or no?"

Perzel: "I know it was a crime. I admitted it. . . I have already admitted my guilt. I have taken responsibility for what I've done."

Neither Tomaselli nor Anthony Painter, an aide who pushed the competing Aristotle software program, was charged. Painter later went to work for Aristotle. Perzel must have known deep down that when Tomaselli and Painter were flipped by the Attorney General's office, it was either a long or short ride downhill to prison.

Perzel never committed to one program over the other for a while and kept both GCR and Aristotle. A participant in the scheme told me that at the state job you would confront a gray area regarding campaigns. It's a judgment call and you agree to do it. Then there's another decision. The gray area becomes larger and larger. Finally, it seems to make no difference because you are already in so deep that one more political move will make no difference. In the end, it's all a gray area.

* * *

John Perzel was so oblivious at first to the 2005 pay raise that even after he helped push it through, he thought he could become governor. He left shortly afterward on a trip to China. Three weeks after the July 7, 2005 middle-of-the-night vote, Perzel took about 20 employees to his campaign office in Philadelphia to watch a presentation on a five-year plan by Tomaselli for Perzel to become governor. Ed Rendell had just been re-elected to his second term in 2006. The seat would be open in 2010, and Perzel had his eye on it. In Philadelphia, unlike central and western Pennsylvania, the pay raise was pretty much a non-issue.

The first I ever heard that Perzel was thinking of running for governor actually came from Rendell. It was surprising to me since Perzel, as a Philadelphia Republican, did not have a formidable statewide base. In some parts of Pennsylvania, the fact that a politician is from Philadelphia might as well be Moscow during the Cold War. Another country, another culture: out to take your money. And so it goes. Rendell was the exception. He rolled up such large margins in Southeastern Pennsylvania as a former Democratic mayor that it didn't matter what the rest of the state did. It's hard to argue that any legislator had more to do with passing Rendell's progressive agenda than John Perzel. He had decided early on that it did him no good whatsoever to quarrel publicly with the popular Rendell.

At the five-year-plan meeting, the first slide presented to the staff was of a casual Perzel with an open-collar shirt, sport coat and khakis, smiling and looking very relaxed in a rustic setting. It was entitled "Road to 2035 North Front Street" — the governor's mansion.

Goal number one wasn't about tax reform, creating jobs or getting tough on crime. It was about "streamlining" fundraising efforts. Goal number two was to develop a "legislative and political plan for 2005 and 2006. The third step was to "raise awareness of John Perzel and to position John Perzel as an effective humanitarian and unique leader."

On October 18, 2011, Joshua Lock cut to the chase: "You presumed, did you not, Mr. Perzel, to run for Governor of Pennsylvania?"

"Did I presume to do it? Yes," Perzel replied.

"You presumed to seek the highest executive branch office in this state while you were continuing to steal state funds, isn't that right?"

"Yes."

* * *

On November 8, 2011, Brett Feese and his secretary, Jill Seaman, were convicted of 40 counts of corruption in the Republican computer case. On February 10, 2012, Feese was sentenced to four to 12 years in state prison; Seaman received a nine- to 23-month sentence. Feese's sentence was precisely the type that Perzel, ever the pragmatist, was trying to avoid with his guilty plea. Brian Preski began the trial as a co-defendant with Feese and Seaman, but he decided in early October to enter a guilty plea.

On March 21, 2012, citing a "shocking and flagrant violation of the public trust," Dauphin County Judge Richard Lewis sentenced 61-year-old John Perzel to two and a half to five years in prison, $30,000 in fines and a million dollars in restitution. He also lost his $85,000-a-year pension. Preski was sentenced to two to four years.

"I have embarrassed myself, my family, my friends and the people of Pennsylvania, and for that I am truly sorry," Perzel told Lewis. Facing the court, the once-powerful Speaker said the electorate had given him "a great honor, and I disgraced them."

Perzel is housed at the dormitory-style State Correctional Institution at Laurel Highlands, near Somerset, which houses inmates from the general population as well as geriatric prisoners and those with illnesses. To this day, I don't believe John thinks he really did anything wrong.

Perzel was a prosecution witness for one trial. Mike Manzo appeared at a series of hearings and trials after his guilty plea, and he would be sentenced less than a month after the Kingfish.

21

Manzo

April 17, 2012

Carl Lee Manzo was a straight-up guy. Things were black and white, no gray. He was a proud member of Steelworkers Local 1211 and worked beside Bill George, who would become president of the state AFL-CIO. Carl carried his lunch bucket to work each day. At age 44, Manzo was crippled in an industrial accident at the former J&L Steel, now LTV Aliquippa, in 1985. Some 23 years later, his only son, Michael, was in trouble, big trouble. Carl always told Michael that what he liked about him was his "resolve." Michael Manzo would need that as he faced 47 criminal charges in Bonusgate. Michael's wife, Rachel, was also charged following a July 2008 grand jury presentment. There were three things that Carl Manzo would ask his son: "Did you do it?" The answer would be yes. "Have you taken responsibility?" The answer would be yes. And he would ask, "Are you taking care of Rachel?" And again Michael would say yes.

Carl Manzo, whom Michael considered his best friend, would get to see his son take responsibility, but he missed the final chapter. Michael C. Manzo (the C is for Carl) agreed to plead guilty in October 2008. His plea deal did set in motion a chain of events that would see Rachel getting probation on misdemeanor charges and Michael Manzo becoming the star witness against former House Democratic Whip Mike Veon and several others. He testified against Veon in two trials and against former representative Bill DeWeese. He made numerous grand jury appearances. By 2012, his string of service for the Attorney General's office was over. Clearly, charging Rachel had been a bargaining chip to jolt Michael into cooperating.

In June 2010, Carl Manzo died at age 67 from a second round of cancer. He had been free of kidney cancer for five years when he began to battle cancer of the lymph nodes. Since his accident, Carl's mobility had been limited, especially near the end, and he frequently used a walker.

The accident at the steel mill had been so bad that Carl Manzo had been given last rites. The event was traumatic for Michael, who was 17 at the time. He would graduate a year later, fourth in his class at Monaca High School, where he played on the baseball team and was a drummer in the marching band. On the same night the family heard about Carl being crushed by a load of four-by-fours, Michael's mother, Michelle, who supplemented the family income by working at a mall jewelry store, was injured in a car accident, suffering a concussion. Michael's world crashed in on him that night.

Michael Manzo began working at 13 and held various jobs, including at a men's clothing store, while in high school. He'd loved politics since reading *All the President's Men* in sixth grade. He also had it in his blood. Carl Manzo had been president of Monaca Borough Council.

At Penn State, Michael majored in marketing with a minor in public relations, while working three jobs to put himself through college. After graduating in 1991, he worked for AT&T and later as a ground agent for U.S. Airways. He met with Mike Veon to get a job in the Pennsylvania House. Veon wanted to hire him at some point. But Manzo received an offer from Wildman Bud George, a gruff-talking state House Democrat from Clearfield County. Veon supported the hire. After a stint with George, Manzo would later become Bill DeWeese's press secretary and rise quickly through the ranks to chief of staff.

* * *

Manzo was a sharp dresser. He'd walk down the capitol hallways thumbing his Blackberry before most people were using them. Reporters loved dealing with him. They would get the truth — what was really going on from his perspective off the record — then good on-the-record quotes for a story. Michael knew policy as well as PR. It was far better than dealing with his quirky boss, Bill DeWeese, who was more concerned about impressing people with his extensive vocabulary. DeWeese had odd habits, such as calling reporters back while winded and huffing on a treadmill. He called a lot of people back at 11:00 p.m. or later. He had an aggravating habit of saying "on the record," talking some more, then changing to "off the record," then "background," adding more to the conversation, then saying "attribute this to a well-placed source in Democratic leadership" and then "on the record" again. It sounded like DeWeese had watched *All the President's Men* once too often. It required saying firmly at the end: Here is what I have on the record and reading it back to him.

I had a chance to sit down with Michael Manzo at the Pennsylvania Society gathering of top politicos in Manhattan in December 2002. I ran into him in the hotel bar, and we took a table. Ed Rendell had been elected in November, and Harrisburg's political energy was focused on what his administration would look like and what it would do. There were rumors that Manzo might become Rendell's press secretary. Too bad for him it didn't work out.

Manzo had a reputation as a lady's man. He was smooth and articulate, but more importantly he was in a position of power. He usually had a wry grin on his face, but he came off as confident, not cocky. The bars of the city were a great place for a single guy, especially one at the pinnacle. It was a high-flying life for someone in his 30s with a big government salary.

At that time, Michael was dating Rachel Hurst, who would later become his wife. It can be said of her that Rachel was a stunning blonde with beautifully angular facial features. She looked more like a model than a research analyst. Michael would later stray from her during their marriage. Worse, his affair would become very public and part of the Bonusgate case. Manzo had placed his mistress, Angela Bertugli, on the payroll in a caucus job — in the South Side office of the Beaver Initiative for Growth — where she did little if any work and was away from the scrutiny likely in Harrisburg, according to the grand jury. Bertugli told investigators that she had "nothing to do 70 percent of the time."

The former beauty queen was paid $45,000 in annual salary, and she received a $7,000 bonus in 2006. Manzo met her at a West Shore bar in 2004. Angela was 21 at the time. He was 35. They had sex in a car that night after a few drinks, according to the grand jury report. She would later move to work in Harrisburg while attending law school at Widener University. She got her degree in 2012.

Manzo testified that he was no longer having sex with Bertugli from the time of his marriage in 2005. But on cross-examination at Veon's trial, he admitted that the affair continued through 2008. Manzo said that while he was still intimate with Angela, they had stopped having intercourse because of his inability to perform. At the 2008 Pennsylvania Gridiron Dinner, an annual spoof of politicians and reporters, a fake ad was shown to the crowd of "Manzo" men's cologne, a scent women could not resist.

On the day of their arraignment, Rachel ran out to get $10,000 in cash for Michael's bail. Once he made his plea agreement, Manzo would testify for the Commonwealth at three major trials. He spent four and a half days on the stand during the Bonusgate trial and was grilled relentlessly by Dan Raynak. He had bronchitis and was running a fever throughout his testimony. He could barely remain focused on the questions. After DeWeese's and Veon's BIG trial in 2012, Manzo's freedom would likely be curtailed.

On April 16, 2012, Judge Lewis sentenced Michael Manzo to 18 to 48 months in prison. It seemed stiff for someone who joined the prosecution team early.

Lewis, however, said Bonusgate was Manzo's "brainchild." But the way he viewed it, under-the-table bonuses had been around on a small scale for years, and he just expanded it, admittedly in a big way, with Mike Veon's approval. People with knowledge of the case from various positions seemed to think that Manzo got hammered. It did not help prosecutors in the long run. What is the incentive to cooperate if the sentence is only slightly less than you would get anyway if you went to trial?

With early parole for nonviolent offenders, Manzo would likely be out in 13 months. The flipside of the argument: 13 months is not a lot for 10 felonies and the illegal use of $1.4 million. His attorneys had argued for no jail time. That had been a longshot. His lawyer, Jim Eisenhower, was a Democrat who unsuccessfully ran for Attorney General against Tom Corbett in 2004.

Manzo took responsibility, as his dad had wanted, at a level beyond that of any of the other Bonusgate defendants. He had prepared for the worst. After all the worrying about prison time, it was far better to know how long it would be and when it would begin. He researched prison entry and incarceration as though it was an issue on which the Democratic Caucus desperately needed an answer. Manzo apologized to the taxpayers of Pennsylvania. "No culture committed this crime, no system committed this crime, I did," he told the judge. Later, talking to reporters outside the courtroom, Manzo expanded his statement, "It was too easy for some people to say, 'It was just the culture, it was just the system, it was the way it worked. I never bought into that. You take responsibility for your own actions."

By spring 2012, Michael and Rachel were divorced. The weight of the Bonusgate episode had just been too much: his affair, his public testimony about it, Rachel's inability to get even a menial job at first with charges hanging over her, the likelihood of Michael going to prison. They both held on, but in the end, the spark was no longer there. They split amicably.

As chief of staff there had been constant demands and little chance to see his family in Monaca. One of the benefits of losing his job and awaiting his sentence was that Manzo was able to spend time with his father in his final weeks.

Several weeks before, while testifying at the BIG trial, Dan Raynak had asked him about making a deal with prosecutors and agreeing to testify against Mike Veon because he was scared of going to prison. "I'm not scared," Manzo said convincingly. After watching your best friend die, very little can scare you. After Carl Manzo died, Michael had a bright blue tattoo inscribed on the inside of his left forearm. It says "RESOLVE" and it runs from below his wrist to just short of his elbow. Carl Manzo, I think, would have been proud.

Next: an odd candidate in the primary election.

22

Primary Election Day

April 24, 2012

Judgment day had arrived for Bill DeWeese. Judge Hoover unintentionally set the date for his sentencing for election day. The sentencing was set for 1:30 p.m. I was running a little late because I would need to stay up to cover statewide elections. I couldn't find a parking place and had to drive past the courthouse. It was 1:15 p.m. There was DeWeese, heading into the courthouse with attorney William Costopoulos. Bill was wearing a navy blue suit, a light blue shirt, a dark tie and an olive green Marines cap. About a dozen still and video cameras greeted them. For the first time in 36 years, he wasn't doing last-day campaigning in his district. But he was still running.

Incredibly, DeWeese filed his nominating petitions for re-election just days after the jury's guilty verdict in February. Under state law, he would not officially become a convicted felon until he was sentenced. He would have to resign his House seat — and he did before arriving at the courthouse — but there was no law preventing him from running again. DeWeese was unopposed in the primary. His hope was to win the general election in November and win his appeal before the new House was seated in November. If he did not get out on bail, he would have to campaign from behind bars.

It bordered on the delusional. Getting a higher court ruling on an appeal in less than eight months was a tall order. Winning his appeal would only result in a new trial, which would take a month or more to schedule and several weeks to complete. Nothing would prevent the Attorney General's office from asking for a postponement until after January 1st. It said a lot about DeWeese's Semper Fi spirit and perhaps his uncontrolled ego. More likely, the combination of these helped him to keep him busy in the darkest hours of his life.

Reporters, curiosity seekers, DeWeese's sister, his girlfriend and former staffers lined up outside the elaborately carved doors of Courtroom 1. No one was allowed in. Judge Todd Hoover was finishing a hearing. A guy was hauled out on a stretcher at the conclusion of the hearing; I have no idea why. Was that an ominous sign? I don't think so. Hoover is quite a civil and reasonable jurist. He can be tough or easy on defendants, I am told, depending on the circumstances. I had no idea what to expect for DeWeese.

Costopoulos put on three witnesses: William Chadwick, former state Inspector General and former acting DA of Philadelphia (and the attorney DeWeese hired to retrieve emails and investigate Bonusgate); John Connelly, a Harrisburg attorney who had done work for the House; and former Acting Attorney General Walter Cohen, who briefly represented DeWeese in his "proffer" to the Attorney General's office and his grand jury appearance. Connelly testified that DeWeese was already losing a pension worth about $2.8 million, based on average life expectancy. Chadwick rebutted prosecution claims that DeWeese didn't cooperate. "Representative DeWeese was trying to do the right thing," he insisted. DeWeese was a pariah in the caucus because some members believed he was on the hunt for scapegoats. Thousands of emails were turned over to the Attorney General.

"He [DeWeese] did not want to see what was turned over before it was turned over," Chadwick added.

Costopoulos also referred to letters written on DeWeese's behalf by conservative Republican state senator Jeffrey Piccola. DeWeese was the only one of the charged legislative leaders for whom Piccola would agree to write a letter. Arthur Rooney, president and owner of the Pittsburgh Steelers, wrote to the court, Costopoulos told Hoover. Another letter of support came from former Attorney General Gerald Pappert. Pappert wrote that he respected the jury's verdict but believed DeWeese's crimes were distinct from the others. He had much to offer society and would benefit from not going to prison, Pappert maintained. Walter Cohen testified that "DeWeese answered every question truthfully, to the best of my knowledge," before the grand jury. This was a heavy-hitting lineup on DeWeese's behalf, especially Pappert, Cohen and Chadwick, three former prosecutors.

Deputy Attorney General Kenneth Brown was pushing for significant prison time. "This defendant was a public official with the public trust who violated that trust over a series of years," Brown argued. "We're not talking about a single error of judgment."

Brown reminded the judge that DeWeese, according to witnesses, said "fucking fire them" when told some of his district office workers did not want to work on his 2006 campaign.

Brown played a video clip (from *Roxbury News*) of DeWeese leaving the courtroom after the jury verdict. He had pretty well escaped the mob of reporters after a brief statement and was heading for an elevator when a persistent reporter asked if the verdict was fair. DeWeese said that he would have fared better with a Western Pennsylvania jury. Instead, he said, "Mr. Fina [a prosecutor] wanted me tried by his peers, not my peers." Judge Hoover had turned down a request to use a Greene County jury for his trial.

This raised an interesting question inherent in the "law of the land" inscription behind the judge on the front courtroom wall and dating back to the Magna Carta. DeWeese's crimes occurred in both Harrisburg (Dauphin County) and Greene County in his district. What was a jury of his peers?

There seems little doubt that DeWeese could have won an acquittal, more or less, in Greene County where he'd delivered millions of dollars and helped connect people to hundreds of jobs. Harrisburg juries, at least in this era, have a tendency to be anti-government. Prosecutors want to win. Why would they use a rural Western Pennsylvania jury, aside from the inconvenience? There would be considerable expense in bringing a Greene County jury pool to Harrisburg and then putting up jurors for several weeks.

Was DeWeese tried by a jury of his peers or, as he suggests, Frank Fina's peers?

I'm not sure that the "law of the land" gives you the right to shop for a jury. Moreover, DeWeese spent a lot of the past 35 years in Harrisburg. It was his second home. But the "law of the land" did deprive Bill DeWeese of his liberty. Judge Hoover sentenced him to two and a half to five years in state prison, fined him $25,000, and ordered him to pay $116,000 in restitution. DeWeese was stoic through the sentencing. For once, Costopoulos had convinced him to say very little in and out of court. In his fantasy world, DeWeese's hope of winning an appeal was not out of the question. What was delusional was the timing: that it could all happen before the next legislature was sworn in and that he could withstand a challenge to a likely lawsuit to remove him from the ballot.

*   *   *

On May 14, 2012, reality came crashing in. On a gloomy day with soaking rain, DeWeese and his girlfriend, Stephanie Lupacchini, showed up at Dauphin County Prison. She held an umbrella. He had none but wore a cap. "Gentlemen," he told reporters gathered outside the gate, "three quick points." He seemed really collected and strong about it, except for an ever-so-slight weakness in his voice. "One, I am going to behave and abide by the protocols of the institution. Two, I am going to stay in tip-top physical condition. Three, I am going to make new friends."

New friends? Did he realize what he was saying?

He kissed Stephanie goodbye. A guard with a rifle slung over his shoulder walked by DeWeese. The ex-lawmaker shook the guard's hand. It was almost instinctual — from the campaign trail. ABC-27's Dennis Owens, who had staked out the prison, offered this final comment in his report: "Yes," Owens said. "He was strip-searched."

Four days later, Bill DeWeese walked out of Camp Hill State Correctional Institution a free man. In an unusual move, the Pennsylvania Superior Court gave him a reprieve to remain out on bail pending a decision on his bail by Judge Hoover. His exit from prison, based on a petition by William Costopoulos, broke on a Friday night and was stunning. Would he go back or not? Four days later, he did go back. Hoover denied bail while the case was appealed. During that little hiatus, DeWeese went to a Harrisburg Senators minor league baseball game. He rode his bicycle, saw his girlfriend and ate Chinese food, DeWeese told *The Inquirer's* Amy Worden. In typical Pennsylvania fashion, he got his temporary reprieve from prison based on a "per curiam" order of the Superior Court — an anonymous ruling without a hint as to which judge or judges had sprung him loose. In Pennsylvania, it's not public record.

Next: there was collateral damage from the Attorney General's prosecution of public corruption.

23

Collateral Damage

May 4, 2012

In a tryout at the age of 15, John R. Zimmerman won a position as a euphonium player in the United States Marine Band. That's like making the NFL as a sophomore in high school. It's unheard of. The physical demands are vastly different, of course. But the Marine Band, like an NFL team, plays at the very highest level. For two centuries, the Marine Band has been the only musical group charged with performing for the president. Thomas Jefferson gave it the name, The President's Own.

John's father, Samuel O. Zimmerman, director of the New Holland Band in Lancaster County, one of the finest community bands in the nation, made him wait two years and finish high school. He was too young to join anyway. After graduating from Garden Spot High School in 1965, John did not need to try out again. He went straight to Washington. Paris Island was not an option for members of The President's Own. They might break a finger or knock out a tooth. At age 17, Zimmerman was the backup euphonium soloist. They went on tour, two concerts a day, seven days a week, for 65 days. To be a soloist at that level, you never took sheet music on a music stand in front of the band. It was all by memory. John had memorized 10 solos. He had to keep those up to performance standards while on tour. His stock-in-trade was "All Those Endearing Young Charms," written by Simone Mantia, a soloist with the Sousa Band. Zimmerman stayed in the Marine Band for seven years, then moved over to the White House operations office, setting up events for the president. He worked under Lyndon Johnson, Richard Nixon, Jimmy Carter and Ronald Reagan. With 20 years service, he retired as a Marine

Corps captain. He had top-secret clearance at the White House. Zimmerman took a job in Pennsylvania state government and did scheduling and advance work for former Republican governor Tom Ridge and later former House speaker John Perzel.

At work on Thursday, November 12, 2009 in the state capitol, Zimmerman received a phone call with stunning news: he was being indicted. "I was just in shock," he said.

He had testified twice before a grand jury and met with agents from the Attorney General's office because he knew he had done nothing wrong. He had nothing to do with the computer scam among House Republicans that Attorney General Tom Corbett was investigating. He was a scheduler, not an IT guy. Surely, they would see this, he thought.

But Zimmerman was dragged along with the sweeping indictment alleging that 10 House Republicans participated in a scheme to buy $10 million in computer equipment, software and voter data to help Perzel and other Republicans win elections and to cover up political work at the capitol. Zimmerman never should have been charged in the Attorney General's investigation of the legislature. Others arguably include Steve Keefer, who was acquitted at the trial of Mike Veon, and secretary Jill Seaman, who was convicted with former Representative Brett Feese in November 2011.

Bonusgate and Computergate were different than the scandals of the 1970s and 1990s because legislative staffers as well as lawmakers were going to jail. A total of 10 of the 12 charged in Bonusgate were current or ex-staffers from the Democratic Caucus. Eight of the 10 people in Computergate were staffers or campaign aides. These scandals were complex conspiracies that, prosecutors argued, required staff to carry them out. I get the difference. But some staffers were charged for the smallest of alleged infractions. In the case of Zimmerman, there was little if any evidence. Jill Seaman was convicted on all counts, swept away by the runaway jury on Brett Feese.

On balance, Tom Corbett and his team of Frank Fina, Patrick Blessington, Marc Costanzo, James Reeder, Laurel Brandstetter, Anthony Krastek, Kenneth Brown, Chris Carusone and Michael Sprowl did an extraordinary job of ridding the state of self-serving Democratic and Republican legislative leaders who acted as if they were above the law. Combined with the feds and the Allegheny County District Attorney's office, they, in effect, enacted reform that the legislature would not do on its own: ending state-financed incumbency protection — at least for a while.

But there was collateral damage.

Zimmerman was named only three times near the end of a 188-page grand jury indictment. He was charged with a felony (hindering apprehension or prosecution, related to "missing boxes") and a misdemeanor (obstructing administration of law or other governmental function). He was accused of taking part in a cover-up of campaign materials that had been placed at the capitol. He allegedly knew of boxes that contained campaign material, which were moved out of the capitol.

Zimmerman reported to the Lower Paxton police station in 2009 for a mug shot and fingerprinting. Most of the defendants were driven individually to the district judge's office where the media was waiting for them to be "perp-walked." It was humiliating. John Zimmerman just stepped outside himself to get through it, a skill he had learned as a soloist. "I put myself in a mind warp. I set myself aside. I realized everyone was just doing their job," he said. He was handcuffed for the first time in his life. "It was surreal," he added. At least the Republicans were cuffed in front and not behind the back like the Democrats, he noted later.

At the end of the Attorney General's news release, it was stated: A person charged with a crime is presumed innocent until proven guilty. That sounds good unless you are really innocent. In the end, nine of the 10 people charged would be convicted, two by a jury and seven, including "Kingfish" Perzel, by entering guilty pleas. There's no arguing with the results. It was a highly effective prosecution.

Only Zimmerman walked away. The charges against him were dropped. They were dropped two years and five days after he was charged. Zimmerman thought that the two-year delay might have been linked to extending the case beyond a statute of limitations in case he would sue. But prosecutors have absolute immunity from facing lawsuits over their charging decisions. For John Zimmerman, it was two years and five days of self-torment, shame, anger and disgust. For the first two weeks, he just beat himself up. He was charged with various crimes, then he got a grip on it, realizing that he "didn't do anything wrong." And then he got angry.

On a recommendation from John Perzel's top aide, Brian Preski, a Perzel co-defendant and an attorney, Zimmerman hired Tom Bergstrom, a criminal defense specialist from Malvern, with Buchanan Ingersoll, who has handled high-profile cases like the murder charge against John DuPont and the trial of Monsignor William J. Lynn, accused of protecting other priests who abused children. Lynn was the first supervisor of priests to be charged with endangering children and conspiracy, according to *The New York Times*. He was convicted on one count of child endangerment and acquitted of conspiracy and another endangerment count.

Bergstrom is a big-leaguer. He filed a habeas corpus petition and a motion to have John Zimmerman's trial severed from the others. Judge Lewis said he'd take the habeas corpus petition — to free him of the charges — under consideration and, in the meantime, severed Zimmerman's case. Just like Sean Ramaley's case in Bonusgate, the approval of severance went a long way to deciding the case.

Zimmerman said he was charged "because I might have been on a phone call and I might have seen some boxes." That appeared to be the entirety of the allegation. In essence, some boxes containing campaign material were found in a basement storage place. Democrats who found them called the Attorney General's office. At Paul Towhey's direction, the boxes were taken to Perzel's office where a secretary, Lori Lochetto, went through them and "extracted the campaign materials," a grand jury report stated. Lochetto was not charged. Towhey, then Perzel's chief of staff, ordered the campaign materials to be taken out of the capitol and moved across the street to the offices of the House Republican Campaign Committee (HRCC). House messengers did the moving. Lochetto, testifying with immunity, said she acted on her own to coordinate the movement of the boxes.

Paul Towhey's action sounds like the right thing, but at this point a criminal investigation was well under way. The right thing would have been calling the Attorney General's office. Towhey was charged with 28 offenses, and he pled guilty to conflict of interest and conspiracy on August 20, 2011. Then 41, Towhey cooperated with investigators and, in March 2012, was sentenced to five years' probation including 500 hours of community service. He was fined $5,000 and was ordered to pay $15,000 in restitution.

The problem occurred when Frank Fina and an agent, armed with a subpoena, came to the capitol about 6:00 p.m. on Friday, February 29, 2008. They were looking for the campaign materials, which had already been moved to the HRCC. They were frustrated after going through boxes of material in Perzel's office and finding nothing. They knew that some campaign material had been identified. And in fact, there had been campaign material: stationery with the letterhead of the Friends of John Perzel. The paper was two years old. The grand jury said there was also "direct evidence of campaign work performed by public employees" (which isn't, on its face, a crime). In any case, Zimmerman said later, the campaign material should not have been at the capitol.

Fina and the agent asked Zimmerman and Towhey if boxes with political material had been moved out earlier. They both denied it. For his part, Zimmerman was not aware of any. The problem was that Towhey was aware. He had actually directed them to be moved. But Zimmerman didn't know that, so he looked like he was lying. That's why he was charged.

"They thought he lied," Tom Corbett said in an interview.

Testimony from a House messenger and video footage from capitol security cameras documented that boxes had been moved from Perzel's office to the HRCC on February 27, 2008 — two days before Frank Fina showed up with the subpoena.

Prosecutors knew that Paul Towhey had lied to them, and they assumed that John Zimmerman had, too. After all, the proximity of his desk in Perzel's office would have given Zimmerman full view of boxes being moved out. Phone records showed that on February 29th, Towhey was in frequent contact with Perzel, Feese, Zimmerman and Lochetto.

No kidding. They worked together.

Phone records showed a call from what they thought was Zimmerman's line to the HRCC on February 27, 2008. What they didn't know, or had overlooked, was that the phone number assigned to Zimmerman rang through to several other people in the office.

In a best case scenario for prosecutors, they would have had to prove that he knew what was in closed boxes that no one saw him handle.

* * *

To me, John Zimmerman was just another name on the computer screen when writing about Tom Corbett's investigation of House Republicans. I feel bad about that now. He was low man on the totem pole with the GOP defendants. He had served as House Republican Right to Know Law Officer at one point, and I'd exchanged emails with him years ago. But I really didn't know him.

Three years after Zimmerman had been charged and almost a year after he got the amazing news from Tom Bergstrom about the case being dropped, he agreed to meet me at the Tom Sawyer diner on 2nd Street.

"What do you look like?"

"I'm 6-1," he replied.

It was May 4, 2012.

Zimmerman had been on an extended vacation in the tropics. Despite heavy use of sun block, his face and neck were lightly tanned. Tom Sawyer's was closed, so we went to Zembie's tavern and restaurant a few doors away. Even then he was leery of going any place frequented by legislative staffers.

As he retold his nightmare, Zimmerman barely touched his hamburger. His gray hair was combed straight back and was a lot longer than might be expected on an ex-Marine. It gave him a casual look. His most prominent feature was his bright blue eyes.

Zimmerman didn't recall making a phone call to the HRCC four years ago. He did not remember seeing any boxes moved that day. It's a common occurrence at the capitol.

He recalled how after he was charged, he was afraid to go to the store and other public places for fear of being recognized: "I was so embarrassed for my friends and family. I was scared to go out in public." He missed his high school reunion and a get-together with his old White House crew in Washington.

I kept thinking, this is a good guy. Why was he charged? As a key Republican staffer who worked with Zimmerman told me: "If you talked to John Zimmerman for even a few minutes, you would realize his mind is incapable of criminal thought."

He thought back to his "proffer" with the Attorney General's office with several prosecutors, including Patrick Blessington and Frank Fina. Blessington was screaming at him, liberally tossing in the F word, Zimmerman recalled. "'You are either the dumbest person I ever met or you are trying to cover up,'" Zimmerman remembered Blessington saying.

Prosecutors claimed that Zimmerman misled them. Thinking back, he said that inside he was laughing at the show put on by Blessington. What wasn't funny was the $75,000 in legal bills. But Tom Bergstrom was worth every penny.

Having his case split from the others was the first step toward freedom. "If I'd been on trial with [Brett] Feese and [Jill] Seaman, I'd be in jail, no doubt in my mind," Zimmerman remarked. That's because Feese and Seaman ran up against a buzz-saw jury that convicted on all counts, just a few days after Jerry Sandusky was charged with sex crimes, creating a "hang 'em high" atmosphere. The verdict came one day after Attorney General Linda Kelly's news conference on Sandusky, broadcast worldwide.

Zimmerman has had a lot of time to think. As a reform in 1978, Pennsylvania voters approved a constitutional amendment to have an independent, elected Attorney General. That meant that the Attorney General would no longer be an employee of the governor. It also meant that the Attorney General would be a politician.

"You've got a political boss over a police force," Zimmerman remarked. Three of the four people who won the office ran for governor: Ernie Preate, Mike Fisher and Tom Corbett. "I believe a non-political Attorney General wouldn't have indicted me."

"The grand jury is an absolute joke," Zimmerman claimed. "It is a tool of prosecutors, period. It offends me that my fellow citizens indicted me. But everything is one-sided. The final statement is prepared by prosecutors. They heard the testimony and knew I didn't do anything wrong." But the case is presented to the grand jury as a package and the grand jurors do whatever the prosecutor wants, he added.

Zimmerman knew Tom Corbett to say hello to from his days as a Ridge staffer. He thought that would give the AG pause to make sure the case was airtight. Corbett said he didn't really know Zimmerman. "I felt badly," Corbett said. "I felt badly about Preski, too. They lose their way." Preski held a fundraiser for Corbett, and Perzel donated $50,000.

* * *

John Zimmerman wasn't the only victim of the investigation. Steve Keefer had his life turned upside down. Keefer should not have been charged, said his attorney, William Fetterhoff. The 16 not-guilty verdicts from the jury are proof of that: "There just wasn't any evidence against him. They claimed he was doing things on state time, but never proved it."

"There's nothing I can do to get my career back," Keefer maintained. He said that he still has a letter from Bill DeWeese stating that he would get his back pay if he was acquitted. Keefer sought $457,000 in back wages, benefits and interest about a month after the verdict. House Democrats said no. Now 43, he is still dealing with the emotion of being falsely accused: "Why me? How did it happen? It took me years. I'm still dealing with the bitterness."

But things were looking up in the spring of 2012. Keefer got married. He was working at a company making truck bodies and moved up to line foreman. That gave him time on evenings and weekends to work on his photography business. His youngest son, age 11 at the time, was traumatized by his father's ordeal, Keefer claimed. Five years later, the son wanted to go to DeWeese's sentencing and confront him. Fortunately for all concerned, that didn't happen. Still, you really can't blame the kid.

*　*　*

During the seven-day preliminary hearing for John Perzel and the Republican defendants in April and May 2010, I came across Jill Seaman eating lunch by herself in the basement cafeteria of the Dauphin County Courthouse. She motioned for me to sit down. We were not supposed to speak to jurors during a trial. Defendants? I didn't think it mattered. Jill is a grandmother from Dauphin, a small borough alongside the Susquehanna River, north of Harrisburg. Aged 59 at the time, she was very polite and friendly. You tend to find that in public corruption cases. You are not dealing with sinister criminals. They are ordinary people. Perzel, Feese, Seaman and the others were held for trial at that preliminary hearing before District Judge William Wenner.

After meeting Jill, I went back to my desk later that day and reread the indictment against Republican defendants to see what Seaman allegedly had done. Even if you took it all to be 100 percent true, she was the most marginal of defendants. On November 8th, election day, Feese and Seaman were each convicted of 40 counts.

I was blown away by the verdicts. I thought Brett Feese might go down on several charges — maybe most of the charges — and that Seaman, who was Feese's secretary, would walk. Or if the jury felt guilty about that, she might get nicked on a minor charge. The grand jury report claimed that she had directed people to do a few political tasks and took notes for Feese at meetings. Prosecutors said some of those notes were later reconstructed to put Feese in a good light and to suggest that he didn't know what was going on was illegal. Seaman clearly knew what Feese knew. But she was a functionary, like many other staffers, doing what she was told.

"I had greater confidence in her case than I did in Keefer's," William Fetterhoff stated. "Women make more sympathetic defendants. Steve was the head of a department, she was a secretary. They [the prosecutors] punished Jill because they wanted her to testify against Feese."

"[Frank] Fina told me the only way she [Seaman] would not be charged was if she testified that Brett Feese was a knowing co-conspirator with Perzel," Fetterhoff remarked several months after the trial during an interview in his law office. If Seaman was guilty of anything, it was of being loyal to a fault.

Jill Seaman was sentenced on January 13, 2012. *The Patriot*'s Matt Miller reported that about 50 supporters of Seaman came to court and stood when Fetterhoff asked them to do so. She said nothing before or after her sentencing. Judge Lewis sentenced her to nine to 23 months in prison, $20,000 in fines and $50,000 in restitution. It was a reasonable sentence given the 40 counts. Fetterhoff noted that she showed no bitterness afterward.

Seaman was offered a job that she could report to through county work release. It is with Pugliese Associates, a lobbying firm. She spent her days there and went back to county prison for evenings and weekends. At the office, she's in the same building, Strawberry Square, that houses the Attorney General's office.

After the verdict, Fetterhoff advised Jill not to appeal. The first consideration for her was the expense, given that she had a large fine and restitution to pay. With her husband, Don, Seaman has two grown children, a daughter and a son. She was born and raised in Ringtown, Schuylkill County, and worked for the House since 1999. In prison, Seaman, who is white, was with much younger women, many of them black. They called her "Miss Jill." She basically ran a "home economics" course for the younger women and was pleased to be able to help them, Fetterhoff said. "'God acts in strange ways and maybe I can make a difference,'" he quoted her as saying.

Next: the investigation to nowhere.

24

Investigation to Nowhere

June 26, 2012

Whatever happened with former state Attorney General Tom Corbett's investigation of Senate Republicans for possible political corruption, says historian Robert B. Swift, is the biggest mystery in Pennsylvania political circles since the disappearance of Jimmy Hoffa.

And yes, there was a Pennsylvania angle to Hoffa's disappearance. Mob enforcer Frank "The Irishman" Sheeran, a hit man for Northeastern Pennsylvania crime boss Russell Buffalino, confessed that he killed Hoffa in *I Heard You Paint Houses*, by Charles Brandt.

In 2007, Corbett pledged to "investigate all four caucuses" of the General Assembly. Indeed, he ripped through the House Democratic Caucus and then the House Republican Caucus, charging 25 people and convicting 22. His Democratic opponent for Attorney General, John Morganelli, criticized Corbett in 2008 for not launching the investigation of all four caucuses simultaneously and for failing to appoint a special prosecutor to handle it because of his political ties to Senate Republicans. Senate GOP leaders had been among Corbett's largest campaign contributors. The size of the House Democratic bonus effort, $2.3 million, and efforts by some Democrats to destroy evidence, necessitated a move on that caucus first, argued Corbett, who was re-elected in 2008.

In 2012, people at the capitol still talked about why Tom Corbett prosecuted no one in the Senate Republican Caucus in the investigation he launched more than five years before. Former Senate GOP leaders authorized the payment of $366,000 in secret bonuses to staff members in 2005 and 2006. In the House

Democratic Caucus, bonuses for campaign work were a central thread of the pros-ecutions. Among House Republicans, they weren't.

Corbett's critics see it as a clear case of the former Attorney General, for political reasons, declining to prosecute his supporters. Bill DeWeese maintained that Corbett laid off Senate Republicans because if he became governor, he'd need them to confirm his nominees, not to mention on other major legislation. It remained in the hands of Corbett's appointed and Senate-confirmed Attorney General Linda Kelly until January 2013. Corbett did investigate the Senate Republican Caucus. The caucus spent $2.5 million on legal fees paid to a private law firm during the investigation. By 2012, the investigation was inactive. Senate records show that the last legal bill was paid on December 28, 2010 to outside counsel, the Conrad O'Brien law firm in Philadelphia.

Prosecutors found no substantial evidence of any caucus-wide scheme like those uncovered among House Democrats and House Republicans, say sources close to the investigation. They could have pursued potential cases among indi-vidual senators, but they would have been "chicken shit," as one source put it. Compared to what was done with House Democrats and Republicans, it would have been laughable.

The reasons that prosecutors didn't file charges are complicated. For one, if there was any wrongdoing, there was no paper trail. Former Senate President Pro Tempore Robert Jubelirer of Altoona, former Senate majority leader David Brightbill of Lebanon, Jubelirer's chief of staff Mike Long and former Senate Republican general counsel Stephen MacNett did not use email to any significant degree. I know for a fact that MacNett did not. I emailed his office once and his secretary said she would print it and give it to him. He would not respond via email, she said. I had to call.

The Bonusgate case was made on incriminating emails and corroborating tes-timony. The Computergate case was made on contracts, emails and testimony. Mike Long had a policy of requiring leave slips before people could campaign. He took part-time pay in combination with leave to work on Robert Jubelirer's 2006 primary race, which Jubelirer lost to John Eichelberger.

From 2004 onward, the Senate Republicans were extraordinarily careful. The Senate GOP leaders were cautious and deliberate on most things. Stephen Mac-Nett took the Jeffrey Habay case seriously. Even before the Habay case, sources say, MacNett was aware that this could become a significant issue.

Top GOP Senate staff knew about problems with members doing campaign work in other states, including Wisconsin's so-called Senate Caucus scandal in 2001-02, which resulted in the convictions of the Senate majority leader and another senator connected to use of state resources for campaigns. Prosecutors said that former Mike Veon aide Brett Cott had worked in Madison for a Democratic figure who was convicted, Senate majority leader Chuck Chvala.

As for the bonuses, the majority of Pennsylvania Senate GOP staffers who received them did not work on campaigns. Substantial bonuses also were given in the previous non-election year. Prosecutors found no linkage to campaigns as there was among House Democrats. Did an upper-level staffer get a slightly bigger bonus for working on a campaign? Perhaps, but there was no proof of it.

The logic of critics, in the simplified version of campaign-speak, goes like this: top Senate GOP staffers got enormous bonuses and they also worked on campaigns, therefore the bonuses were tied to campaign work. The problem is that no credible evidence ever surfaced making that link. It is legal to work on campaigns on one's own time.

There was, however, evidence viewed by prosecutors that from Jeffrey Habay forward, Senate Republicans got better at separating campaigns and stood out when compared to House Democrats and Republicans. That probably got them points with Corbett, who used Habay as the standard and couldn't believe that other leaders continued to ignore the reality from the Ethics Commission case.

Mike Long's base salary in 2006 was $127,283. His bonus that year was $22,500. Over a two-year period, for the 2005–06 session, Long received $41,000 in bonuses, the highest of any staffer in the General Assembly. In 2006, Long took about six weeks of leave to work on Robert Jubelirer's intense primary campaign. He was on part-time pay during the first half of the year.

Stephen MacNett, the top lawyer, also received a $22,500 bonus in 2006 in addition to a $150,021 salary. MacNett worked for David Brightbill. MacNett was treasurer for the Senate Republican Campaign Committee, but he was not a hands-on campaigner. The next highest bonuses went to non-campaigners, former Secretary of the Senate Mark Corrigan and Senate clerk Russell Faber at $20,676. They served the institution of the Senate.

Another top GOP lawyer, Andrew Crompton, who worked for Jubelirer, received a $19,467 bonus in 2006 in addition to a $101,523 salary. He spent more than three months on the unsuccessful gubernatorial campaign of Republican Lynn Swann that year. He took 14 weeks of leave in 2006. Jubelirer aide David Atkinson got a $20,000 bonus, and Erik Arneson, Brightbill's chief of staff, got $15,000. They took leave to work on 2006 campaigns

In November 2007, Ed Rendell teed off on Corbett and the Senate Republicans. He did so as watchdog groups called on Bill DeWeese to resign as Democratic leader as the bonus scandal unfolded. Rendell would only say that DeWeese had some "explaining to do" to his caucus.

Rendell said he didn't want the corruption investigation to become a distraction, which, of course, it already was. But he told reporters that he thought the attention focused on Democrats by the Attorney General's investigation and the news media was out of balance. Rendell pointed to Andrew Crompton's $19,000 bonus while working for the candidate who was trying to unseat him as governor.

Maybe, Rendell suggested, Crompton should have gotten a bonus from the Swann campaign. "That's the only place he should have gotten a bonus," the former governor remarked. Senate Republicans responded that it was a cheap shot.

To Corbett's critics like the blog Casablancapablogspot.com, Crompton was the "poster boy" for his easy treatment of Senate Republicans. Casablanca was an anonymous anti-Corbett blog believed to be written by Brett Cott and/or his wife, Tess Candori.

In 2006, when Republicans again kept control of the Senate, 16 Senate staffers were awarded $179,544 in bonuses. They ranged from Long's $442 to MacNett's $22,500. Eight of the staffers had some campaign ties with four showing "moderate to extensive" involvement based on campaign reimbursements, according to a December 17, 2007 story by *The Post-Gazette*. The other four were marginal, the story claimed. So the majority, 12 of 16 bonus recipients, were not active campaigners.

Senate officials said the bonuses were for legislative work. Stephen MacNett told *The Patriot-News* in August 2008 that Andrew Crompton and other staffers put enormous amounts of work into a property tax bill. McNett held that Mike Long was key in guiding the Senate Republicans through a leadership transition after Robert Jubelirer lost.

*   *   *

It would be wrong to say that the Senate Republican investigation is closed. Prosecutors won't say that. It's why prosecutors still refuse to comment publicly. It is inactive. The statute of limitations, apparently, has expired. But there are extensions that can be added to prosecute elected officials.

Chief Deputy Attorney General Frank Fina, questioned by reporters on several occasions in the first half of 2012 after other trials and hearings, said he could not comment on why no one was charged in the secret grand jury investigation of Senate Republicans. Asked if he could clear people in the former Senate GOP caucus leadership and in top staff positions, Fina said he could not do so. Prosecutors aren't in the business of clearing people, he added. A key piece of evidence could come in later, at least theoretically, that could change the entire picture. As much as he may have wanted to do so, Matt Haverstick, who led a team of Conrad O'Brien lawyers defending the Senate, could not comment on the dormant Senate GOP investigation.

A joint statement by Senate President Pro Tempore Joe Scarnati and Senate majority leader Dominic Pileggi in September 2011 stated that 55 current and former caucus employees were interviewed by the private law firm the caucus retained. Scarnati and Pileggi were not members of the leadership during the period that bonuses were paid. They had nothing to do with it.

MacNett voluntarily appeared before the grand jury on two occasions. Erik Arneson, David Brightbill's spokesman, said no one was subpoenaed. But there were other current and former Senate employees who went without subpoenas to testify voluntarily before the grand jury, and agents interviewed several people as well.

A practice among Senate Republicans was to delete emails after three days. But as the investigation unfolded, a tech brought news that there was a server in the capitol basement with everything on it. Even if they had wanted to, they could not get rid of it. MacNett's instructions were to keep everything. Tens of thousands of documents were turned over to the Attorney General's office, Pileggi and Scarnati both claimed. Every effort was made to cooperate, they insisted.

In 2008, Stephen MacNett said that documents had been subpoenaed. It was a "formalization of an information gathering and sharing process that has gone on for some time," he added. In July 2011, MacNett joined the Philadelphia law firm of Conrad O'Brien, the same firm that represented the caucus during the grand jury investigation. As general counsel, he oversaw Conrad O'Brien's work for the Senate GOP.

* * *

Four senators were charged with crimes, but not by the Attorney General. Republican senator Jane Orie was prosecuted by Allegheny County district attorney Stephen Zappala. Democratic senators Vincent Fumo, Ray Musto and Bob Mellow were charged by the FBI. While Fumo and Mellow were convicted, the bribery-related charges were still pending against Musto as of February 2013. Mellow pleaded guilty in 2012 to mail fraud and filing a false tax return. He was accused of using Senate staff to work on his campaigns. The FBI branched out since it had a foothold in the Senate Democratic Caucus with the Fumo investigation, which began in 2004.

Jane Orie was an anomaly because the intern who reported suspected campaign work on state time says that a receptionist in the Attorney General's office referred her to the Allegheny County DA. The Orie and Corbett conspiracy theorists viewed the intern as a "plant" by the Democrats and the referral as proof that the AG had punted on a Senate Republican probe. It was a heck of a coincidence that Jennifer Rioja was referred to Orie by former Democratic senator Sean Logan of Plum in the Pittsburgh suburbs. But there is no proof of either theory. Rioja insists that she never met Sean Logan.

* * *

When John Eichelberger joined the Senate and the Republican Caucus in January 2007, there was a chill within the GOP caucus. "It was very difficult," Eichelberger recalls about his transition. "It was really unpleasant." Here was a guy who defeated Robert Jubelirer, the leader of the caucus, who was assured of his place in history after three decades in the Senate. "Several people were polite, cordial perhaps," Eichelberger remembers. "There was a sense of demonization of myself and Mike Folmer." In the same 2006 primary, Folmer defeated Brightbill.

"When we walked in the door, everyone had an opinion of us, and it wasn't good," Eichelberger said in an interview. They were viewed as uncompromising ideologues.

"It was very uncomfortable," Folmer noted.

The tension was real, Eichelberger recalls. "You could feel it from members."

In 2006, Robert Jubelirer was defeated by the pay raise as much as by John Eichelberger. Despite leading the repeal effort, Jubelirer was closely linked to initiation of the 2005 raise. As any politicians would, Eichelberger and Folmer ran on it and pledged reform. Eichelberger wasted no time after *The Patriot-News* broke the Bonusgate story, shortly after he took office. He asked Attorney General Corbett to investigate. As a former Blair County commissioner, Eichelberger had seen Mike Long, David Atkinson and Jubelirer's district aide Jim Gregory in his own race and other local contests over the years.

When he won his Senate race, Long was still the caucus chief of staff, and Eichelberger had to call him to set up his office and staff.

"Jubelirer's office was closed. They never turned one record over to me. They were destroyed," Eichelberger claimed. That is not unheard of in other House and Senate districts. Mike Veon, for instance, left not a shred of paper to his successor, Representative Jim Marshall.

"I've never been interviewed," Eichelberger stated. In 2007, he could name times and places where he'd seen Jubelirer aides. He concedes that it's a lot fuzzier in 2012.

Eichelberger's claim of not being interviewed was challenged by prosecutors. "They did talk to [consultant Jeff Coleman], who worked in my campaign," Eichelberger noted. Seeing someone at an event is proof of nothing, especially if someone had leave to be out of the office.

"It's kind of surprising" that no Senate Republicans were prosecuted, Mike Folmer remarked. Many GOP senators knew nothing about the bonuses in 2005 and 2006, Folmer added.

When Linda Kelly was unanimously confirmed by the Senate, she made the customary rounds to meet with each senator. "I talked to Linda Kelly when she was going through the confirmation process," John Eichelberger recalled. "I asked her, 'Will you continue this investigation?' She said, 'Well, I've been asked that but never that bluntly. I really can't say. It's sealed. I haven't had access to that.'" Since then, senators and staff have been more accepting, he added.

The final decision not to prosecute was political, Eichelberger concluded. After all these years, he doesn't buy the Attorney General's claim that "we can't discuss it."

"Someone should clear up the Senate side of the building and say 'we didn't have evidence,'" Eichelberger remarked.

We may never know.

Over the course of several years, I had come to know Frank Fina. If there was any kind of scheme in that caucus, he would have filed charges. If Tom Corbett, as an elected official, had resisted for political reasons, Fina would have gone across the street from Strawberry Square to the U.S. Attorney's office to file charges against him.

Fina was disliked by so many at the capitol for his apparent belief that they were all crooks. But it seemed, at times, that he was all that stood between the contending legions. Nonetheless, I still have substantial questions about how the Senate GOP got off the hook. It's hard to believe that they couldn't have filed at least some charges. Some who worked with him say Fina, first of all, was a loyalist. I suspect that means loyal to Corbett.

*   *   *

By 2012, Robert Jubelirer was working the capitol as a lobbyist. He was a partner with Obermayer, Rebmann, Maxwell & Hippel and served as the firm's government affairs director. David Brightbill, who was "of counsel" with the law firm of Stevens & Lee, was also a registered lobbyist.

After leaving the Senate, Mike Long, Jubelirer's former political guru, was a lobbyist with two firms he founded, Long, Nyquist & Associates and Commonwealth Strategic Solutions, which also runs the campaigns of Senate Republicans. They are both located at 121 State Street. Long was the campaign manager for Joan Orie Melvin's successful Supreme Court bid in 2009. Stephen MacNett, with Conrad O'Brien, is the lawyer for Long, Nyquist & Associates.

MacNett was often called the 51st senator. He knew virtually everything about the General Assembly. He was one-stop shopping for journalists covering Harrisburg — a treasure house of legislative, historical and political information. Stephen MacNett was the master of the legislative chess game. On an annual basis, he was often the Senate Republicans' MVP.

Several Senate GOP staffers work for Mike Long, including Todd Nyquist, Joe Scarnati's former chief of staff. Nyquist co-founded Long, Nyquist with Long in 2009. He wasn't part of the leadership staff in 2005-06. Long is one of the top political strategists in Pennsylvania. Behind the scenes, he directed the campaign against then Democratic governor Robert Casey's tax reform plan in 1989, which was defeated 3-1 by the voters. No one is more responsible for keeping the Senate in Republican hands for more than two decades, save for a brief period from November 1992 to March 1994. Except for that period when Democrats briefly ruled, Robert Jubelirer has been president pro tem since 1984.

*   *   *

As a young reporter in the 1980s, I remember seeing stories by *Patriot-News* veterans John Scotzin and Carmen Brutto referring to Mike Long as Jubelirer's political director in the Senate. I remember asking Scotzin how that could be. Wasn't he a state-paid staffer? Wasn't he effectively Jubelirer's chief of staff as "majority staff administrator"? It just seemed odd. I was told essentially that's just the way it is. In those days, no one thought twice about doing political work in state offices.

There seems little doubt that in the past, when no one was paying attention, Senate Republicans used state resources like the other caucuses. Some people with ties to the caucus have told me that. "The same thing as the House," a GOP source, in a position to know, assured me. Staffers spent long lunch hours stuffing envelopes. Large groups of staffers traveled to districts for special elections.

John Morganelli, the Northampton County DA who ran against Tom Corbett for Attorney General in 2008, may have hit on the two reasons that eventually determined why Senate Republicans weren't charged — timing and resources. Morganelli said an investigation of each of the four caucuses should have begun at the same time. Seeing a bigger problem with House Democrats and Republicans, Corbett started there, leaving the Senate Republicans last. By 2011, the Sandusky probe was in high gear. By 2012, the statute of limitations had expired on most Senate officials investigated in Bonusgate. It may also be why there were so few resources for the investigation of a serial child rapist named Jerry Sandusky. The Senate Republicans had plenty of time to prepare for the pending investigation.

The resources of the Attorney General's office had been stretched too thin. Corbett seemed more than happy to let the feds investigate the Senate Democrats. In *On the Front Lines of Pennsylvania Politics: Twenty-Five Years of Keystone Reporting,* John Baer asks why "Corbett, who investigated the same sort of misdeeds by other lawmakers, didn't investigate [Republican senator Jane] Orie and why didn't the Allegheny County district attorney turn over the case to the Attorney General's office. . . ."

"The answers I got were fuzzy and leaned on things like 'original jurisdiction,'" Baer wrote.

Robert Jubelirer was defeated before Bonusgate. All of Mike Long's political tricks were not enough to combat the negative karma that emanated from the pay raise. Jubelirer's prints were all over it. Even the repeal was not enough.

Mike Long has never said much about it publicly. In December 2007, he told the *Post-Gazette:* "The Senate Republican Caucus was very careful when people worked on campaigns that they would go off the payroll. We had discussions with staff and caucus members over the years to be very clear that during campaigns people should leave the payroll if they were going for protracted periods of time and get their reimbursements from campaign funds."

One conclusion that might be drawn from the way the Senate Republicans reacted to the Jeffrey Habay case: They were just smarter.

Next: a family tragedy

25

A Family Tragedy

June 4, 2012

As an attorney and former prosecutor, Jane Orie was not intimidated by courtrooms. Wearing blue high heels, Orie strode confidently to the witness stand. She proudly wore a gold crucifix on a necklace. A brilliant American flag lapel pin adorned her blue pinstripe dress. The still-sitting senator from suburban Pittsburgh had been waiting for this moment to vindicate herself to end the nightmare that had enveloped her since late October 2009, when an intern complained to the Allegheny County district attorney that Orie was using her Senate staff for her sister Joan Orie Melvin's statewide Supreme Court campaign.

Orie was the defendant at her own trial — for the second time in a little more than a year.

For Jane Orie to be charged with crimes was a lot like Mother Teresa being arrested for streetwalking. The fact that Jane and two of her sisters would be charged with public corruption was unlike anything that political analyst Terry Madonna had seen in three decades of Pennsylvania politics.

With perfectly coifed but dyed blond hair, Jane was the "Barbie Senator." At age 50, she kept trim simply by eating very little, and she ran to stay in shape. Single, she lived with her father, Dr. John R. Orie. She was the populist, conservative darling of Pittsburgh's North Hills voters. She was so popular that she was re-elected in 2010 while under indictment for using her staff and other resources for her own campaigns and Melvin's. Jane had carefully nurtured her public image as a former sex crimes prosecutor who fought gaming, higher taxes and higher state spending under Governor Ed Rendell. She championed stronger sex crimes laws, pushed reform of the Turnpike Commission and the Gaming Control Board, and opposed the 2005 pay raise. She was a devout Roman Catholic, raised by a mother who went to Mass every day.

Jane and her sister Janine were charged in April 2010 for using Orie's Senate staff to support Joan Orie Melvin's successful Supreme Court race and for Jane's races. Janine Orie worked for Melvin while she was a Superior Court judge. The first trial ended in a mistrial.

Allegheny County Common Pleas judge Jeffrey Manning declared a mistrial on March 3, 2011 after the discovery of forged documents submitted by the defense. Manning cleared Orie's lawyer, William C. Costopoulos, of that fiasco. Still, somehow doctored documents became part of the defense exhibits. The forgeries were so blatant that "Ray Charles could see that the signature was doctored," an angry Manning had remarked. Jane Orie was charged with evidence tampering for the second trial. The forgeries had helped put her case in a better light

On March 19, 2012, in Jeffrey Manning's courtroom in the Allegheny County Courthouse, Jane took the stand in her second trial as she had a year before. Manning was a no-nonsense former federal prosecutor who headed the criminal division. He does not suffer fools or sloppy work by lawyers. Had he presided in Bonusgate, Dan Raynak would have been jailed the first day. On the witness stand, Jane Orie frequently spoke directly to the jury, and she used her hands and arms to explain answers to questions asked by her lawyer, the *Tribune*'s Bobby Kerlik reported. As the paper's former court reporter, Kerlik was there for the first and second trials. His steady, unbiased reports gave insight to the trials and the players.

"I did everything in my power as best as I could that all my directives were complied with according to the ethics law, according to the Senate rules and according to the laws of Pennsylvania to keep political work separate," said Orie, 48 at the time. She testified that election supplies were paid for out of her campaign account or the Republican campaign committees.

Speaking in calm, smooth tones on the 16th day of the second trial, Orie staunchly denied fixing any documents to make them more favorable to her defense. As Bobby Kerlik reported, Orie became combative under questioning by Assistant District Attorney Lawrence Claus.

"I have absolutely no idea who did it," Orie said of the forgeries. "I did not do that," she testified.

MOB HIT

Jane Orie once worked with Lawrence Claus in the Attorney General's office, and early on in the case, she claimed that he had a grudge against her because she supposedly helped speed his departure from the AG's office. The DA's office denied any conflict and the case moved forward. In the bigger picture, the Ories claimed that the charges were a vendetta against Jane by District Attorney Stephen Zappala because she criticized the Zappala family's ties to the casino industry as part of her continuing battle for gambling reform. On numerous occasions, Zappala denied any such motive.

"This is a case of good versus evil, David and Goliath," her brother Jack Orie, an attorney, told Pittsburgh reporters after Jane and sister Janine were charged. "The case has all the earmarks of a Mafia hit."

WOMAN OF GOD

Joan Orie Melvin was elected to the Pennsylvania Supreme Court in her second attempt. She wasn't one to wear poof hair-dos. She was a working mother of six, solid and seasoned on the bench. She would later describe herself as "a woman of faith." Joan struck me as the toughest of the Orie sisters. She'd been a judge most of her adult life, and she had an air about her of being in charge. She served on the Superior Court before her election to the highest court. Jane, Joan, Janine and Jack were four of nine siblings all with first names beginning with "J"— the children of John and Jean Lally Orie. Like Jane, most of them were overachievers. They were descended from Polish and Irish immigrants.

I knew Jane Orie well and covered her in the state Senate. I had the opportunity to meet Joan twice and, for a while, I stayed in touch with her. I first met her as a candidate for the state Supreme Court. I'd talked to her long before that in a phone interview when she turned down the 2005 pay raise and later sued the court system for making her take the increase, pay taxes on it, and then send the money back to the treasury. That was a sure sign that she was eyeing the Supreme Court after losing a statewide bid in 2003. Other judges despised her. To varying degrees, the justices that Joan would serve with felt the same. Gamesmanship? Maybe. But it is a tough stand to take, and I respected her for it.

Jane voted against the pay raise and refused it. At her trial, Jeffrey Manning ruled that Orie could not bring up the pay raise or the alleged animus between the Ories and the Zappalas. Those were arguably two strong issues for her. It's somewhat like the Dauphin County pretrial ruling that prevented Mike Veon from bringing up Tom Corbett's political motivation. The reasoning behind those decisions? Relevance. Even if they were true, the defendant either committed the crimes or did not. I get that. But the judgments of Jeffrey Manning and Richard Lewis in Dauphin County show how decisions by the trial judge can subtly steer the outcome of a case.

Manning's ruling tied the hands of William Costopoulos in defending Jane Orie. It would be raised as an issue on appeal. In the end, a long line of former Senate staffers would testify about campaign work they were told to do or that they observed in Jane Orie's district office. So there was no question — she did it. There is a question as to how big a deal her political work was, at least compared to Mike Veon's or John Perzel's. Seeing all the photos of the Ories dodging photographers in Pittsburgh before and after trial didn't bother me. One that did was a 1978 picture of six of the Orie kids in the *Post-Gazette* with their mom.

Judy was 25 and about to graduate from the University of Pittsburgh Medical School. Joan, 21, would soon graduate from Notre Dame with a 3.84 average. Jane was just a teenager, and as the kids looked at a family portrait, Jane stood with her head tilted to the side as a young girl might be prone to do. There was so much promise.

ANOTHER DIMENSION

To understand Jane Orie, a longtime observer noted, one must think in the spiritual realm. The Orie sisters were often a step or two out of this world, dabbling in the supernatural. During one period in their lives, Jane and Janine regularly saw their "angel ladies," two blond Greek Orthodox psychics who dressed in pink. They advised them on decisions, from the ordinary to the life-changing. There came a point in Jane's life when she depended on the angel ladies for every decision. The angel ladies apparently were part mediums and part psychics who claimed to hear from actual angels.

Charlotte Ramsey and Eileen Miller of North Hills were the angel ladies.

People who have been to them swear that they know things only close family friends could know. Whether they communicated with angels or not, the Ories trusted them. Jane and Joan also communicated with the Philadelphia clairaudient Carolann Sano and considered her an angel lady, according to *The Pittsburgh Gazette's* Dennis Roddy. Sano describes herself as a "spiritual channel." She poses questions and hears them answered in her right ear.

Prosecutors became aware of the Ories' interest in the angel ladies through emails obtained in a search warrant. The angel ladies didn't come up at trial.

Court records suggest that Joan and Jane consulted Sano on what District Attorney Stephen Zappala would decide after the sisters sent an intermediary to meet with him in November 2009. The middle man with ties to organized labor met with Zappala and informed him of the all-out PR assault the sisters would launch against him if he proceeded with the case. Zappala reportedly didn't blink.

There's too much of a tendency among secularists to dismiss a faith-based belief in angels and mystics. According to their critics, it meant that the Orie sisters were crazy. I am not judging their belief in the supernatural. Jane was a bit squirrelly to begin with, but no more so because of the angel ladies. Psychics have been used by the police, sometimes with success, to find missing kids and cadavers.

Like many public officials, Jane Orie had a public side and a vastly different private side. The trial was about the "two faces of Jane Orie," prosecutor Lawrence Claus told the jury. The alleged threat to take on Zappala showed that the Ories were hardball players. They had a reputation since childhood of being scrappers and later political street fighters. They would appear in one setting to be sweet, churchgoing ladies. But off the record and in private, Jane and Joan might drop the F-bomb, acquaintances claimed. The Orie family was tight, almost a clan. For them, nothing superseded family, not even the law.

THE GATEKEEPER

The Commonwealth had numerous staffers who would take the stand and talk about their political work in Jane Orie's office. But the lead domino was Jamie Pavlot, who was Jane's chief of staff. Back in 2009, when I heard that she had been interviewed for six hours by detectives and that she was cooperating, I knew that Jane was probably going down. Others would follow as witnesses upon hearing that Pavlot was cooperating. She knew everything.

In a way, Jamie even looked like Jane and Janine, and she was also into the angel ladies. Jamie was the key person in whom Jane confided.

In her role as a senator, Jane set up a virtual Chinese wall for reporters trying to get through to her. There was an intense paranoia on her part about the media and a fear of outsiders penetrating the veil. After winning a special election in 2001, she immediately burned through her new Senate staff. There was almost a complete turnover. Jane Orie was a controlling personality and a micro-manager. Jamie was her shield and her operative.

I have many memories of calling downstairs to her Senate office and being routed by her nervous Harrisburg aides to the McCandless office, where the call would eventually end up with Jamie, who wanted to know in great detail what the story was about. Pavlot screened all calls. Jane's paranoia made her ripe for conspiracy theories. She was always looking over her shoulder and had a huge mistrust of the media.

Many reporters who covered her mistakenly thought that Jane was dumb, but she was politically astute. Jane was inarticulate, which is hard to believe for a lawyer and former prosecutor. She became tongue-tied when speaking extemporaneously. When Jane spoke at news conferences or in committees, her remarks were prepared in advance, and they were well rehearsed. Everything was written out for her.

There was a dichotomy about Jane. While extremely untrusting, she was also careless, a former staffer remembered. She sent a lot of information in emails, believing that they were secure. She used all caps even for routine emails, and they were almost always in blue. I received a few; they were cautious at first, and always began with the words OFF THE RECORD.

THE PRIZE

Shortly after Pennsylvania Supreme Court Chief Justice Ronald D. Castille administered the oath of office to Joan Orie Melvin, her husband, Greg, helped her into the black robe that she highlighted with a multicolored, V-shaped cowl that she pulled over her head. The "robing" was part of the official ceremony. In many respects, it was an extraordinary ceremony on stage at the Forum, a building catty-corner to the state capitol. There was a strong sense of foreboding. It was Friday, January 8, 2010, and it may have been the high water mark of Melvin's legal and judicial career.

The event was packed with big-name Republicans including Attorney General Tom Corbett. Jackie Evancho, a 10-year-old with a full woman's voice, sang the National Anthem. Evancho, a resident of Jane Orie's district, was bound for stardom, but as yet was largely unknown. In November 2009, Joan Orie Melvin concluded a hard-fought campaign by defeating Democrat Jack Panella 53 to 47 percent. The Republican establishment had backed her. Melvin's victory gave the GOP a four-to-three edge on the court.

Something was amiss here. A former Allegheny County judge who battled her way to the Superior Court, Joan said at the ceremony marking her first day on the high court that she was determined to "remove the stealth nature of the judiciary." She was ripping the lid off the Supreme Court she was about to join, a court that oversees the entire state judicial system and jealously guards its right to govern the practice of law in Pennsylvania.

"In the wake of unethical back-room deals, pay raises, public corruption and scandals in the judiciary, people are demanding reform," Melvin declared while sitting beside six stone-faced justices: "It is my mission to remove the stealth nature and the mystery from the judicial branch of government by bringing reform, accountability and transparency. Let the sunshine in."

Seated in the front row was Jane Orie's first criminal defense attorney, Jerry McDevitt, a Pittsburgh litigator of high-profile cases. He was not a familiar face to many at the Forum, but he was well known to those in attendance from the Allegheny County legal community. McDevitt was a dead giveaway that something out of the ordinary was up.

Agents from the Allegheny County District Attorney's office had raided Jane Orie's district Senate office less than a month before Joan Orie Melvin's swearing in. The investigation into using taxpayer resources for campaigns began a few days before the election. That was the pall cast over Joan's big day. Most of the politically connected people here knew that this would not end well. It was clear that Joan was the prize.

Within a two-year span, three Orie sisters — Jane, Janine and Joan — would each be charged with crimes for using public resources for campaigns. The activity by Jane and Janine, prosecutors say, was for Joan's two bids for the Supreme Court. Jane also allegedly used her staff from her own campaigns. Essentially, the accusation was that Joan with her sisters' help had cheated to get on the high court. Within that time period, another sister, Dr. Judith Orie, was a cardiologist who died at age 59 in 2011. The oldest of nine siblings, Jack Orie, a Pittsburgh attorney, faced a foreclosure motion on his house less than a week after Jane and Janine were charged with crimes. This was later resolved. It was the first time Jack missed a payment and he received no notice. Jack Orie suspects that back-channel political pressure was put on the bank to squeeze him. He made the rest of the payments and resolved it. What happened to that family was tragic.

Within Pennsylvania it was unprecedented for three sisters to be charged with public corruption: one a state senator, another a Supreme Court justice and the third a judge's former state employee. This was the view of G. Terry Madonna of Franklin and Marshall College. It was unheard of for a justice to speak out the way Joan did at her swearing-in ceremony. It's why I liked Joan. Regardless of the motivation for her pay raise stunt and for criticizing the court, it took guts to do that. Joan was despised by other members of the judiciary for making them look bad. On the day Jane was sentenced in June 2012, I kept wondering what had happened to this once-powerful family, how it came about and especially what would happen to Joan the justice.

STOIC

Jeffrey Manning called the day he became aware of fraudulent documents in the case doubtless "the most disturbing and disheartening day in my nearly 24 years on the bench." State Senate aides in Harrisburg recall the day as well. Knowing Jane, it sounded exactly like something she'd do. Judge Manning told Orie: "I came to the realization that I had sent 12 unwary citizens to deliberate, to perform the most solemn duty of citizenship, with fraudulent documents — documents you identified, authenticated and offered into evidence."

"Today [June 4, 2012] is the second most disturbing and disheartening day, for it falls upon me to penalize you for the ultimate lawyer's transgression — fraud on our system of justice," Manning added.

Jane was stoic at her sentencing, reporter Jeremy Boren indicated in his account in the *Tribune-Review*. He saw no tears. Manning sentenced her to two and a half to 10 years in prison, a much longer sentence than she would have received for merely using state resources for campaigns. The cliché about the cover-up being worse than the crime came up over and over again in interviews about Jane Orie.

"KIDS FOR CASH"

The legal battle that continued with Joan's case pitted two of Pittsburgh's most powerful families against each other, the Ories and the Zappalas, from the Republican and Democratic Parties, respectively. Allegheny County District Attorney Stephen Zappala Jr., son of former Supreme Court Chief Justice Stephen Zappala, filed the charges against the three Ories. The first round came after Jane Orie, as a state senator, had gone after the Zappala family's ties to the gambling industry. The younger Zappala denied it was a vendetta. But if thwarting an opponent was the reason, then it was likely about Joan, not Jane.

Jack Orie claimed that Stephen Zappala stated to public officials: "Anyone who fucks with my family, I will indict them." He claimed that Zappala also said, "These bitches are going down."(Zappala denied making these statements.)

Orie's Senate inquiry focused on the Pennsylvania Casino Association. Michele Zappala Peck, the former chief justice's daughter, served then as the association's operations director. The senior Zappala chaired the group. He had been the executive director. Orie claimed that the association at one point had not disclosed the Zappalas' ties. Formed in 2007, the association was "virtually invisible" even though it was run by the powerful Zappalas, according to a 2009 story by Tracie Mauriello of the *Post-Gazette*. The Zappalas' names weren't on incorporation papers or tax filings, the story claimed. Zappala, the district attorney, denied any connection between the charges and Orie's pursuit of the gambling issue.

The association was a trade group for three casinos and had not done any extensive lobbying, Philadelphia lawyer Richard Sprague, part owner of Sugar House casino, told a legislative panel. If the Ories were viewed as a threat to the Zappalas, that perceived threat came from the "Kids for Cash" case, in my opinion, not from gambling.

As a Supreme Court candidate, Joan Orie Melvin came down hard on the judicial discipline board's failure to do anything about the Luzerne County judges who sent kids to a private detention center built by a contractor who paid $2.6 million in bribes to the judges. A complaint had been dismissed internally. Jack Panella, who was Joan's 2009 opponent, had been a member of the Judicial Conduct Board. Melvin aired a negative TV ad blasting Panella for the board's inaction in stopping Judges Mark Ciavarella and Michael Conahan. Both the board and Panella denied it.

Conahan, the president judge, closed a county-owned juvenile center and signed an agreement with PA Child Care, LLC. Ciavarella, meanwhile, was railroading kids by sending them to the center at hearings without benefit of legal counsel. In an extraordinary order in 2009, the Pennsylvania Supreme Court dismissed or expunged virtually every juvenile case Mark Ciavarella had handled.

Robert Mericle, the builder of PA Child Care in Luzerne and Butler Counties, made payoffs to the judges through Robert Powell, a Luzerne County lawyer who co-owned the private detention centers with Gregory Zappala, son of the former justice and brother of the DA. Gregory Zappala bought out Powell and became the sole owner. Mericle and Powell entered guilty pleas. A letter from a federal prosecutor in Philadelphia stated that Zappala's company was not a target. Gregory Zappala, an investment banker, has not been accused of any wrongdoing or charged with any crimes. I spoke with him once, briefly, and he denied any impropriety.

Still, the Zappala vendetta theory has been the centerpiece of both Jane and Joan's defense. In July 2012, Melvin filed a motion with the judicial board to remove a member because of that person's alleged ties to the Zappalas. It just makes more sense that *if* there were a vendetta, protecting Gregory Zappala from potential attacks by Melvin as a high court justice would be far more important than Jane's effort to embarrass the casino association. The Court of Judicial Discipline suspended Melvin without pay pending the outcome of the criminal case.

*   *   *

Being charged with crimes by Democratic district attorney Stephen Zappala fit perfectly into the conspiracy theories of the Ories. Jane Orie, in her position as a senator, had gone after the Zappala family's ties to the gambling industry. Some portrayed it as a long-running feud. Maybe they didn't like each other, who knows? But it was not one of the legendary Pittsburgh political feuds like the battle between former coroner Cyril Wecht and Sheriff Eugene Coon, or between Commissioner Tom Foerster and Mayor Richard Caliguiri.

THE INTERN

The problem with these theories is that the case apparently fell into Stephen Zappala's lap. On October 30, 2009, the Friday before the November 3rd election in which Melvin vs. Panella was the premier race, Jennifer Rioja, an intern for Jane Orie, reported the state-paid work being done for Joan Orie Melvin's election to the district attorney.

At the time, Rioja was 26 and a graduate student at the University of Pittsburgh. She had applied for work at several senators' offices. Unbeknownst to Jennifer, Senator Sean Logan, a suburban Pittsburgh Democrat, had referred Rioja to Orie with a handwritten card because Rioja then lived in Ross Township, part of Orie's district.

Rioja had tried to report the work to the Attorney General. She was referred to the local DA's office. This, of course, fueled speculation that Tom Corbett, who was then AG, was tanking the case because Jane Orie was a Republican senator — his senator as a resident of Glenshaw. Rioja spoke with a receptionist, not an agent.

Was Jennifer Rioja a "plant" by the Democrats? That was the Orie theory. I have to admit that at the time this theory surfaced, it seemed plausible because of Logan's referral and the fact that Rioja, in a blog, had referred to herself as a "commie liberal." Granted, she was a college student, and to some that may have typecast her as a liberal Democrat.

Rioja's husband, Brandon, drove her to Dormont to make the complaint. If Zappala wanted to play real hardball, he could have announced or leaked before the election that there was a complaint involving allegations against Melvin, but he did not. Still, if Rioja were placed in Jane Orie's office by Democratic operatives, the entire case would have been suspect. Sean Logan had political ties to Stephen Zappala.

No evidence ever surfaced along those lines. And after the trial, while Jennifer Rioja would not consent to an interview, she did agree to an "email interview" that spanned several weeks. She was eager to put to rest any suggestion that she was a plant or was used by anyone. Rioja was not defensive about it; she seemed to be straightforward. Logan had passionately denied it at the time.

"I've never met Sean Logan," she stated. "I've never been to his office. I sent a cover letter and résumé to his office, to Senator Orie's office and to three other legislators' offices. I had no idea Senator Logan's office sent my letter on to Senator Orie's office until it came out in the paper that it happened. . . . No, Sean Logan wasn't using me. . . . There is no chance he was using me. . . . To go one step further, there is no chance anyone was using me. . . . I was acting on my own volition because what was happening in Orie's office was wrong."

Indeed, that may be exactly what happened. In the end, there was no evidence of any targeting of the Ories by the Zappalas.

Meanwhile, crimes against the taxpayers go on.

26

Seven Years After

July 7, 2012, 2:00 a.m.

Just like the "Watergate babies," the Democrats elected to Congress in the wake of the scandal that felled a president, John Milliron rode a wave of reform into the state House in 1974. Milliron, an Altoona Democrat, would serve two terms before losing his seat to Republican Rick Geist.

Geist, elected in 1978, would eventually serve as the House transportation chairman. His ardent belief in the need for taxes and fees to provide money for the state's infrastructure played into the hands of a Tea Party-type candidate backed by money from the Citizens Alliance of Pennsylvania. Republican John McGinnis knocked off Geist in the April 2012 primary.

Just as Milliron won with a national trend providing a tailwind, McGinnis benefited from the mood stimulating conservative Republican voters across the nation along with Geist's support of large tax increases. Milliron went on to become a successful lobbyist. The firm he founded in 1980 eventually became Milliron Associates LLC, and it represents clients from the Pennsylvania Society of Anesthesiologists, the American Red Cross, and the Pennsylvania Amusement and Music Machine Associates to the Pennsylvania Motor Truck Association.

I'd known Milliron for years, primarily quoting him whenever another push emerged to legalize video poker machines. An attorney, Milliron was extremely knowledgeable on his issues, articulate and trustworthy. You could take what he told you to the bank. Milliron and I were speakers at an informal event for medical students sponsored by the Pennsylvania Medical Society in April 2012. We'd been asked to give the students an idea of what was going on at the capitol. I gave them a rundown on the criminal cases involving legislative leaders.

"The place does not change," John Milliron asserted. He said it several times during his remarks.

Seven years after the 2005 pay raise, after thousands of promises, a special reform commission and scores of new members, Milliron was right. Not much had changed. It's true that for several years there were no more middle-of-the-night sessions to wear members down so they would vote for any bill placed in front of them. Voting records were posted on the Internet. A new state law required online expenditures of agencies and the legislature on a state web page.

New House rules prevented lawmakers from being affiliated with nonprofits that get state grants, but that provision was not cemented in state law. Supposedly, "gut and replace" legislation was no longer allowed. That is the tactic of taking a harmless bill like state police background checks for horseracing and turning it into legislation creating a multi-billion-dollar casino industry, as occurred in 2004. During his first two years in office, Governor Tom Corbett would not consider traditional WAMs, though other discretionary grants still flowed. The House cut back per diems by $1.7 million but still spent $3.5 million in 2011-12. Representative Dan Truitt, a West Chester Republican, filed a bill to eliminate per diems. It died in the Rules Committee in 2012, and he refiled it in 2013. The House in particular has been far more open about Right to Know (RTK) requests of late. Still, legislative expense material — and the governor's travel and mansion costs — should be on the highly touted state web page.

A recent example of the old ways of thinking still prevailing was a request to the Senate for senators' mileage paid for with tax dollars. It produced a long "pdf" document, a useless format that can't be used to produce totals for each member. The House provided the totals. When totals for each senator were specifically requested, the Senate's chief clerk responded that under the RTK law, agencies are not required to "create a record" where one doesn't exist. In other words, forget about it.

There has been no talk of a pay raise since the 2005 debacle. The truth is that legislators, top state officials and jurists get one virtually every year anyway, based on cost-of-living increases, thanks to the automatic pay hike bill John Perzel had helped usher through. A lawmaker's basic salary rose to $83,801 by the end of 2012.

Just as in the old days, lawmakers complained again that there was no time to read bills rammed through in the closing hours before recess. In the House, they suspended the rules to meet past 11:00 p.m. Gut and replace legislation again became one of the standard practices. House members had to start contributing one percent of their pay toward health care, as the Senate had been doing. One percent. Gradually, some of the old ways crept back.

All of that said, I've known plenty of honest, hard-working legislators. Each day they're at the capitol, however, makes them more vulnerable to the culture, the willingness to cut corners and tolerate leaders focused primarily on maintaining or grabbing power. There are some new leaders with integrity. But over time, the system will eat away at them like coastal erosion ravages a shoreline. John Milliron saw people who came in as reformers go on to become leaders and, in some cases, inmates. As leaders became entrenched, the drive to hold onto power was as ingrained as the need to eat, drink and sleep.

INVESTIGATING THE PROSECUTOR

As Attorney General, Tom Corbett rode the anti-legislative furor that Bonusgate helped create. He defeated Democrat Dan Onorato in the gubernatorial race of November 2010.

Ed Rendell backed Onorato, of course, but he knew that Corbett would win. He virtually said so on several occasions. To Rendell, the political landscape and the mood of the electorate were obvious.

*   *   *

There is no doubt that the bonus scandal on the whole was hugely beneficial to Corbett politically. It was a major factor in his visibility, his image and ultimately his election. Still, no one has been criticized more than Corbett for the Bonusgate and Computergate prosecutions, of which he won 22 of 25 cases — 23 of 26 if Mike Veon's second conviction in the Beaver Initiative for Growth affair is counted. Some of those cases were tried under his successor, Attorney General Linda Kelly, but they were known and viewed as Corbett's cases. He was hammered, at first, for prosecuting only Democrats. Defense attorneys tried to frame their cases as a political prosecution by a Republican running for governor. It *was* unprecedented for an Attorney General and major GOP candidate for governor to be prosecuting former top Democrats as he campaigned for the state's highest office.

Defense lawyers and defendants tried to claim that Corbett had done the very same things their clients were accused of doing — having a state-paid driver chauffeur him to campaign events, talking to state-paid workers on his campaign/personal cell phone, and moving key staffers back and forth from the office to the campaign. The driver was for security, his office claimed, and past AGs used them. Moving workers off staff to campaign payrolls — and back — should not be permitted. It is certainly not comparable to giving state employees bonuses to work on campaigns. Still, it's an area too cozy and ripe for abuse.

A resign-to-run law for top state officials would solve much of the problem. It should be in place, especially for the Attorney General.

Corbett said he did not plan on running for governor in 2007, when Bonusgate was launched, or most of the next year. His strong showing in the November 2008 re-election campaign for Attorney General eventually convinced him, he stated. Apparently, Corbett is also not someone who set out to make a name for himself by taking down powerful legislative leaders. Newspapers handed him Bonusgate. He could have done a minimal amount and taken a pass. Critics believe it was all by design: taking out powerful legislative leaders to strengthen his hand when he became governor.

To his credit, Corbett is the first Attorney General in state history to take on public corruption. Perhaps one reason is that he is not afraid to lose. He recalls his days as a young assistant district attorney in Allegheny County when at the outset he lost several cases. "I wasn't afraid to try anything," he said. "I didn't grow up a politician," Corbett told WITF radio's *Smart Talk*. "I grew up as a prosecutor."

Walter Cohen, the former acting Attorney General who represented John Perzel and Bill DeWeese while they were under investigation, questioned the validity of Corbett's "corruption" cases.

"Not a single person charged during this period took cash payments in return for legislation," said Cohen. What happened did not meet that traditional quid pro quo for public corruption, he suggested in an interview.

Told of former Ethics Commission director John J. Contino's testimony, during the Vince Fumo trial, that crimes against democracy are worse than bribery, Cohen remarked, "He [Contino] says that because that's what he does." There's a need for clear rules on what legislators can and cannot do, Cohen added.

In my view, the Jeffrey Habay case established those rules. If observers had any sense, they knew it in 2004 when the Habay case was decided by the Ethics Commission. They certainly knew it by 2007 when the Superior Court ruled on Habay. Stacking the deck in elections is probably worse than taking a payoff because the consequences are far-reaching.

*   *   *

Tom Corbett's place in history isn't likely to be determined by his public corruption prosecutions as Attorney General or even his record as governor. The Jerry Sandusky case and the Penn State cover-up will define his legacy. Passions run strong and every Pennsylvanian is in the know due to 24-7 news coverage. Corbett's investigation nailed Sandusky on 45 counts. The cover-up at Penn State continues to unravel. As of this writing, the verdict isn't in on how Corbett handled it. Sandusky, the 68-year-old serial predator, was sentenced to 30 to 60 years in prison for abusing 10 young boys over a period of 15 years.

The 33 months it took to arrest Sandusky became fodder for Democratic Attorney General nominee Kathleen Kane in 2012. She held that using a statewide grand jury investigation slowed it down. A former sex crimes prosecutor in Lackawanna County, Kane said she never used a grand jury on a child abuse case. The statewide grand jury meets one week per month, which inherently delays a complex investigation.

Kane didn't create the public furor about the length of the investigation. It was already a question ordinary folks were talking about. Kane struck a nerve when she started to emphasize it. She told the *Times-Tribune* in Scranton that Corbett had "probably" played politics with the investigation and pledged a full investigation into how the Sandusky case was investigated by the Attorney General's office. It was one of the main reasons Kane won, outpolling President Obama and Senator Bob Casey in November 2012. Pennsylvanians wanted answers, as did the Penn State nation. Penn State claims to have the world's largest dues-paying alumni association and boasts 560,000 graduates among hundreds of thousands of other Nittany Lions fans.

"People want us to move on and forget it," said former Pittsburgh Steeler Franco Harris, a star running back under Joe Paterno. "Penn Staters are not going to do that." Kane carried Centre County, where Penn State's main campus is located, by even larger margins than her stunning statewide rout.

Tom Corbett had a lot invested in the race. He cleared the Republican primary field for Cumberland County DA David Freed, son-in-law of still-potent GOP power lawyer LeRoy Zimmerman, the first elected Attorney General. Corbett raised money for Freed through the Republican National District Attorneys Association. Zimmerman had been chairman of the Hershey Trust, which was under civil scrutiny by the Attorney General's office for several multi-million-dollar land deals, including the purchase of a golf course. The golf course was losing money; an original investor had been CEO of the Hershey Company.

The entire purpose of the Hershey Trust is to provide a school for disadvantaged students. The school already had three golf courses when the trustees paid $17 million for the Wren Dale golf course and clubhouse, according to superb reporting by *The Philadelphia Inquirer's* Bob Fernandez. His articles were instrumental in triggering the investigation. David Freed said it was a conflict for him, and he would have appointed a special prosecutor. Still, as Kathleen Kane noted, the special prosecutor would ultimately report to Freed.

On November 6, 2012, Kane became the first woman and first Democrat elected Attorney General since the statewide elective office was created three decades ago. Even untested and unproven, she was as close as it gets to a superstar in state politics.

Before taking office, Kane would choose Adrian King as her first deputy. A widely respected former top staffer for Ed Rendell, King was the brother-in-law of John Estey, who was a vice president of the Hershey Trust and Rendell's first chief of staff. They were both lawyers from the Philadelphia law firm of Ballard Spahr. Kane said she would wall King off on Hershey Trust matters. She had also taken a $100,000 contribution from a former trust board member, Robert Reese, grandson of the originator of Reese's peanut butter cups.

The gist of the Sandusky undercurrent was this: Had Corbett deliberately taken his time and, by understaffing the investigation, put off the bombshell that erupted at Penn State until after the November 2010 gubernatorial election? Had he devoted more resources to Bonusgate than to a serial pedophile? Was the investigation mismanaged?

To die-hard Penn State fans, the perception that former head coach Joe Paterno had been dragged through the mud was the worst sin of all. Paterno wasn't charged by Corbett. In fact, he appeared to have been treated with enormous deference in a brief grand jury appearance.

The Freeh report, in July 2012, included Paterno among the top officials who participated in a "conspiracy of silence." As a member of the Penn State Board of Trustees, Corbett urged Paterno's firing and recommended former FBI director Louis Freeh to head the university-paid investigation. In November 2011, after Jerry Sandusky's arrest and Joe Paterno's firing, the campus was in chaos.

Was the Sandusky case understaffed? Initially, there was one trooper and one supervisor from the state police and one agent and one supervisor from the Attorney General's office. This information from State Police Commissioner Frank Noonan came to light months after the controversy stirred by Sara Ganim's reporting. In other words, there were essentially two investigators in the field. And there was just one trooper on the ground, just as Ganim reported.

In the 2012 book *Silent No More*, Sandusky victim Aaron Fisher ("Victim No. 1") described a tag-team of four troopers assigned to his case over a course of almost three years. Each trooper, one at a time, had to start from scratch with Fisher's story, and more importantly, had to win his trust. This was a kid who thought no one believed him because of the length of the probe. Fisher says he considered killing himself at one point because of the slow pace of the investigation. In February and March 2010, Fisher, his psychologist and those close to him anticipated an indictment of Sandusky on several occasions. To their frustration, it didn't happen.

I never realized until reading Aaron Fisher's book that the anticipated period for indictment was smack in the middle of Mike Veon's trial, which already posed a potential embarrassment for Corbett if the Attorney General lost. Fisher's book (written largely by his psychologist, Mike Gillum) says former Deputy Attorney General Jonelle Eshbaugh was telling Fisher that it was Corbett's call whether to proceed with the presentment.

"Jonelle promised us there would be an arrest in the middle to third week of March [2010]," Gillum wrote. It didn't happen.

At that time, Corbett was running for governor and the Veon jury was deliberating. He was convicted on March 22, 2010.

"I was convinced Corbett felt that arresting Sandusky would interfere with his chances of being elected," Gillum wrote, arguing that Corbett didn't want to alienate Penn State fans till after the election. Corbett states emphatically that the prosecution was not delayed for political reasons.

Fisher's fragile emotional state, including a meltdown before the grand jury, suggests why Corbett may have been insisting on finding more victims who were willing to testify. Could Fisher, as the only victim, withstand a blistering cross-examination from Sandusky's lawyer, Joe Amendola?

Frank Noonan, who pumped up the resources for the Sandusky investigation when he took over the state police in January 2011, said in retrospect that he didn't think initially that there was a need for more personnel. Noonan previously headed investigations for the Attorney General.

Investigators didn't find former assistant coach Mike McQueary until December 2010, following an Internet tip to a local prosecutor. McQueary, a former quarterback under Paterno, reported the 2001 incident he believed was of a sexual nature involving Sandusky and a boy of about 10 in a Penn State locker room shower. He didn't see a sexual act, but the "slapping sounds" he heard suggested sex. Over and over, the question from the press became: Why has the investigation taken so long? Corbett said the media was obsessed with its length. By the fall of 2012, Corbett had negative performance ratings in a Quinnipiac University poll.

"There's not one person out there that's going to say I told them to hold that case up," Corbett said at an October news conference while responding to Kathleen Kane. He was visibly angry on July 12, 2012 when *The Inquirer*'s Angela Couloumbis asked respectfully if the Freeh report in retrospect suggested in any way that the investigation could have been expedited. Corbett exploded and slammed his palm on the lectern, rebuking Couloumbis for the question.

"We do not hold up investigations for anything," Corbett declared. "You are disparaging the reputations of men and women in that [Attorney General's] office who have worked very hard to take a monster off the street." To continue to ask the question is "out of line," he added.

The brusque firing of Joe Paterno and the NCAA sanctions against the Nittany Lions football team infuriated alumni across the state. Paterno was fired on November 9, 2011. He died of lung cancer on January 22, 2012. By July 2012, his seven-foot statue would be removed from the front of Beaver Stadium.

Thomas Baldino, a political science professor at Wilkes University in Wilkes-Barre, theorized that voters angry about Penn State and Paterno's treatment "merged" those thoughts with questions about the length of Corbett's investigation and directed their discontent at Tom Corbett.

"I know I didn't commit any criminal act. None. Zero," Corbett said in November after Kathleen Kane's election and her investigation (of his investigation) was a certainty. It was a stunningly unsophisticated comment for a top-level politician. No one had accused him of a crime. It's indicative of his style: blunt and straightforward.

Corbett said the grand jury was needed to compel testimony of victims and because of the complexity of proving a cover-up. Moving on one victim's testimony would have been a mistake, he argued. Imagine the outcry, Corbett has suggested, if he hurried the investigation, charged Jerry Sandusky based on one victim's testimony — and lost.

In September 2012, a Franklin and Marshall poll found 65 percent of Pennsylvanians thought Corbett did a poor or only fair job on the Sandusky investigation. It didn't help that a lot of average folks seemed to be aware of news accounts that Corbett, while running for governor, had taken thousands of dollars from board members of the Second Mile charity founded by Sandusky. It was created to help underprivileged kids, but became Sandusky's hunting ground for prepubescent boys to groom as victims.

In July 2011, four months before Sandusky's arrest, Governor Corbett personally approved a three-million-dollar grant for the state's portion of a new building for the Second Mile. It was part of a batch of building projects initiated by lawmakers under former Democratic governor Ed Rendell. It was three months after the *Patriot-News'* Sara Ganim first reported on the Sandusky investigation. Even loyal Corbett supporters asked me: *What was he thinking?*

Corbett believed that refusing to approve the grant, based on what he knew as Attorney General, would have compromised the investigation and alerted the Second Mile and others as to what law enforcement was doing, said his spokesman, Kevin Harley. "He couldn't block that [grant] from going forward because of what he knew as Attorney General," Harley added. "He couldn't let on to anyone [including the governor's office] what he knew." Corbett simply could have denied it for vague legal reasons, period. It happens all the time in state government.

Aaron Fisher's mother, Dawn Daniels, out of frustration with the lack of progress, even went to the FBI. Aware of Corbett's probe, the FBI declined to look at it, but told her they would do so if no charges were brought against Sandusky.

In early February 2013, Kathleen Kane brought in a special deputy Attorney General to conduct the investigation. The findings could range from assertions that:

- The Sandusky investigation was botched and prolonged, not only by use of the grand jury, but as a result of understaffing. Sara Ganim's November 14, 2011 story quotes a source close to the investigation as saying, "It was completely mishandled. I know these investigations take time, some of them, but someone should have been on this day and night from the beginning because of the severity of the allegations." Sandusky's home wasn't searched until the summer of 2011 — two and a half years after the investigation began, Ganim also reported. Yet a former supervisor from the Attorney General's office told *The New York Times* that Corbett "had nothing to do with slowing anything down."

- Other kids potentially were at risk during the period when the investigation progressed at a slow pace.
- Someone in the AG's office put the brakes on the investigation; worse — someone did so, or attempted to do so, for political reasons and obstructed justice.
- Corbett's investigation is vindicated by the internal review. That appears unlikely, but Kane said she will be willing to say that nothing was wrong with Corbett's probe.

It has been a tightrope for Kathleen Kane. As Attorney General, Kane took over the prosecution of three former PSU officials: former president Graham Spanier, former athletic director Tim Curley and former administrator Gary Schultz, whose duties included overseeing the campus police. They maintain their innocence. Kane must prosecute them while trying not to unravel the investigation. If she appears to be acting in a partisan manner, it will hurt her public standing.

Tom Corbett's reputation was built upon being a hard-nosed prosecutor. Kane's investigation goes at that directly. Corbett, if necessary, will dismiss it as a partisan document from a political prosecutor. As of this writing, there is no evidence of prosecutorial misconduct. Still, it could come down to a judgment: the view of one prosecutor versus another on how it should have been handled. Meanwhile, Sandusky is spending the rest of his life in prison.

In a sign of the likely disputes ahead, Corbett said he would cooperate and sit down with Kane's investigators unless he perceives the investigation is "political." In an interview, when asked whether the investigation took too long, Corbett paused and answered the question with a question: "How long should it have taken?"

WHY THE CYCLICAL NATURE?

Here's the bottom line. Corruption tends to be brought out by prosecutors from the party opposing those in power in Harrisburg or Washington, D.C. Of the major Pennsylvania corruption cases since the 1970s, a U.S. Attorney, Attorney General or district attorney of the opposing party typically prosecuted the pols suspected of corruption. It was far more common than prosecutors of the same party launching investigations of their own high-profile politicos.

Republicans Dick Thornburgh in Pittsburgh and David Marston in Eastern Pennsylvania uncovered corruption in the Democratic Milton Shapp administration and among Democratic legislators. Some token Republicans were convicted. Later, going against this trend, Thornburgh protégé James West, as a deputy state Attorney General and acting U.S. Attorney, prosecuted Republican R. Budd Dwyer. West and Republican Attorney General LeRoy Zimmerman charged Al Benedict, a Democrat and former Auditor General. David Barasch, a Democrat and top federal prosecutor in the Middle District, took down Republican Ernie Preate. Republican Patrick Meehan, former U.S. Attorney and now congressman, oversaw the investigation of Democrat Vincent Fumo. Republican Tom Corbett helped convict 10 Democrats in Bonusgate and nine Republicans in Computergate.

Some argue that John Perzel and his crew were out of power and expendable. Democratic governor Ed Rendell and many Republicans initially criticized Corbett for the inequity of charging only Democrats. People were screaming for GOP heads to roll. It was inevitable. Corbett charged "enough Republicans to quell the relentless cries of partisanship arising from his theretofore exclusive prosecution of Democrats," defense lawyer Josh Lock, who represented Brett Feese and former Representative Steve Stetler, argued in a lengthy motion alleging prosecutorial misconduct against Corbett. The motion was denied by Judge Richard Lewis. Stetler, former House Democratic policy chairman, was convicted in June 2012 of six felony counts of using public resources for campaigns.

Allegheny County district attorney Stephen Zappala, a Democrat, prosecuted and convicted Republican senator Jane Orie and charged her sister, Supreme Court justice Joan Orie Melvin, a Republican elected statewide, and Joan's aide, her sister Janine. Against the trend: Peter Smith, the Democratic U.S. Attorney in Harrisburg, charged former Senate Democratic leader Bob Mellow, who pleaded guilty to one count of conspiracy for income tax fraud and using state resources for campaigns.

Prosecutors from the opposing party have the motive to look harder at political targets. It doesn't mean that they're wrong or that all the defendants are *innocent*. Most trial prosecutors I know would go after anyone, regardless of political affiliation. Their bosses, more prone to the political winds, call the shots. Combined with backsliding over time, it may explain the cyclical pattern, or rather the cyclical *discovery*, of corruption.

Just when it appeared that corruption allegations were slowing down, a statewide grand jury, in March 2013, announced widespread corruption at the Pennsylvania Turnpike Commission. Tom Corbett began the investigation as Attorney General in 2009. Kathleen Kane inherited it and, to her credit, enthusiastically pursued it even though an alleged multi-million-dollar pay-to-play scheme on state contracts involved Democrats, including Robert Mellow. Eight people accused of wrongdoing allegedly used the agency to "line their pockets and to influence elections," Kane remarked. This is, after all, Pennsylvania. The fact that the grand jury heard allegations of secret gifts of cash, travel and entertainment, and the payment of contributions to elected officials, should come as no surprise to anyone, especially the readers of this book.

The crimes against the taxpayers go on.

* * *

On November 30, 2012, Robert Mellow, a Scranton Democrat, was sentenced to 16 months in federal prison. Mellow's conviction made him the fourth convicted ex-leader with a portrait in the capitol because he had served briefly as president pro tempore. He became the eighth ex-leader to go to prison from 2009 to 2012. By early 2013, all were imprisoned *simultaneously*.

Mike Veon, Bill DeWeese, Jane Orie, Brett Feese and Steve Stetler have appeals pending. An Allegheny County jury convicted Joan Orie Melvin and Janine Orie in February 2013.

27

Changing Harrisburg

Policymakers and political observers were asked to make three recommendations for cleaning up the state capitol, particularly the legislature. They are a varied group made up of former prosecutors, ex-governors, reformers and academics. This chapter is concerned with their views.

> **Robert P. Strauss** is Professor of Economics and Public Policy at the H. John Heinz III College of Carnegie Mellon University in Pittsburgh.

"Most observant adults who move into Pennsylvania from outside the original colonies usually gasp at the general stasis and ethical and moral vacuum that characterizes governance in the Commonwealth.

"First, one has to be realistic. The underlying fact is that Pennsylvania's 'system' of political and economic elites likes the status quo and cares not that it impedes improvements in our standard of living and unduly limits our liberties. Why? Because an unfettered public sector appropriates through taxes, regulation or outright taking of private property if it chooses to, and is under no obligation to give anything in return vis-à-vis public services. That is, we do not have honest graft in Pennsylvania.

"Being limited to three changes is thus unlikely to make a difference because the 'system' will adapt in other ways to return to the current equilibrium that embraces pay-to-play by elected state and local officials and the squandering of public monies along with a failure to produce much for despondent taxpayers with the lucre that is grabbed from us. So, while I'm not optimistic that just three changes will make a difference, that is 'cash for kids,' public suicides of statewide-elected treasurers on TV, or the tribal incarceration of one family of elected officials by another family of appointed/elected officials (e.g., the Zappalas vs. the Ories) will end with the adoption of my favorite three changes, here goes:

"Take certain kinds of money out of the electoral process so that honestly inclined individuals can run for office without making promises to the devil that necessarily result in changing one's mind about keeping promises made upon swearing in. The campaign finance reform I have in mind comes in two flavors. The first is a revised version of what Howard Baker of Tennessee opined some years ago, as related to me by the late James C. Cannon III: 'No candidate for elected or appointed office in Pennsylvania may receive, directly or indirectly, any monies or other considerations for such campaigns unless they are made by a natural person who is legally eligible to vote in that election.'

"Move from an elected judiciary at the state *and* local level to an appointed-for-life judiciary through a confirmation process; make judicial pay at the 95th percentile of the distribution of state taxable income statewide; require annual public disclosure of the tax return of each judge and his immediate family, and require that in that disclosure would be not only income but the lot and block number and photograph of each judge's personal residence. This will not completely prevent judges from being 'bought' as many now conjecture, but it will reduce the distractions and temptations by orders of magnitude that campaigning leads to, and hopefully improve the amount of impartial justice that gets served out each year.

"My third change involves the oath of office that each elected local school board director and appointed school official must swear to. Circa 1968, the Pennsylvania School Code was amended so that elected school directors were no longer prohibited from engaging in indirect self-dealing. For those who understand human nature (e.g., greed) and ingenuity, the removal of this safeguard goes very far in explaining both why we pour more and more money into public education and these vast sums result in no discernible, positive effect on learning.

"I would obligate elected school directors and appointed school managers (e.g., superintendents, principals, etc.) to affirm as follows:

"I [name], a duly elected or appointed school board director or senior education leader, do solemnly swear: To support the Constitution of the United States and to support the constitution and laws of this state; to allocate school resources and effect educational policy solely for the purpose of ensuring that each student learns to his or her intellectual capacity; and to discharge these duties loyally, honestly, impartially, and with diligence and care, so help me God."

Former Republican representative John Kennedy of Camp Hill was a railroad laborer who founded his own railroad construction company, Kennedy Railroad Builders. He is chairman of Citizens Alliance of Pennsylvania, a nonprofit group committed to government reform.

"Three things I would like to see changed about the General Assembly:

Limit terms served in each chamber: House, four two-year terms, and Senate, two four-year terms.

Eliminate pensions for legislators and compensate them in accordance with the state constitution (i.e., only salary and travel expense).

Stop exempting legislators from laws they enact. "Citizens Alliance of Pennsylvania (CAP) believes empowering the Commonwealth's employers and taxpayers will help break state government's 'Iron triangle of career politicians, bureaucrats and big government lobbyists.' It will, over time, ignite a Pennsylvania comeback, making our commonwealth more competitive and a model for other states to follow. Though headed by a Republican, CAP targets liberal Republicans in press releases and advertisements to expose their union connections and their votes for higher spending and taxes. It is patterned after the national Club for Growth except that the focus is on state legislative candidates.

"*The Patriot-News* reported recently that our General Assembly is irrevocably broken, and CAP agreed and is on its way to fixing the process by electing a new breed of citizen legislators who will serve with *no pension rights* while pushing a pro-business and pro-government reform agenda."

Former Republican governor Dick Thornburgh was U.S. Attorney for Western Pennsylvania, U.S. Attorney General and Assistant Attorney General for the Criminal Division of the U.S. Department of Justice.

Thornburgh says Pennsylvania needs:

"Statutes that provide for transparent and accountable government; an independent, nonpolitical judiciary — with judges chosen on merit — to decide corruption and other criminal cases; a strong, sustained and visible commitment by political leadership to the integrity of all governmental operations."

> **Former Auditor General Jack Wagner** was a Democratic state senator from Pittsburgh's South Side, president of Pittsburgh City Council and an unsuccessful candidate for governor in 2010.

Wagner's three recommendations before leaving office, in January 2012, were these:

> "Shrink the size of the 253-member General Assembly. The Auditor General should audit the legislature; currently, a state law specifically protects the legislature from audits by the independently elected fiscal watchdog. Overhaul the reapportionment process."

> **Former governor George Leader,** a onetime chicken farmer and Democratic state senator from York, helped establish Country Meadows and Providence Place retirement homes.

Leader's recommendations are as follows:

> "People in government tend to reflect the moral and ethical standards of society. We cannot hope to improve the standards of performance in government until we improve the standards of modern society.
>
> "We can make an effort to improve government by selecting the cream of the crop. This is a very difficult task, but try we must. In fact, it is virtually impossible until we put our loyalty to our country above the loyally to our party and then overcome selfishness and greed in all walks of life — including, of course, our government.
>
> "How sad it is that our talk is so far superior to our performance both on the part of the people in government and those who elect them."

> **Gene Stilp,** Harrisburg activist and government reformer, was a recent Democratic candidate for the state and U.S. House. He won a lawsuit allowing people who file ethics complaints to talk publicly about the allegations and not be fined. He is the creator of the "Pink Pig" for public protests.

Here are Stilp's recommendations:

> "The entire legislature must be included in a strengthened Open Records Act to give citizens access to every aspect of the legislature, including the legislative budget.

"The financial connection between lobbyists and the legislature must be eliminated. No gift should be allowed, no matter how small.

"No one who does contracting business with the state, or who has pending legislation before the legislature that directly benefits their business, should be allowed to contribute to political campaigns, directly or through agents or lobbyists who represent the contracting parties or through family members."

Russ Diamond, Lebanon businessman, led the charge against the 2005 pay raise.

Diamond had these ideas:

"Part-time legislature limited to 30 to 45 session days per year (or better yet, every other year); prohibition of all campaign contributions other than from individuals within the represented district; abandoning the partisan primary system in favor of a nonpartisan qualifier that sends the top two vote-getters to the general election."

Former Republican governor Mark Schweiker previously served as lieutenant governor and Bucks County commissioner, and headed the Greater Philadelphia Chamber of Commerce.

His recommendations include the following:

"Pennsylvanians want and expect a clean and transparent state government. While there are countless remedies, the time has come to seriously consider three:
1. Campaign contribution limits must be enacted to prevent what has become a system throttled by special interests.
2. Aid the discussion of innovative ideas and the ascension of thoughtful members of the legislature by enacting reasonable limits on caucus and committee leadership positions.
3. Provide for the merit selection of state appellate court judges to ensure the best people assume seats on the bench, rather than those operating the biggest fundraising machines."

Tim Potts is co-founder and former president of Democracy Rising Pennsylvania. He spent more than 21 years in the executive and legislative branches of government. He is now chairman of the Majority Party Pennsylvania PAC.

Here are his three ideas:

1. "A constitutional convention that can re-engage citizens in making policy decisions about the government they want. The only time Pennsylvania citizens directly decide public policy is at a referendum on proposed amendments to the state constitution. Everything else is derivative, meaning that someone else decides, with or (most often) without fealty to the desires of the public, who are the owners of the government under the American system.

   "It's hard to get people interested in issues that they cannot affect. It's much easier when citizens know that their opinions count.

   "The Constitution, being the fundamental law on which all other laws are based, creates opportunities for direct citizen participation. First, a convention only happens when citizens approve a referendum to create one. Second, the procedure for selecting delegates to a convention can give ordinary citizens the chance to participate as delegates in unique and important debates. Third, before any recommendation from a convention can take effect, it must be approved by voters at another referendum.

   "All evidence suggests that a veto-proof majority of Pennsylvania citizens are eager for such an opportunity. At the time of the pay raise, only 24 percent of Pennsylvania voters favored having a constitutional convention. Now it's 72 percent."

2. "A level playing field for all candidates to get on the ballot, regardless of political affiliation, which would increase the number of competitive elections and thereby mitigate gerrymandering. In the absence of initiative, referendum and recall, elections are the only way citizens have to hold their elected officials accountable. When there is no competition, there is no accountability."

3. "Strengthen watchdog agencies with greater authority, adequate dedicated funding (not annual appropriations by the legislature) and true operational independence from the three branches of state government. The State Ethics Commission, whose board is appointed by the legislature, has been conspicuously absent from high-profile prosecutions, as have inspectors general, the auditor general and others whose duty is to prevent and pursue public corruption.

   "Public integrity agencies are chronically underfunded. As more and more corruption has been discovered, budgets for the agencies have shrunk. No legislation has been enacted to expand their authority, clarify any ambiguity in the law, and provide the funding required to ensure compliance with our weak laws.

   "It is frankly silly to have the budgets of integrity agencies depend upon the most criminally prosecuted legislature in America."

Eric Epstein is co-founder of Rock the Capital; chairman of Three Mile Island Alert, Inc.; president of EFMR Monitoring Group, Inc.; teacher of adult education for 18 years and Visiting Assistant Professor of Humanities at Penn State University, Harrisburg, where he co-authored the *Dictionary of the Holocaust* in 1997.

These are Epstein's views:

On ballot access:
"The electoral process is rigged and dominated by two parties and big money. . . the threshold for third-party participation is absurdly high."

On nonpartisan redistricting:
"Partisan redistricting has resulted in the creation of career 'safe districts' for incumbents."

On voter initiative and referendum:
"Pennsylvanians deserve the right to change laws without depending on a middle man."

David Taylor is executive director of the Pennsylvania Manufacturer's Association (PMA), a statewide trade organization representing the interests of manufacturers; a former staff assistant to Senator Rick Santorum; and a member of the board of directors of PMA, the Lincoln Institute for Public Policy and the Pennsylvania Leadership Council. He is outspoken on reform issues.

Taking aim at the "self-dealing culture of corruption," Taylor recommends:

- "Transparency — online access to all state government documents, including all state contracts, public employee compensation records and government expenditures.
- "Limits on government power — how much of the private economy can be consumed by government through taxes and spending.
- "Greater public involvement.

"Intense transparency increases the risk of getting caught and should minimize that temptation. More citizen participation by individuals, private-sector groups and the media could use the increased transparency to focus on those bright-line limits on government power to keep it in check."

> **Jerry Sterner**, foreman of the 28th Investigating Grand Jury, which issued a stinging critique of the Pennsylvania General Assembly in 2010, spent 32 years in manufacturing, including the role of plant manager. He then worked as a management/union consultant.

The recommendations are Sterner's, not necessarily those of the grand jury.

"Legislators would serve one six-year term and then return to the private sector. Each year, one-sixth of the positions would be up for election, ensuring fresh thoughts and experience at the same time, and no need to establish a very lucrative pension plan.

"Establish oversight! There appears to be none in the budgeting, appropriation and spending plans. Require annual outside audits of all budgeting accounts.

"Eliminate the caucuses and create bipartisan service departments such as human resources, printing, mail and information technology."

> **Barry Kauffman** has been executive director of Common Cause of Pennsylvania for 25 years. Prior to joining Common Cause, Kauffman was a citizens' advocate in the Governor's Action Center.

His views are detailed below.

"There are so many reforms that the legislature needs to adopt that it is virtually impossible to limit them to three. I have listed the three game changers that could really make the legislature more open and accountable to the people:

- Campaign finance reform
- Redistricting
- Initiative and referendum

"*Campaign Finance Reform.* Pennsylvania will never obtain a legislative body that is accountable to the voters until it changes the way its elections are financed. Currently, Pennsylvania is one of just 11 states that have no limits on campaign contributions. Thus any lobbyist, any special interest seeking favors or public policy changes from state government, or any other person can give unlimited amounts of campaign cash to the people who will be the decision-makers. Pennsylvania's campaign finance system has been characterized by many pundits as being nothing short of legalized bribery. The current system diminishes the relevance of voters because it makes campaign contributors, rather than the voters, the primary constituency to which it caters. The current system not only helps special interests manipulate the legislative process, it also perpetuates incumbency. It is almost universally recognized that large campaign contributors get, at a minimum, privileged access to lawmakers. Campaign contributions can affect the prioritizing of issues to be addressed, introduction of legislation, introduction of amendments, determining whether a bill is assigned to a friendly or hostile committee, determining whether a bill is ever brought to committee vote, whether an amendment is sequenced in such a manner as to make it irrelevant based on other amendments, whether leadership will press for passage of a bill or allow rank-and-file lawmakers to vote their conscience, whether it is tabled, whether it is recommitted to committee, or whether it is scheduled for a final vote. Along with campaign contribution limits, Pennsylvania must require full and timely disclosure of all independent expenditures and require corporations that spend money on 'independent' political expenditures in Pennsylvania's political races to present that information to their stockholders and get stockholders' consent. Pennsylvania also must move toward expenditure limits for, and public financing of, its elections.

"It would require candidates to run based on their values, goals, commitment, intellect and energy, rather than their ability to tap wealthy donors for funds. If Pennsylvania is to have elections that are competitive, and encourage a broader range of people to run for office, then the state must retake ownership of the elections by financing them and provide candidates with a base level of resources necessary to run a viable campaign.

"*Redistricting.* Like campaign finance reform, redistricting reform is essential to achieve accountability for public officials. The current system is designed to enable senior legislative leaders to predetermine the logical victors of legislative political campaigns long before any election is held. The current system generally guarantees one party will be dominant in each legislative district. That makes the primary election the real election. This, to a large degree, disenfranchises voters not registered with the dominant party since they cannot vote in that party's primary.

"*Initiative and Referendum (I&R).* Pennsylvanians deserve a safety valve in the legislative process. This would require a constitutional amendment. Article I, Sections 2, 20 and 25 of the Pennsylvania Constitution essentially provide the rights of I&R; however, the legislature has not created the mechanisms to implement those rights. When the legislature fails to address key issues, for self-serving or any other reason, or if lawmakers implement policies that are repugnant to substantial numbers of citizens, the citizens should have the right to address the issue on their own by drafting an alternative and presenting it at the ballot box. Many of the most critical social and government reforms our nation has seen either started or got momentum in initiative states because citizens finally said 'enough is enough.' An I&R system must be carefully structured to prevent abuse. It can be neither too easy to use, thus diminishing the real value of representative and deliberative decision-making of the legislature, nor can it be difficult to use, thus making it irrelevant. If the General Assembly has the citizens looking over its shoulder, with the ability to take action, they are more likely to responsibly address issues of importance to the people."

Matthew Brouillette is president and CEO of the Commonwealth Foundation.

Brouillette's thoughts are given below:

"When the number-one political objective is re-election in order to receive a salary that is more than double the median salary in Pennsylvania, as well as health care, retirement and other fringe benefits that exceed those found in the private sector, it is understandable why the longer members stay in office, the more apt they are to bend or violate the rules. For many, this is the best job they've ever had or will ever get. So the incentive to hold onto their seat at any and all costs is high. To help restore a citizen legislature:

"*Term Limits:* Pennsylvania currently limits the number of terms a governor can serve. Term limits should also be placed on the General Assembly, such as currently exist in 15 other states. Term-limiting committee chairmanships would be a meaningful first step.

"*Session Limits:* Pennsylvania is one of only four "full-time" state legislatures with an unlimited number of session days. Limiting the number of session days, coupled with limited terms, will return Pennsylvania to a citizen-led legislature. Texas, for example, has nearly double the population of Pennsylvania, yet its legislature meets for only a limited period every other year.

"*Compensation Limits:* The annual salary for rank-and-file Pennsylvania legislators (about $82,000) is the fourth highest in the country, trailing only those in California, Michigan and New York. However, the total cost to taxpayers for each legislator includes much more than salary. Perks and benefits for Pennsylvania lawmakers include: health, dental, vision and prescription drug coverage valued at over $16,000; a pension that is among the most generous in America; lifetime post-retirement health care; and tax-free per diem payments of $163 per day when lawmakers are attending legislative committee meetings or in session. Many legislators have bought homes near the capitol while collecting per diems for their lodging. In contrast, consider the case of Texas. The Lone Star State has twice the population of Pennsylvania and is four times the size of the Keystone State geographically. Yet the Texas legislature meets once every two years for 140 days to produce a biennial budget. When Texas lawmakers need to deal with emergency situations or revise their budget, they return for a limited, special session. During its 2007 session, Texas' legislature passed 1,672 bills, while Pennsylvania's full-time General Assembly passed less than one-fifth that number. There is convincing evidence that restoring the General Assembly to part-time, term-limited, reasonably compensated legislature would result in lower taxes, more efficient government and less corruption."

U.S. Representative Patrick Meehan, a Republican, was the former U.S. Attorney for the Eastern District of Pennsylvania. He launched the investigation of state Senate powerbroker Vincent Fumo. He's the former District Attorney of Delaware County.

Here are Meehan's recommendations:

"A stronger and better-funded state Ethics Commission that can catch things as they're happening and handle smaller offenses with civil penalties.

"Demonstrate real leadership at the top. If the top elected official makes clear what is acceptable and unacceptable, many will follow.

"A moral compass. All the laws enacted won't keep people from breaking them."

Former acting governor Mark Singel served as lieutenant governor under the late Democratic governor Robert Casey. A former state senator, he now heads The Winter Group, a lobbying and management/strategic consulting firm in Harrisburg.

Singel has these recommendations:

"The first two require individual effort; the third is a collective need.

"1. Conscience: Every elected official understands the political realities of the votes and actions he or she takes, but few ask themselves the question: 'Is it the right thing to do?' Legislators are so obsessed with their own re-election that they fall in line with leadership or with the prevailing public whim and do not consult their own consciences.

"2. Communication: In those instances when the 'right thing' contradicts popular opinion or political demands, legislators must explain themselves. They should present their case often and effectively to their voters. A working relationship with editors and public opinion leaders to help get their story told is invaluable in this regard.

"3. Culture: Governors, legislative leaders, political power brokers, the media and the public must actively encourage a culture of cooperation and compromise. They must reject the current 'dumbing down' of the political discourse and commit to conduct public business with the dignity that the forefathers intended."

John Milliron is a lobbyist and a former Pennsylvania House member.

He sums up the problem in this way:

"The place does not change."

Epilogue

ROBERT B. SWIFT

A theme running through Brad Bumsted's *Keystone Corruption* is the century-long parade of Pennsylvania elected officials either ignoring or bending laws to suit their own ends and purposes. Bumsted demonstrates that corruption is cyclical in nature, just as is public outrage over acts of corruption. The opportunity to shake the plum tree, as 19th-century political boss Matthew S. Quay put it, is a strong temptation for individuals having the power to control political machines, shape state budgets and steer public contracts.

The Capitol Graft Scandal of 1907; the wave of post-Watergate prosecutions of county political chairmen, state lawmakers, state cabinet secretaries and congressmen during the 1970s; and the Bonusgate investigation, starting in 2007, into legislative branch misuse of public money for political purposes are all documented in Bumsted's book.

These periodic breaches of the public trust show that only constant vigilance can ward off the corruption that robs democracy of its vitality and spirit.

Bumsted's book appears just after the 40th anniversary of the Watergate scandal, resulting from the break-in of Democratic National Committee headquarters in Washington by men working for President Richard Nixon's re-election team. The botched burglary was the catalyst for a federal investigation of a host of high crimes that led to a president's resignation and prison time for his top aides. One of the great questions posed during the Watergate crisis was whether the rule of law had any place left in American life.

On the night he was sacked by Nixon as Watergate special prosecutor midway through the crisis, Archibald Cox gave this statement: "Whether ours shall continue to be a government of laws and not of men is now for Congress and ultimately the American people to decide."

The rule of American law prevailed with Nixon's resignation in August 1974, ahead of certain impeachment and removal from office, but what of Pennsylvania's laws considering that the length of the Bonusgate investigation exceeded that of Watergate?

Pennsylvania historically doesn't get good marks in surveys weighing the effectiveness of its anti-corruption laws. A survey in 2012 by the Center for Public Integrity gave Pennsylvania a C- minus grade for corruptibility. Pennsylvania's campaign and ethics disclosure laws are considered weak due to the lack of spending limits and high monetary thresholds for reporting outside income. The response of the General Assembly to the parade of legislative leaders going to prison in the past few years hasn't been to pass a lot of tough new laws.

Lawmakers have passed two sunshine laws since 2007, updating an open record statute that had been in effect since the 1950s and authorizing creation of an online site to post information about spending. Yet on the crux issue of looting the public treasury to underwrite campaigns and enlisting legislative staffers to stump for candidates on the public's dime that defined the Bonusgate prosecution, lawmakers have not passed new laws to try to deter this activity from happening again in the next cycle. The Senate approved a rule barring political activity on legislative time, but made itself the enforcing agent, and the House adopted a set of policies. Many think much more needs to be done to guard against corruptibility.

The final chapter of *Keystone Corruption* contains suggestions from individuals who have some experience in this arena — either carrying out reforms themselves as public officials or as activists prodding for change from the outside. Some of these suggestions call for a cultural change in the way we think of government. Others are practical, commonsense proposals that can be implemented in short order if the political will exists.

Former state Auditor General Jack Wagner said a law is needed to give the Auditor General's office authority to conduct a real audit of legislative spending — the kind that verifies if money was spent for the stated purpose.

Jerry Sterner, the foreman of the 28th investigative grand jury, and Barry Kauffman, executive director of Common Cause of Pennsylvania, both list outside audits of the legislature as a necessary reform. Oversight agencies like the state Ethics Commission and the state Office of Open Records need to have true independence and a dedicated stream of funding, said Tim Potts, co-founder of Democracy Rising Pennsylvania. He has put out an "integrity budget" showing how these agencies fare in the annual state budget process.

Former governors George Leader and Dick Thornburgh stress the importance of rebuilding democratic institutions to reflect better civic values. Thornburgh advised that an independent, nonpolitical judiciary is needed to keep a rein on corruption.

Setting term limits for lawmakers just like the governor has is a suggestion that is frequently heard. Setting term limits for committee chairs would be a meaningful first step in the view of Matthew Brouillette, CEO of the

Commonwealth Foundation. So would term limits for legislative leaders who wield great power affecting all Pennsylvanians, but are often little known outside their districts.

If changes along these lines are not made, Pennsylvanians will continue to be at the mercy of the attitude expressed by Frank Hague, boss of Jersey City in the 1930s, forgotten about today except for his infamous remark: "I am the law."

Bibliography

References are listed by chapter. Some entries cover more than one chapter. This list contains many old newspaper stories that are not necessarily on the Internet. Headlines to help identify the articles have been provided where possible. Please note that web sites sometimes change addresses and therefore links may change over time.

INTRODUCTION

Belson, Ken, Questions on Sandusky Are Wrapped in a 2005 Mystery, *New York Times,* November 8, 2011.

http://www.nytimes.com/2011/11/09/sports/ncaafootball/questions-on-sandusky-wrapped-in-2005-gricar-mystery.html?_r=0

Pearson Sophia, Ex-Penn State President Charged with Sandusky Cover-up, Bloomberg, December 7, 2011.

http://www.bloomberg.com/news/2012-11-01/ex-penn-state-president-charged-with-sandusky-cover-up.html

The Freeh Report: http://progress.psu.edu/the-freeh-report

Bronstein, Hugh, Colombian Soldiers Convicted in Massacre of Police, Reuters, February 18, 2008.

http://mobile.reuters.com/article/worldNews/idUSN1817945720080218?i=1

Harman, Danna, The War on Drugs Ambushed in Jamudi, *Christian Science Monitor*, September 27, 2006.

http://www.csmonitor.com/2006/0927/p01s04-woam.html

Bronstein, Hugh, Dozens of Colombia Politicians Killed Ahead of Vote, Reuters, September 28, 2007.

http://uk.reuters.com/article/2007/09/28/uk-colombia-elections-idUKN2844701220070928

Colombia Sentences Soldiers for Murder of Civilians, British Broadcasting System, November 30, 2011: http://www.bbc.co.uk/news/world-latin-america-15978134

Colombian Soldiers Paid $500 for Victims to Boost Kill Counts: Testimony, *Colombia Reports,* December 5, 2011.

http://colombiareports.com/colombia-news/news/20890-false-positives-recruiter-received-500-per-victim.html

CHAPTER 1

Roxbury, James, Computergate Sentencing: John Perzel. . . 30-60 months, *Roxbury News* video, August 31, 2011.

http://www.roxburynews.com/index.php?a=4793

http://www.roxburynews.com/index.php?a=4792

Bumsted, Brad, Disgraced State House Leaders Cash Out, *Pittsburgh Tribune-Review,* August 19, 2012.

http://triblive.com/home/2403973-74 system-paid-convicted-money-retirement-state-pension-restitution-defendants-former#axzz2M0IJGh9e

Bumsted, Brad, Debra Erdley and Mike Wereschagin, Shockwave Shatters Pa. Politics, *Pittsburgh Tribune-Review*, October 3, 2005.

http://triblive.com/x/pittsburghtrib/news/regional/s_454821.html#axzz2M0IJGh9e

Bumsted, Brad, Another Late Budget and Unrepentant Pols, Pittsburgh Tribune-Review, July 9, 2006.

http://groups.yahoo.com/group/pacleansweep/message/13314

Bumsted and Erdley, Analysis: State Probe Angling for Dem Leaders, *Pittsburgh Tribune-Review*, November 16, 2007.

Bumsted and Erdley, Pennsylvania Legislative Payroll Is Bigger Than Ever, *Pittsburgh Tribune-Review*, November 12, 2009.

http://triblive.com/x/pittsburghtrib/news/regional/s_731584.html#axzz2M7Nj1M6c

Bumsted and Erdley, More Checks Than Balances, *Pittsburgh Tribune-Review*, June 4, 2006.

http://triblive.com/x/pittsburghtrib/news/regional/s_456614.html#axzz2M0IJGh9e

Bumsted and Erdley, 28th Statewide Grand Jury, Report Number 1: Investigative Report on "Time Warp" in Pa. Legislature, May 24, 2010; Sent to House and Senate: Judge Pay Irks State Lawmakers, *Pittsburgh Tribune-Review*, November 1, 2009.

http://triblive.com/x/pittsburghtrib/news/regional/s_472207.html#axzz2M7Nj1M6c

Bumsted, Brad, Prison, Pension Forfeiture Await Perzel, *Pittsburgh Tribune-Review*, August 31, 2011.

http://triblive.com/x/pittsburghtrib/news/regional/s_754361.html#axzz2M7Nj1M6c

Bumsted, Brad, Status Quo? Try Non-Pro, *Pittsburgh Tribune-Review*, July 24, 2011.

Bumsted, Brad, John Perzel, Rat No. 1, *Pittsburgh Tribune-Review*, September 4, 2011.

http://triblive.com/x/pittsburghtrib/opinion/columnists/bumsted/s_754793.html

Bumsted, Brad, *Pittsburgh Tribune-Review*, October 23, 2011.

http://triblive.com/x/pittsburghtrib/opinion/columnists/bumsted/s_763129.html#axzz2M0IJGh9e

Erdley, Debra, and Richard Gazarik, Various Stories Regarding Dawida Grant and WAMs, *Pittsburgh Tribune-Review, 1999.*

Dawida Withdraws from Business Group, Associated Press, *Beaver County Times*, December 15, 1999.

Roxbury, James, John Perzel, Guilty, *Roxbury News,* September 4, 2011. www.Roxburynews.com

Bumsted, Brad, The Kings of Perks, *Pittsburgh Tribune-Review*, February 27, 2005.

Heller, Karen, Taxpayers Should Not Foot the Bill for Jazz Festival, *Philadelphia Inquirer*, July 7, 2010.

http://articles.philly.com/2010-07-07/news/24964091_1_newport-jazz-festival-festival-attendees-state-grants

McCoy, Craig R., and Emilie Lounsberry, Testimony Ends in Fumo Trial, *Philadelphia Inquirer*, February 25, 2009.

http://articles.philly.com/2009-02-20/news/24984754_1_fumo-testimony-ends-witness

Scolforo, Mark, Perzel Among 10 Charged in PA Bonusgate Case, Associated Press, November 12, 2009.

http://www.dailypress.com/wpmt-pmnews-bonusgate-harrisburg-11-12-09,0,2367495.story

Couloumbis, Angela, Perzel Pleads to Abuse of Public Funds, Apologizes, *Philadelphia Inquirer*, August 30, 2011.

Pennsylvania Attorney General's News Release on Bonusgate Charges (in next link — also containing Grand Jury Report); 28th Statewide Investigative Grand Jury Reports (link on bottom of web page).

http://www.attorneygeneral.gov/press.aspx?id=3771

Pennsylvania Office of Attorney General, News Release, Computergate.

http://www.attorneygeneral.gov/press.aspx?id=4835

Statewide Grand Jury Presentment Against State House Republicans, November 12, 2009.

United States of America v. Vincent Fumo, Grand Jury Indictment, February 6, 2007.

U.S. Department of Justice News Release on Fumo's Indictment.

http://www.prnewswire.com/news-releases/state-senator-vincent-fumo-indicted-along-with-three-aides-54467237.html

DeWeese, Bill, et al., Motions on Resentencing Fumo by Prosecutors and Defense, October 2011 (Guidestar); Statewide Grand Jury (Separate) Presentment Against Democrats, December 15, 2009.

Epstein, Eric, Pay Raise, 2005-11 (booklet), *Rock the Capital*, 2011. National Conference of State Legislatures' web page: ncsl.org.

Kurtz, Karl, and Brian Weberg, The State of Staff, *NCSL*, July-August 2009.

Letter from Bill DeWeese to Bonus Recipients, December 2006 (from copy of actual letter).

Pork Spending, Commonwealthfoundation.org, February 18, 2011.

Murphy, Jan, and Charlie Thompson, Pennsylvania Lawmakers Unlikely to Repeal Automatic Raises for Lawmakers, *Patriot-News*, Harrisburg, November 27, 2011.

www.pennlive.com/midstate/index.ssf/2011/11/pennsylvania_lawmakers_unlikel.html

Ackerman, Kenneth D., *Boss Tweed: The Corrupt Pol Who Conceived the Soul of Modern New York*, New York, Viral History Press, 2011.

Thomas, Frank, Indepth: Benefits Available to Legislators, *USA Today*, September 23, 2011.

http://usatoday30.usatoday.com/news/nation/story/2011-10-11/state-legislators-pensions-records/50523328/1

Bumsted and Erdley, 3500-Plus State Employees Earn $100,000 or More, *Pittsburgh Tribune-Review (via Patriot-News), May 15, 2011.*

Bumsted and Erdley, Shadows of Greed Darken State Capitol, *Pittsburgh Tribune-Review,* November 18, 2007.

CHAPTER 2

Beers, Paul B., *Pennsylvania Politics Today and Yesterday: The Tolerable Accommodation,* University Park, The Pennsylvania State University Press, 1980.

Davenport, Walter, *Power and Glory: The Life of Boies Penrose,* New York, AMS Press, 1931.

Miller, Randall M., and William Pencak, *Pennsylvania: A History of the Commonwealth,* University Park, The Pennsylvania State University Press, 2002.

Pennsylvania General Assembly, *The Pennsylvania Capitol,* Harrisburg, n.d.

Kehl, James A., *Boss Rule in the Gilded Age: Matt Quay of Pennsylvania,* Pittsburgh, University of Pittsburgh Press, 1981.

Bowden, Robert Douglas, *Boise Penrose: Symbol of an Era,* Books for Libraries 1937.

Crist, Ronald G., *Pennsylvania Kingmakers,* Pennsylvania Historical Studies Series, University Park, Pennsylvania Historical Association,1985.

Arrests for Graft in PA Scandal, special to the *New York Times,* September 19, 1907.

Graft Used to Pay Politicians' Notes, special to the *New York Times,* August 5, 1907.

http://query.nytimes.com/mem/archive-free/pdf?res= F10C13FF3C5A15738DDDAC0894D0405B878CF1D3

Arrests for Fraud in Graft Scandal, special to the *New York Times,* September 19, 1907.

http://query.nytimes.com/mem/archive-free/pdf?res=F40715F9385512738DDDA00994D1405B87 8CF1D3

Capitol Sentenced Delayed, special to the *New York Times,* May 14, 1909.

Huston Guilty of Fraud, special to the *New York Times,* April 30, 1910.

Graft Sentences Upheld (Snyder and Shumaker), *New York Times,* March 7, 1910.

Huston's Conviction Holds, *New York Times,* March 4, 1911.

Pennsylvania Capitol Preservation Committee web site: http://cpc.state.pa.us/cpcweb/

CHAPTER 3

Pennsylvania Historical Museum Commission: http://www.phmc.state.pa.us/bah/dam/mg/ mg397.htm

Kury, Franklin, *Clean Politics, Clean Streams: A Legislative Biography and Reflections,* Bethlehem, PA: Lehigh University Press, 2011.

Thornburgh, Dick, *Where the Evidence Leads: An Autobiography,* Pittsburgh: University of Pittsburgh Press, 2003.

Carocci, Vincent P., *A Capitol Journey: Reflections on the Press, Politics, and the Making of Public Policy in Pennsylvania,* University Park, The Pennsylvania State University Press, 2005.

Thornburgh, Dick, Crises in Integrity (speech), Thornburgh Papers, Pittsburgh: University of Pittsburgh Library, March 31, 1977.

Anderson Jack, Pa. Probe Opens Pandora's Box, The Washington Merry-Go-Round, *Washington Post*, January 17, 1976.

CHAPTER 4

Madonna, G. Terry, and Michael Young, *Benediction,* Politically Uncorrected, Franklin and Marshall College, September 25, 2003.

http://www.fandm.edu/politics/politically-uncorrected-column/2003-politically-uncorrected/benediction

Bumsted, Brad, Last Call at the Bum Steer, *Pittsburgh Tribune-Review,* September 21, 2003.

Livingood, Ben, Knoll Making 2nd Bid for Treasurership, *Morning Call,* Allentown, April 3, 1984.

Livingood, Ben, Statewide Grand Jury Presentment Against John Kerr, November 1983 (paper copy); Six Democrats Vie for State Treasurer Job, 1984 Election Pennsylvania, April 3, 1984; Lie Detector Clears Him, Says Benedict, *Morning Call,* January 26, 1984.

Drachler, Stephen, Benedict Pleads Guilty to Racketeering, Tax Fraud, Former Auditor Admits Bribes, *Morning Call,* Allentown, January 15, 1988.

http://articles.mcall.com/1988-01-15/news/2621520_1_bribery-no-bid-contracts-benedict

Witnesses Testify They Bought State Jobs, Associated Press, *Indiana Gazette*, Indiana, PA, June 22, 1984.

Criminal docket sheet, Benedict, CR 88-00003, U.S. District Court, January 8, 1988.

Cuddy, Jim Jr., Benedict, Dwyer: Trade Scandal Charges in Debate on Telephone, *Pittsburgh Press*, October 10, 1984.

http://news.google.com/newspapers?nid=1144&dat=19841010&id=KTkgAAAAIBAJ&sjid=_WEEAAAAIBAJ&pg=2175,4637989

U.S. Department of Justice, press release, January 14, 1988.

Benedict, Al, Obituary, legacy.com:

http://www.legacy.com/obituaries/erietimesnews/obituary.aspx?n=al-benedict&pid=1364822&fhid=3691

Prosecutor Says Investigation into Bribe Scheme Not Over, Associated Press, *Reading Eagle,* October 24, 1984.

CHAPTER 5

Morris, David, R. Budd Dwyer Shoots Self Dead, Associated Press, *The Herald,* Sharon, PA, January 23, 1987.

Swift, Robert, First Person Account of PA Treasurer Suicide, Ottoway News Service, *The Daily Item,* Sunbury, January 23, 1987.

Vathis, Paul, Eyewitness Account of AP Photographer, Associated Press, *The Titusville Herald,* Titusville, PA, January 23, 1987.

Stevens, William, Official Calls in Press and Kills Himself, *New York Times,* January 23, 1987.

Keisling, William, *The Sins of Our Fathers*, 2nd Ed., Airville, PA, Yardbird Books, 2011.

Dirschberger, James, *Honest Man: The Life of R. Budd Dwyer* (DVD documentary), EightyFour Films, December 10, 2010.

Slimed Dwyer Seeks Re-election in Year of Controversy, Associated Press, *Indiana Gazette,* October 9, 1984.

Dwyer suicide video: http://www.youtube.com/watch?v=dtUA4w7TO5o

Abbreviated version: http://www.youtube.com/watch?v=Od9aftM22m0

CHAPTER 6

Cusick, Frederick, The Last Dark Days of Budd Dwyer, *Philadelphia Inquirer,* June 1987.

Dwyer, R. Budd, Final Statement (paper handed out at news conference), January 22, 1987.

Package of *Philadelphia Inquirer* stories on Dwyer, before and after:

http://articles.philly.com/keyword/budd-dwyer

Dracher, Stephen, Terms as Legislators Swelled Dwyer's Pension, *The Morning Call,* Allentown, April 19, 1987.

Miller, Matt, State Prison Term Ordered for William Trickett Smith in Fraud Case, *Patriot-News,* Harrisburg, November 23, 2010.

Bumsted, Brad, Asher Drives GOP Success in Pennsylvania, *Pittsburgh Tribune-Review,* December 5, 2010.

Collection of Dwyer stories, *Philadelphia Inquirer:* http://articles.philly.com/keyword/budd-dwyer

CHAPTER 7

The following stories were provided as printouts by Peter Shelly, courtesy of the Harrisburg *Patriot-News.* The headlines as they appeared in the newspaper were not readily available.

Shellem, Pete, and Peter J. Shelly, *Patriot-News,* Harrisburg, April 4, 1993.

Shellem and Shelly, *Patriot-News,* Harrisburg, July 29, 1993.

Shelly, Peter J., *Patriot-News,* Harrisburg, March 31, 1994.

Shellem and Shelly, *Patriot-News,* Harrisburg, April 7, 1994.

Shellem and Shelly, *Patriot-News,* Harrisburg, May 6, 1994.

Shelly, Peter J., *Patriot-News,* Harrisburg, September 24, 1994.

Shellem and Shelly, *Patriot-News,* Harrisburg, December 2, 1994.

Shellem and Shelly, *Patriot-News,* Harrisburg, March 30, 1995.

Shelly, Peter J., *Pittsburgh Post-Gazette,* November 7, 1995.

PA's No. 3 Official Prepares to Plea on Mail Fraud, *New York Times,* June 10, 1995.

http://www.nytimes.com/1995/06/10/us/pennsylvanias-no-3-official-agrees-to-plea-on-mail-fraud.html

Preate, Ernie, Law firm web page: http://www.preate.com/Firm%20Info/Lawyers/1816773.aspx

Reeves, Tim, Crime Probe of Preate Branded Anti-Italian, *Pittsburgh Post-Gazette*, May 12, 1993.

http://news.google.com/newspapers?nid=1129&dat=19930512&id=16kkAAAAIBAJ&sjid=0G4DAAAAIBAJ&pg=2541,6348054

Preate biography, *Gettysburg Times,* June 14, 1995.

Zausner, Robert, Protests and Preate's Porchetta Italians Take on Crime Commission, *Philadelphia Inquirer,* May 26, 1993.

http://articles.philly.com/1993-05-26/news/25964835_1_italian-american-attorney-general-ernie-preate-porchetta

Cattabiani, Mario, The Sleuth (a profile of Pete Shellem), *American Journalism Review,* June-July 2007.

Bumsted, Brad, Ex-Lawmakers Recall Jail Stints as 7 Prepare to Hear Their Fates, *Pittsburgh Tribune-Review,* March 20, 2012.

http://triblive.com/x/pittsburghtrib/news/regional/s_787329.html#axzz2M0IJGh9e

Neri, Albert, Preate, Mezvinsky Wage Costly Campaigns, *Pittsburgh Post-Gazette,* November 1, 1988.

Cusick, Frederick, and Russell Eshelman, Report Says Preate Took Illegal Businesses' Money: Video Poker Interests Escaped Prosecution After Making Donations, The Crime Commission Says, *Philadelphia Inquirer,* April 12, 1994.

Cusick, Frederick, FBI, Too, Investigated Allegations Against Ernie Preate; The Probe Ended with the Death of His Key Accuser; The Pa. Crime Commission Cited Similar Allegations, *Philadelphia Inquirer,* June 2, 1993.

Collection of stories on Ernie Preate by *The Morning Call,* Allentown:

http://articles.mcall.com/keyword/attorney-general-ernie-preate/recent/5

CHAPTER 8

Drexler, John A., and Eric Epstein: *Rock the Capital's Pay-Raise Voter Guide:* Who voted for it and which members kept "unvouchered expenditures" and didn't pay it back. Harrisburg, Rock the Capital booklet, 2006.

Diamond, Russ, *Tip of the Spear,* published by *Raintree,* November 2007.

Pennsylvania Legislative Pay Raise (assorted stories), *Philadelphia Inquirer,* starting in 2005.

http://www.philly.com/philly/news/special_packages/inquirer/pa_pay_raise/

Bumsted, Brad, Lawmakers OK 16 Percent Pay Hikes, *Pittsburgh Tribune-Review,* July 8, 2005.

The Legislative Pay Raise: A Public Shafting (editorial), *Pittsburgh Tribune-Review,* July 8, 2005.

Bumsted, Brad, Hiding the Pay Grab, *Pittsburgh Tribune-Review,* July 10, 2005.

Worden, Amy, Pay-Raise Opponents Stripped of Posts, *Philadelphia Inquirer,* July 28, 2005.

White, Bill, Illegal Pay Raise (blog), *The Morning Call,* Allentown, July 18, 2005.

Erdley, Debra, and David Brown, Lawmaker's Limo White Lie, *Pittsburgh Tribune-Review,* October 13, 2005.

Cattabiani, Mario, Perzel in a Hornet's Nest: Questions about pay hike, limo mar school visit, *Philadelphia Inquirer,* October 18, 2005.

Epstein, Eric, *Pay Raise, 2005-2011,* Harrisburg, Rock the Capital, July 7, 2011.

Epstein, Eric, *Rock the Capital: Anniversary Edition,* Harrisburg, Rock the Capital, July 6, 2010.

Bumsted, Brad, Lawmaker's Bill Calls for Pay Raise Repeal, *Pittsburgh Tribune-Review,* August 24, 2005.

Potts, Timothy, The Pay Raise, *DR News,* Democracy Rising PA, March 3, 2013.

http://www.democracyrisingpa.com/index.cfm?organization_id=66&section_id=1011&page_id=4088

O'Neill, Brian, Convention is Overdue to Remodel State House, *Pittsburgh Post-Gazette,* December 13, 2005.

Bumsted, Brad, and Debra Erdley, Capital Cash Grab Series, *Pittsburgh Tribune-Review,* September-December 2005.

Bumsted and Erdley, Judges Uphold Their Raises, *Pittsburgh Tribune-Review* September 15, 2005.

Wereschagin, Mike, Pay Raise Ends with Apology, *Pittsburgh Tribune-Review,* November 17, 2005.

Bumsted, Brad, The Reformers, *Pittsburgh Tribune-Review,* March 25, 2007.

http://triblive.com/x/pittsburghtrib/opinion/columnists/bumsted/s_499440.html#axzz2MKJ7l25A

Bumsted, Brad, Height of Arrogance by Pay-Jacker, *Pittsburgh Tribune-Review,* December 23, 2006.

http://triblive.com/x/valleyindependent/opinion/s_485581.html#axzz2MKJ7l25A

Wereschagin, Mike, Leader Cracked, Pay Hike Crumbled, *Pittsburgh Tribune-Review,* November 20, 2005.

Bumsted, Brad, Analysis: Rendell Erases Pay Raise, *Pittsburgh Tribune-Review,* November 17, 2005.

http://triblive.com/x/pittsburghtrib/news/specialreports/capitalcash/s_395394.html#axzz2M0IJGh9e

Bumsted, Brad, Pay-jacking Pay Back, *Pittsburgh Tribune-Review, January 29, 2012.*

http://triblive.com/x/pittsburghtrib/opinion/columnists/bumsted/s_778768.html#axzz2MKJ7l25A

Cattabiani, Mario, Perzel Rousing Ire in Party Faithful, *Philadelphia Inquirer, May 28, 2006.*

Cattabiani, Mario, From Perzel, the Last Word on the Pay Raise, *Philadelphia Inquirer,* June 20, 2006.

CHAPTER 9

Acton, Robin, Scandals Engrained in State Government History, *Pittsburgh Tribune-Review,* July 13, 2008.

Roddy, Dennis, Druce Negotiating Plea Bargain, *Pittsburgh Post-Gazette,* August 31, 2000.

Thomas Druce Released from Prison, Associated Press via WPVI-TV, March 13, 2006.

Worden, Amy, Ex-lawmaker wants sentence overturned: Thomas Druce's lawyers say the judge who sentenced him in a fatal hit-and-run was biased, *Philadelphia Inquirer,* May 16, 2003.

Roddy, Dennis, How the World Fell Apart for a Politico with Plans, *Pittsburgh Post-Gazette,* October 24, 2000.

http://news.google.com/newspapers?nid=1129&dat=20001024&id=ZedRAAAAIBAJ&sjid=)8DAAAAIBAJ&pg=7117,3689300

Pa. Court Upholds Sentence of Former Rep. Druce, Associated Press, *Insurance Journal,* May 3, 2004.

Bauder, Bob, Friends Recall Convicted Legislator Gigliotti's Good Qualities, *Pittsburgh Tribune-Review,* August 12, 2011.

McNulty, Timothy, Obituary: Frank Gigliotti: "Old-style politician" became a political force in the city and state, *Pittsburgh Post-Gazette,* August 11, 2011.

http://www.post-gazette.com/stories/local/obituaries/obituary-frank-gigliotti-old-style-politician-became-a-political-force-in-the-city-and-state-309878/#ixzz2MERQ7pIL

Hopey, Don, Senator Gets Jail Time for Dumping Sewage, *Pittsburgh Post-Gazette,* May 10, 2000.

http://old.post-gazette.com/regionstate/20000510slocum6.asp

Slocum, William, State Sen. Slocum Answers Critics (op ed), *Punxsutawney Spirit,* March 7, 2000.

Baer, John M., *On the Front Lines of Pennsylvania Politics: Twenty-Five Years of Keystone Reporting,* The History Press, 2012.

Shellem, Pete, Sen. Loeper to Plead Guilty, *Patriot-News,* Harrisburg, October 25, 2000.

Strawley, George, Senate Leader Resigning, Associated Press, *Pittsburgh Post-Gazette,* October 25, 2000.

Dilanian, Ken, and Tom Fitzgerald, Loeper Will Resign Over Tax Charges, *Philadelphia Inquirer,* October 25, 2000.

http://articles.philly.com/2000-10-25/news/ 25585568_1_loeper-municipal-tax-bureau-nicholas-panarella

Durantine, Peter, Delp's Social Life Raises Concerns, *Observer-Reporter,* Washington, PA, July 26, 1997.

Durantine, Peter, Delp Will Stay on Job Despite Charges, Associated Press, *Pittsburgh Post-Gazette,* September 30, 1998.

Durantine, Peter, Delp Escaped Most Serious Charge, Associated Press, *Observer-Reporter,* Washington, PA, June 14, 1998.

http://news.google.com/newspapers?nid=2519&dat=19980614&id=oWpeAAAAIBAJ&sjid=V2ENAAAAIBAJ&pg=1377,4482541

Mamula, Kris, Associated Press, *Pittsburgh Post-Gazette,* May 13, 2000.

Hayes, Kristen, Former State Rep. Seyfert Sentenced to Six Months in Prison, Associated Press, *Pittsburgh Post-Gazette,* August 8, 2000.

Dilanian, Ken, and Tom Fitzgerald, Loeper Will Resign Over Tax Charges, *Philadelphia Inquirer,* October 25, 2000.

http://articles.philly.com/2000-10-25/news/25585568_1_loeper-municipal-tax-bureau-nicholas-panarella

Dilanian, Ken, Tom Fitzgerald et al., Loeper Leaves Majority Leader's Post After Felony Plea (collection of articles on Loeper by various reporters), *Philadelphia Inquirer,* November 14, 2000.

http://articles.philly.com/keyword/majority-leader/recent/5

Baer, John, *Philadelphia Daily News,* February 7, 2000.

Bumsted, Brad, and Debra Erdley, Shadows of Greed Darken State Capitol, *Pittsburgh Tribune-Review,* November 18, 2007.

Strader, Jim, Associated Press*, Pittsburgh Post-Gazette,* December 11, 1998.

CHAPTER 10

Pennsylvania State Ethics Commission decision in re: Jeffrey Habay, Order No. 1313, March 11, 2004.

DiRienzo, Dominick, Habay Ex-Staffers Told Panel of Political Work, *Pittsburgh Tribune-Review,* June 18, 2004.

Bumsted, Brad, and Andrew Conte, Rep. Habay Fined $13,000 for Using State Workers to Campaign, *Pittsburgh Tribune-Review,* June 18, 2004.

Roddy, Dennis, Habay Takes Stand in His Own Defense, *Pittsburgh Post-Gazette,* December 9, 2005.

http://www.post-gazette.com/stories/local/breaking/habay-takes-stand-in-his-own-defense-614039/

Roddy, Dennis, Habay Trial Takes Detour, *Pittsburgh Post-Gazette,* December 10, 2005.

http://www.post-gazette.com/stories/local/neighborhoods-north/habay-trial-takes-detour-614120/?print=1

Keat, Brandon, Habay Trial Gets Started, *Valley News Dispatch,* Tarentum, PA, December 8, 2005.

http://triblive.com/x/valleynewsdispatch/s_402144.html#axzz2M9e5kkoK

Wereschagin, Mike, Habay Aides Detail Threats, *Pittsburgh Tribune-Review,* December 9, 2005.

Kerlik, Bobby, Habay to Serve Four to Eight Months in County Jail, *Pittsburgh Tribune- Review,* August 1, 2008.

http://triblive.com/x/pittsburghtrib/news/regional/s_580493.html

Keat, Brandon, and Reid R. Frazier, Jeff Habay Was Once GOP's Rising Star, *Pittsburgh Tribune-Review,* April 1, 2005.

http://triblive.com/x/pittsburghtrib/news/pittsburgh/s_319470.html#axzz2M9e5kkoK

Commonwealth of Pennsylvania v. Jeffrey E. Habay, Pennsylvania Superior Court, Colville opinion, October 10, 2007.

http://law.justia.com/cases/pennsylvania/superior-court/2007/s43004-07.html

CHAPTER 11

Reeves, Tim, Behind the Scenes, Not a Household Name to Many: Mike Veon '79 is emerging as one of Pennsylvania's leading political figures, Tim, *Allegheny: The Allegheny College Magazine,* Vol. 12, No. 1, Winter 1992.

Cattabiani, Mario, House Democrats to Veon: You Are on Your Own, *Philadelphia Inquirer,* January 31, 2010.

Politics PA Yearbook, PoliticsPA.com, 2001.

Roddy, Dennis, A Political Reformer's Rise and Fall, *Pittsburgh Post-Gazette,* June 29, 2008.

http://www.post-gazette.com/stories/local/state/a-political-reformers-rise-and-fall-400383/

Erdley, Debra, Next blow to one-time 'rising star' Mike Veon, *Pittsburgh Tribune-Review,* July 11, 2008.

http://triblive.com/x/pittsburghtrib/news/regional/s_577065.html#axzz2M9e5kkoK

Roddy, Dennis, and Tracie Mauriello, 12 Face Charges in Bonus Scandal, *Pittsburgh Post-Gazette,* July 11, 2008.

Cattabiani, Mario, Bonusgate's Round 2 Is Test for Veon and Corbett: Alleged Leader's Trial Is to Start Tomorrow, *Philadelphia Inquirer,* January 31, 2010.

Barnes, Tom, Defeated Rep. Veon Now Tobacco Lobbyist, *Pittsburgh Post-Gazette,* March 17, 2002.

Bumsted, Brad, and Debra Erdley, Democratic Panel Pays Off Veon's Debt, *Pittsburgh Tribune-Review,* February 21, 2008.

Bumsted and Erdley, Democrats' Gift to Veon Campaign Faces Growing Criticism, *Pittsburgh Tribune-Review,* February 22, 2008.

http://tribune-review-pittsburgh.vlex.com/vid/democrats-gift-veon-faces-criticism-192632363

CHAPTER 12

Thompson, Charles, and Jan Murphy, Democrats Give Some Staffers Bonuses, *Patriot-News,* Harrisburg, January 27, 2007.

http://www.pennlive.com/midstate/index.ssf/2008/07/archive_democrats_give_some_st.html

Barnes, Tom, Senate Halts Bonus Practice, *Pittsburgh Post-Gazette,* February 1, 2007.

Bumsted, Brad, Assembly Staff Got Over $1M Bonus Pay; Senate Leaders Disclosed Over $363 K in Bonuses, *Pittsburgh Tribune-Review,* February 1, 2007.

Murphy, Jan, Senate Slaps Down Bonuses, *Patriot-News,* Harrisburg, October 18, 2007.

Thompson, Charles, Plans, Profiles and Politics, *Patriot-News,* Harrisburg, October 17, 2007.

Mauriello, Tracie, 33 House Staffers Were Paid Over $100,000, *Pittsburgh Post-Gazette,* February 17, 2007.

http://www.law.com/jsp/pa/PubArticleFriendlyPA.jsp?id=900005492022

Roddy, Dennis, and Tracie Mauriello, Democratic Offices Searched in Harrisburg, *Pittsburgh Post-Gazette,* August 30, 2007.

Cattabiani, Mario, PA Probe of House Bonuses Widens, *Philadelphia Inquirer,* October 15, 2007.

Bonusgate Timeline, *Pittsburgh Post-Gazette,* February 12, 2007.

http://www.post-gazette.com/pg/08162/888801-178.stm

Bumsted, Brad, Tom Corbett's Conundrum, *Pittsburgh Tribune-Review,* December 11, 2009.

Bumsted, Brad, A Hint of an Expanded Probe? *Pittsburgh Tribune-Review,* August 31, 2009.

CHAPTER 13

Vincent Fumo blog, *Philadelphia Inquirer:* http://www.philly.com/philly/news/special_packages/inquirer/fumo/

United States of America v. Vincent J. Fumo, indictment, *Philadelphia Inquirer,* February 6, 2007.

http://inquirer.philly.com/rss/News/2007fumoindictment.pdf

PA Senator Indicted on 139 Counts, Associated Press, *USA Today*, February 6, 2007. http://www.usatoday.com/news/nation/2007-02-06-fumo_x.htm

Carocci, Vincent, *A Capitol Journey: Reflections on the Press, Politics, and the Making of Public Policy in Pennsylvania*, University Park, The Pennsylvania State University Press, 2005.

McCoy, Craig R., Vincent Fumo resentencing: Live blog, *Philadelphia Inquirer*, November 8 and 9, 2011.

Fumo Announces His Retirement, Fumo.com: http://www.fumo.com/Press_Releases/VJFRetire3-12-08.htm

DeCoursey, Pete, Senator Fumo Bids Farewell to State Senate, Capitolwire.com, July 7, 2008.

Pearson, Sophia, and Christopher Yasiejko, Ex-Senator Fumo Sentenced to 55 Months, *Bloomberg News*, July 14, 2009.

Bumsted, Brad, Bully's Club Fortified Fumo's Charm, *Pittsburgh Tribune-Review*, March 1, 2009. http://triblive.com/x/pittsburghtrib/news/s_613954.html

Bumsted, Brad, Fumo, Ruthless Master of Power, *Pittsburgh Tribune-Review*, September 7, 2008.

Bumsted, Brad, Through the Eyes of an Angry Taxpayer, *Pittsburgh Tribune-Review*, August 2, 2009.

Philly Clout, *Philadelphia Daily News*, August 12, 2009.

CHAPTER 14

Bumsted, Brad, Lawyer: Ex-Rep. LaGrotta Talks with Prosecutors, *Pittsburgh Tribune-Review*, November 15, 2007.

Presentment No. 7: The Twenty-Sixth Statewide Investigating Grand Jury State Employees Retirement System (SERS) web page on forfeiture act: http://www.portal.state.pa.us/portal/server.pt?open=514&objID=593234&mode=2

Scolforo, Mark, Ex-legislator Charged with Giving Family Members No-show Jobs, Associated Press, Centredaily.com, State College, PA, November 14, 2007.

Police Criminal Complaint, *Commonwealth of Pennsylvania v. Frank LaGrotta*, Dauphin County Court, unsigned and undated copy given to press, November 14, 2007.

Grand Jury Presentment No. 7 against LaGrotta, sister and niece, in the Allegheny County Court of Common Pleas, prior to November 14, 2007; sent to Supervising Senior Judge Barry Feudale.

Vidonic, Bill, LaGrotta Expected to Enter a Plea, Timesonline.com, *Beaver Valley Times*, January 31, 2008.

Walter, Kory, Ex-lawmaker, Relatives Arraigned for Ghost Employee Charges, Herald Standard. com, November 16, 2007.

Roxbury, James, Frank LaGrotta Guilty, Roxbury News video, February 4, 2008. http://www.roxburynews.com/index.php?p=search

Bumsted, Brad, Ex-Rep. LaGrotta Sentenced, *Pittsburgh Tribune-Review*, February 5, 2008.

Ex-legislator LaGrotta Pleads Guilty in Prescription Case, Associated Press, *Pittsburgh Tribune-Review*, April 8, 2011.

Bowling, Brian, Former Lawmaker LaGrotta Finally Sentenced to Jail, *Pittsburgh Tribune-Review*, June 15, 2011.

Bowling, Brian, Sentence Confirmed for Former Lawmaker, *Pittsburgh Tribune-Review* June 16, 2011.

Former Rep. LaGrotta Falls Ill During Drug Charge Sentencing, *Pittsburgh Tribune-Review,* June 13, 2011.

http://triblive.com/x/pittsburghtrib/news/regional/s_742285.html#axzz2M9e5kkoK

Roddy, Dennis, Checks to Legislators Probed, *Pittsburgh Post-Gazette,* April 11, 2008.

Bumsted, Brad, and Debra Erdley, Casino Probe Targets Campaign Finances, *Pittsburgh Tribune-Review,* April 18, 2008.

Press release, Office of the Pennsylvania Attorney General, November 14, 2007.

LaGrotta will Collect $36,000 Annual Pension Plus, Associated Press, Pennlive.com, February 29, 2008.

CHAPTER 15

Bumsted, Brad, Judge Postpones Former Lawmaker Ramaley's Trial, *Pittsburgh Tribune-Review,* August 31, 2009.

Bumsted, Brad, Arguments to Begin Ex-Lawmaker's Trial, *Pittsburgh Tribune-Review,* December 9, 2009.

Bumsted, Brad, Defense Rests in Corruption Trial without Putting Ramaley on the Stand, *Pittsburgh Tribune-Review,* December 9, 2009.

Bumsted, Brad, Ex-Pennsylvania Lawmaker Ramaley's Defense Stresses Honesty, *Pittsburgh Tribune-Review,* December 9, 2009.

Bumsted, Brad, Jury Acquits Ramaley of Six Felony Charges, *Pittsburgh Tribune-Review,* December 11, 2009.

http://triblive.com/x/pittsburghtrib/news/regional/s_657123.html#axzz2M9e5kkoK

Mauriello, Tracie, Ramaley Acquitted in Corruption Trial, *Pittsburgh Post-Gazette,* December 11, 2009.

Cattabiani, Mario, First Bonusgate Defendant Not Guilty: Former State Rep. Sean Ramaley was among a dozen charged in the Pa. corruption scandal, *Philadelphia Inquirer,* December 11, 2009.

CHAPTER 16

Mauriello, Tracie, Two More Aides to Testify on Democratic Bonuses, *Pittsburgh Post-Gazette,* October 16, 2007.

Attorney General's Release on Arrest of 12 Democrats: News release, July 10, 2008 (handout at news conference).

Bumsted, Brad, Veon, Ramaley Charged in Bonus Scandal, *Pittsburgh Tribune-Review,* July 11, 2008.

Roddy, Dennis, and Tracie Mauriello, 12 Face Charges in Bonus Scandal, *Pittsburgh Post-Gazette,* July 11, 2008.

Thompson, Charles, and Jan Murphy, Bonus Busts, *Patriot-News,* Harrisburg, July 11, 2008.

Andren, Kari, Democracy Was the Victim, *Patriot-News*, Harrisburg, July 12, 2008.

Mauriello, Tracie, Five in Bonusgate Scandal Agree to Cooperate, *Pittsburgh Post-Gazette,* October 23, 2009.

Cattabiani, Mario, Ex-Beauty Queen in Bonusgate Scandal Is Still on State Payroll, *Philadelphia Inquirer,* July 19, 2008.

Cattabiani, Mario, Trial Opens for Veon, 3 Others: One lawyer blamed Bonusgate on State Rep. Bill DeWeese, *Philadelphia Inquirer,* February 2, 2010.

http://articles.philly.com/2010-02-02/news/25220011_1_campaign-work-defense-strategy-bonuses

Scolforo, Mark, PA Attorney General's Public Corruption Trial Gets Underway Against Rep. Veon, 3 Aides, Associated Press, *Star Tribune,* Minneapolis, February 1, 2010.

Mauriello, Tracie, Veon Loads Double-Barreled Defense Team, *Pittsburgh Post-Gazette,* January 19, 2010.

Bumsted, Brad, Judge Denies Mistrial Request in Veon Case, *Pittsburgh Tribune-Review*, March 22, 2010.

Scolforo, Mark, Jury Deliberations Resume in Trial of Veon, Aides, Associated Press, Connellsville, PA, *Daily Courier,* March 16, 2010.

Scolforo, Mark, Veon's Fate Rests in Jury's Hands, Associated Press, *Patriot-News,* Harrisburg, March 13, 2010.

Bumsted, Brad, Veon Trial Witness Admits to Creating Fake Taxpayer-Financed Job, *Pittsburgh Tribune-Review*, February 6, 2010.

Scolforo, Mark, Veon Jury Gets Case After AG Sums Up Allegations, Associated Press, *Chicago Tribune,* March 12, 2010.

Scolforo, Mark, Veon Case Expected to Go to Jury Today, Associated Press, *Patriot-News,* Harrisburg, March 12, 2010.

Bumsted, Brad, Veon Jury to Start Anew, *Pittsburgh Tribune-Review,* March 20, 2010.

Scolforo, Mark, Veon Convicted, Associated Press, *Patriot-News,* Harrisburg, March 23, 2010.

Veon and 2 Aides Guilty in Scheme to Fund Campaign, *Pittsburgh Post-Gazette,* March 22, 2010.

Bumsted, Brad, Attorney General Corbett Thinks Veon Will Serve Prison Time, *Pittsburgh Tribune-Review*, March 23, 2010.

Bumsted, Brad, Mistakes Cost Former Lawmaker 6-14 Years, *Pittsburgh Tribune-Review*, June 18, 2010.

http://triblive.com/x/pittsburghtrib/news/regional/s_686668.html#axzz2MK83L7Vv

Roxbury, James, Brett Cott — 21 to 60 months, *Roxbury News,* March 23, 2010.

http://www.roxburynews.com/index.php?p=search

Mauriello, Tracie, Bonusgate: How the Statewide Public Corruption Case Unfolded, *Pittsburgh Post-Gazette*, February 12, 2012.

Collection of Mike Veon stories on Philly.com (*Philadelphia Inquirer*): http://articles.philly.com/keyword/mike-veon

CHAPTER 17

Bumsted, Brad, Disgraced State Senator: I Will Repay All These (Expletive) Some Day, *Pittsburgh Tribune-Review,* November 6, 2011.

http://triblive.com/x/pittsburghtrib/news/regional/s_765825.html

McCoy, Craig R., Vincent Fumo Resentencing: Live blog, *Philadelphia Inquirer,* November 8 and 9, 2011.

Bumsted, Brad, Fumo Sentencing Hearing Begins in Philadelphia, *Pittsburgh Tribune-Review,* November 9, 2011.

Bumsted, Brad, Fumo's Sentencing Hearing Goes into Second Day, *Pittsburgh Tribune-Review,* November 9, 2011.

Gorenstein, Nathan, and Craig R. McCoy, At Sentencing Hearing, Fumo Faces Up to 17 Years, *Philadelphia Inquirer,* November 10, 2011.

Government's Memorandum Regarding Resentencing, U.S. District Court, Criminal No. 319-03.

Bumsted, Brad, Fumo Skates Again, *Pittsburgh Tribune-Review,* November 13, 2011.

Bissinger, Buzz, Judge: A Total Fumo Suck Up, Philly.com, November 15, 2011.

CHAPTER 18

Schmedlen, Hearn Jeanne, *Speakers of the House,* Pennsylvania House of Representatives, Armstrong Printery, Inc., 1998.

Conte, Andrew, State Officials Join the Jet Set, *Pittsburgh Tribune-Review,* December 1, 2005.

Thompson, Charles, Democrats Purge 7 Top Aides in House, *Patriot-News,* Harrisburg, November 14, 2007.

Thompson, Charles, Bonus Storm Swirls Around DeWeese, *Patriot-News,* Harrisburg, November 19, 2007.

Thompson, Charles, It's Been a Very Difficult Lesson, *Patriot-News,* Harrisburg, December 20, 2007.

Bumsted, Brad, and Debra Erdley, Ex-Aide Accuses DeWeese in Probe, *Pittsburgh Tribune-Review,* October 9, 2008.

Cattabiani, Mario, Records Show DeWeese Knew of Staff Misdeeds, *Philadelphia Inquirer,* April 6, 2009.

Attorney General Corbett Announces Additional Charges in Ongoing Public Corruption Investigation: News release, Office of the Attorney General:

http://www.attorneygeneral.gov/press.aspx?id=4919

Bumsted, Brad, DeWeese, Two Others Charged with Politicking with PA Money, *Pittsburgh Tribune-Review,* December 16, 2009.

http://triblive.com/x/pittsburghtrib/news/regional/s_657829.html#axzz2M9e5kkoK

Bumsted, Brad, Email May Tie DeWeese to Scandal, *Pittsburgh Tribune-Review,* March 16, 2009.

http://triblive.com/x/pittsburghtrib/news/regional/s_616264.html#axzz2M9e5kkoK

Defendant's Motion to Dismiss All Charges Because the Conflict of Interest Statute Is Unconstitutionally Vague; filed by William C. Costopoulos in Dauphin County Court, April 19, 2010.

Gilliland, Donald, Pennsylvania lawmaker Bill DeWeese featured in Merriam-Webster's Word of the Day, *Patriot News,* Harrisburg, July 6, 2011.

Bumsted, Brad, Former DeWeese Aide Says He Worked on Campaign on Taxpayers' Dime, *Pittsburgh Tribune-Review,* January 23, 2012.

Bumsted, Brad, State-paid Staffers Made Bill Happy, *Pittsburgh Tribune-Review,* January 24, 2012.

http://triblive.com/x/pittsburghtrib/news/s_778054.html#axzz2M9e5kkoK

Olson, Laura, DeWeese's Former Top Aide Testifies, *Pittsburgh Post-Gazette,* January 25, 2012.

Miller, Matt, Bill DeWeese Attorney William Costopoulos Grills Ex-Aide Kevin Sidella as Corruption Trial Enters Third Day, *Patriot-News,* Harrisburg, January 25, 2012.

Bumsted, Brad, Ex-Coordinator Says DeWeese Demanded Help, *Pittsburgh Tribune-Review,* January 27, 2012.

Bumsted, Brad, DeWeese on Trial: "I Didn't Do Anything Wrong," *Pittsburgh Tribune-Review,* February 2, 2012.

http://www.pittsburghlive.com/x/pittsburghtrib/news/regional/s_779528.html

Miller, Matt, DeWeese Is "Servant Who Earns His Pay," Supporter Says, *Patriot-News,* Harrisburg, February 1, 2012.

Bumsted, Brad, DeWeese Trial Set To Go Thursday, *Pittsburgh Tribune-Review,* February 1, 2012.

Bumsted, Brad, No Verdict Yet: DeWeese Jury Will Resume Deliberations Friday, *Pittsburgh Tribune-Review,* February 2, 2012.

Bumsted, Brad, Jury Finds DeWeese Guilty of Five Felonies, *Pittsburgh Tribune-Review,* February 7, 2012.

DeWeese Free on Bail Days After Reporting to Prison, *Pittsburgh Tribune-Review,* May 19, 2012.

Epstein, Eric, *Pension Projection* (booklet), Harrisburg, Rock the Capital, February 8, 2012.

CHAPTER 19

Bumsted, Brad, and Debra Erdley, BIG Conflict of Interest, *Pittsburgh Tribune-Review,* February 26, 2006.

Bumsted and Erdley, State Officials Seek Records of Beaver Non-Profit, *Pittsburgh Tribune-Review,* October 11, 2008.

Bumsted and Erdley, Former State Rep. Veon Charged with Stealing Taxpayers' Money, *Pittsburgh Tribune-Review,* March 26, 2009.

http://triblive.com/x/pittsburghtrib/news/regional/s_617864.html#axzz2M9e5kkoK

Attorney General Corbett Announces Public Corruption Charges Against Former House Member and Staffer: News release, Office of the Attorney General, March 25, 2009.

Bumsted and Erdley, House Dems Abruptly Cancel Deal with Delta Development, *Pittsburgh Tribune-Review,* March 27, 2009.

Bumsted, Brad, Ex-Senator: BIG Was Completely Under Veon's Control, *Pittsburgh Tribune-Review,* September 4, 2009.

Mauriello, Tracie, Beaver Nonprofit Behind on Audits, *Pittsburgh Post-Gazette,* March 27, 2009.

Thompson, Charles, For Now "It's a Good Day" for Veon, *Patriot-News,* Harrisburg, May 22, 2009.

Bumsted, Brad, Van Horne Provides Damaging Testimony Against Ex-Rep. Veon, *Pittsburgh Tribune-Review*, May 21, 2009.

Mauriello, Tracie, Veon and Aide Ordered to Face Trial, *Pittsburgh Post-Gazette*, September 5, 2009.

Bumsted, Brad, Jury Selection Begins in 2nd Veon Trial, *Pittsburgh Tribune-Review*, February 13, 2012.

Bumsted, Brad, Nonprofit Exec: Checks Meant Trouble, *Pittsburgh Tribune-Review*, February 17, 2012.

http://triblive.com/x/pittsburghtrib/news/regional/s_782074.html#axzz2M9e5kkoK

Jackson, Peter, Conflicting Views of Veon Emerge at Trial, Associated Press, *Johnstown Tribune-Democrat*, February 16, 2012.

Bumsted, Brad, Trying John Gallo, *Pittsburgh Tribune-Review*, February 26, 2012.

Bumsted, Brad, Witness Veon Gave Law Firm $4,000 Per Month, *Pittsburgh Tribune-Review*, February 23, 2012.

Bumsted, Brad, Lawyer Calls Veon Prosecution "Political Assassination," *Pittsburgh Tribune-Review*, March 26, 2009.

Bumsted, Brad, Ex-BIG Exec: Veon Non-Profit, Legislative Funds Were Intertwined, *Pittsburgh Tribune-Review*, February 22, 2012.

Miller, Matt, Brothers to Square Off at Ex-Rep. Mike Veon's Corruption Trial; Jeff Foreman Likely Will Testify Tomorrow, *Patriot-News*, Harrisburg, Pennlive.com, February 22, 2012.

Bumsted, Brad, New Witness, Defense Rests; Web Update, Triblive.com, February 29, 2012.

Mauriello, Tracie, Bonusgate Witness' Affair Described, *Pittsburgh Post-Gazette*, February 10, 2012.

Bumsted, Brad, Inmate Veon Convicted of Felony Theft, *Pittsburgh Tribune-Review*, May 23, 2012.

http://triblive.com/x/pittsburghtrib/news/s_784928.html#axzz2M9e5kkoK

Jackson, Peter, Veon Convicted in 2nd Corruption Trial, Associated Press, March 5, 2012.

Bumsted, Brad, Prosecutors Seek More Prison Time for Veon, *Pittsburgh Tribune-Review*, May 23, 2012.

Bumsted, Brad, Veon Gets Additional Prison Time for Misusing Taxpayers' Money, *Pittsburgh Tribune-Review*, June 19, 2012.

http://triblive.com/news/2034846-74/veon-prison-judge-office-beaver-six-state-democratic-midland-money#axzz2M9e5kkoK

Bumsted, Brad, PA's Rogue's Gallery, *Pittsburgh Tribune-Review*, June 23, 2012.

http://triblive.com/opinion/2072176-74/veon-deweese-former-state-prison-perzel-charged-convicted-orie-republican#axzz2M0IJGh9e

CHAPTER 20

Bumsted, Brad, and Debra Erdley, More Checks Than Balances, *Pittsburgh Tribune-Review*, June 4, 2006.

http://triblive.com/x/pittsburghtrib/news/regional/s_456614.html#axzz2M9e5kkoK

Thompson, Charles, Bonus Probe Turns to House GOP, *Patriot-News*, Harrisburg, September 10, 2008.

Cattabiani, Mario, Republicans Called to Testify in Bonusgate, *Philadelphia Inquirer,* October 21, 2009.

Bumsted, Brad, Corruption Total Will Be Stunning, Corbett States, *Pittsburgh Tribune-Review,* February 23, 2009.

Pennsylvania Office of the Attorney General, press release: "Attorney General Corbett Announces Criminal Charges in Second Phase of Legislative Investigation: 10 Suspects Charged," November 12, 2009.

Cattabiani, Mario, Living Testimony From a Pa. Ghost Employee, *Philadelphia Inquirer,* November 22, 2009.

Couloumbis, Angela, Corruption Case Opens in Harrisburg, *Philadelphia Inquirer,* March 21, 2012.

Bumsted, Brad, Perzel's Chief of Staff May Testify Against Him, *Pittsburgh Tribune-Review,* August 20, 2011.

Couloumbis, Angela, Perzel to Plead Guilty to Corruption, *Philadelphia Inquirer,* August 31, 2011.

Bumsted, Brad, Three Aides to Plead Guilty to Misusing Public Money for Political Purposes, *Pittsburgh Tribune-Review,* August 15, 2011.

Thompson, Charles, John Perzel's Astonishing Fall from Grace, *Patriot-News,* Harrisburg, September 1, 2011.

http://www.pennlive.com/midstate/index.ssf/2011/09/john_perzel_s_astonishing_fall.html

Jackson, Peter, Preski Pleads Guilty in Corruption Case, *Patriot-News,* Harrisburg, October 6, 2011.

Bumsted, Brad, Perzel Testifies: Knowledge of Corruption Case Reached Top of the House, *Pittsburgh Tribune-Review,* October 18, 2011.

Miller, Matt, Wait Begins for the Verdicts, *Patriot-News,* Harrisburg, November 2, 2011.

Jackson, Peter, Ex-Rep. Brett Feese Convicted in Scheme to Spend Millions of Taxpayer Dollars on Campaigns, *Delaware County Times,* November 9, 2011.

Bumsted, Brad, Prison, Pension, Forfeiture Await Perzel, *Pittsburgh Tribune-Review,* September 1, 2011.

Editorial: Perzel Isn't Exactly the Model of Contrition, *Philadelphia Inquirer,* September 1, 2011.

http://www.philly.com/philly/blogs/inq_ed_board/?month=8&month=8&year=2011&year=2011

Bumsted, Brad, Ex-Speaker Perzel Gets Up to 5 Years, *Pittsburgh Tribune-Review,* March 22, 2012.

Baer, John, Baer Growls, *Philadelphia Daily News,* June 5, 2012.

http://www.philly.com/philly/blogs/growls/Perzel-DeWeese-Stir-Crazy-Pols.html

Nolan, Jim, and John Baer, Hispanics Remain Angry at Rep. Perzel's Remark, *Philadelphia Daily News,* March 28, 1995.

Collection of Philadelphia Inquirer articles on John Perzel at Philly.com: http://articles.philly.com/keyword/john-perzel

CHAPTER 21

Carl Lee Manzo (obituary), *Pittsburgh Post-Gazette,* June 29, 2010.

Couloumbis, Angela, Sentenced to prison, a Bonusgate defendant blames only himself, *Philadelphia Inquirer,* May 28, 2010.

Roddy, Dennis, Pennsylvania Bonus Scandal: Michael R. Veon, former House Democratic Whip, *Pittsburgh Post-Gazette*, July 10, 2008.

Bumsted, Brad, The Manzo Example, *Pittsburgh Tribune-Review*, May 13, 2012.

Prose, J.D., Former Beauty Queen Was "Smart, Active" as College Student, *Beaver Valley Times*, July 12, 2008.

Detrow, Scott, Veon Trial: Day Two, State House Sound Bites (blog), WITF, Harrisburg, February 2, 2010.

Mauriello, Tracie, Bonusgate Defense Attorneys May Seek Mistrial for Veon, *Pittsburgh Post-Gazette*, March 28, 2010.

Former Bill DeWeese Aide to Be Last Sentenced in Bonusgate, *Patriot-News*, Harrisburg, April 16, 2012.

Boren, Jeremy, Toilet Seat Tactics an Issue in Monaca Council Race, *Beaver Valley Times*, November 1, 2003.

Package of Manzo stories from the *Patriot-News*, Harrisburg, on Pennlive:

http://topics.pennlive.com/tag/Michael%20Manzo/index.html

Mauriello, Tracie, and Dennis Roddy, Ex-aide Implicates DeWeese on Bonuses: Manzo testifies boss knew of campaign work, *Pittsburgh Post-Gazette*, October 9, 2008.

Bumsted, Brad, Witness: Nonprofit's South Side office was empty, idle, *Pittsburgh Tribune-Review*, February 24, 2012.

CHAPTER 22

Owens, Dennis, ABC 27-TV Harrisburg, May 14, 2012:http://www.abc27.com/story/18371037/deweese-to-report-to-prison-monday

Bumsted, Brad, DeWeese to Learn His Fate Today, *Pittsburgh Tribune-Review*, April 23, 2012.

Bumsted, Brad, DeWeese Sentenced to as Much as Five Years, *Pittsburgh Tribune-Review*, April 24, 2012.

Miller, Matt, Ex-state Rep. Bill DeWeese sentenced to 30 to 60 months in state prison in corruption case, expected to forfeit $2.8 million in pension payments, *Patriot-News*, Harrisburg, Pennlive.com, April 24, 2012.

Couloumbis, Angela, Commonwealth Confidential (live tweets), *Philadelphia Inquirer*, April 24, 2012.

Olson, Laura, Despite Conviction, DeWeese Will Remain on Primary Ballot, *Pittsburgh Post-Gazette*, April 20, 2012.

Baer, John, Perzel and DeWeese: Stir Crazy Pols, Baer Growls blog, *Philadelphia Daily News*, June, 5, 2012:

http://www.philly.com/philly/blogs/growls/Perzel-DeWeese-Stir-Crazy-Pols.html

CHAPTER 23

Mauriello, Tracie, Press release: Office of the Attorney General, Harrisburg, November 12, 2009.

Mauriello, Tracie, GOP Defendant Held for Trial, *Pittsburgh Post-Gazette*, May 26, 2010:

http://www.post-gazette.com/stories/local/state/gop-defendant-held-for-trial-248380/

Murse, Tom, County Native Who Worked for Perzel Charged in Probe, Lancaster Online, November 12, 2009:

http://lancasteronline.com/article/local/244915_County-native-who-worked-for-Perzel-charged-in-probe.html

New Holland Band website, "History": http://newhollandband.org.

Miller, Matt, Jill Seaman Sentenced to 9 to 23 Months in Prison for Computergate Case Convictions, *Patriot-News*, Harrisburg, January 13, 2012.

Couloumbis, Angela, Preski interrupts Computergate trial to plead guilty, *Philadelphia Inquirer*, October 6, 2011.

Buchanan Ingersoll and Rooney web page: Profile of Tom Bergstrom, "Of counsel":http://www.bipc.com/thomas-a-bergstrom/

CHAPTER 24

Brandt, Charles, *I Heard You Paint Houses: Frank "The Irishman" Sheehan and the Inside Story of the Mafia, the Teamsters and the Last Ride of Jimmy Hoffa*, Hanover, NH, Steerforth Press, 2004.

Bumsted, Brad, Sources: GOP Senators in Clear, *Pittsburgh Tribune-Review*, July 11, 2012.

Thompson, Charles, and Brett Lieberman, Is State Bonus Probe Partisan? *Patriot-News*, Harrisburg, August 3, 2008.

Mauriello, Tracie, and Dennis Roddy, Bonuses Spread Over Party Lines in Legislature, *Pittsburgh Post-Gazette*, December 17, 2007:

http://www.post-gazette.com/stories/local/uncategorized/bonus-pay-spread-over-party-lines-in-state-legislature-515354/

Thompson, Charles, Tom Corbett and Bonusgate: Did Senate Republicans Get a Break? *Patriot-News*, Harrisburg, February 27, 2013.

Mauriello, Tracie, AG to review Senate GOP records in bonus probe, *Pittsburgh Post-Gazette*, February 13, 2008.

Bumsted, Brad, Eichelberger Seeks to Ban Bonuses, *Pittsburgh Tribune-Review*, February 26, 2007.

Morganelli, John, Candidacy statement for Attorney General, January 24, 2008, provided by the John Morganelli campaign.

Long Nyquist & Associates web page: http://longnyquist.com/

Statement from Senators Scarnati and Pileggi, January 31, 2007, distributed by the Senate Republican Committee, Harrisburg.

Statement from Senators Scarnati and Pileggi: made upon request to *Pittsburgh Tribune-Review*, September 12, 2011.

List of Senate Republican bonuses, 2005-06, released by the Office of Senate President Pro Tem Joseph Scarnati.

Barnes, Tom, *Pittsburgh Post-Gazette*, Sentencing Memo for Brett Cott, issued by the Attorney General's Office, March 12, 2012.

Patser, Rachel, Caucus Scandal Tarnishes Wisconsin Politics, *The Badger Herald*, Madison, September 17, 2002.

Bumsted, Brad, Assembly Staff Got Over $1 Million in Bonus Pay, *Pittsburgh Tribune-Review*, February 1, 2007.

CHAPTER 25

Acton, Robin, Orie's Colleagues Reward Her Ethics, *Pittsburgh Tribune-Review*, December 31, 2009.

Orie biography, *Pennsylvania Manual*, Pennsylvania General Assembly, 1997-98.

Orie biography, *Pennsylvania Manual*, Pennsylvania General Assembly, 2009-10.

Orie, Jane, News release on Government and Gaming Reform, January 14, 2010.

Bumsted, Brad, and Bobby Kerlik, Records in Orie Office Seized by Allegheny County DA, *Pittsburgh Tribune-Review*, December 24, 2009.

http://triblive.com/x/pittsburghtrib/news/regional/s_659204.html#axzz2M8HpZ2u0

Roddy, Dennis, Senator Orie Facing Inquiry, *Pittsburgh Post-Gazette*, December 24, 2009.

http://www.post-gazette.com/stories/local/state/senator-orie-facing-inquiry-372997/

Roddy, Dennis, Orie's Staff to Be Summoned Before Grand Jury, *Pittsburgh Post-Gazette*, December 25, 2009.

Roddy, Dennis, Orie Sisters Ordered to Face Trial, *Pittsburgh Post-Gazette*, July 22, 2010:

http://www.post-gazette.com/stories/l/state/orie-sisters-ordered-to-face-trial-256415/?print=1

Bumsted, Brad, and Debra Erdley, Sister's Use of Orie Office for Election Denied, *Pittsburgh Tribune-Review:*

http://triblive.com/x/pittsburghtrib/news/regional/s_659976.html#axzz2M8HpZ2u0

Kerlik, Bobby, Habay Case Didn't Deter Orie, Ex-Aide Testifies at Her Trial, *Pittsburgh Tribune-Review*, February 16, 2011.

Wilson, Linda, It's Graduation Days at the Orie House, *Pittsburgh Post-Gazette*, May 18, 1978.

http://news.google.com/newspapers?id=_cpRAAAAIBAJ&sjid=TW0DAAAAIBAJ&pg=2820%2C2828085

Application for Search Warrant, County of Allegheny, Detective Lyle C. Graber, December 11, 2009.

McDevitt, Jerry S., letter to District Attorney Stephen Zappala, December 14, 2009.

Lord, Rich, Joan Orie Melvin Claims Political Vendetta, *Pittsburgh Post-Gazette*, May 22, 2012:

http://article.wn.com/view/2012/05/22/Joan_Orie_Melvin_claims_a_political_vendetta/

O'Neill, Brian, Zappalas/Ories Play Public Feud, *Pittsburgh Post-Gazette*, January 31, 2010.

Ward, Reed, Bank Files Foreclosure Notice on Orie's Brother, *Pittsburgh Post-Gazette*, April 14, 2010.

Judge Declares Mistrial in Orie Case, KDKA, CBS Pittsburgh, March 3, 2011.

Kerlik, Bobby, Doctored Documents Lead Orie Judge to Declare Mistrial, *Pittsburgh Tribune-Review*, March 3, 2011.

Kerlik, Bobby, More on the Line for Sen. Jane Orie as Second Trial Gets Under Way, *Pittsburgh Tribune-Review*, February 26, 2012.

Kerlik, Bobby, Orie Corruption Retrials at Opposite Ends, *Pittsburgh Tribune-Review*, March 1, 2012.

Kerlik, Bobby, Orie's attorney calls charges against her a smokescreen, *Pittsburgh Tribune-Review*, March 2, 2012.

Kerlik, Bobby, Sen. Jane Orie's Testimony Gets Tense at Corruption Trial, *Pittsburgh Tribune-Review*, March 21, 2012.

Pace, Laura, Realm of Spirits Draw Closer as Leaves Fall, *Pittsburgh Post-Gazette*, October 26, 2006.

Ward Reed, Paula, Jane Orie Sentenced to Prison, *Pittsburgh Post-Gazette*, June 4, 2012.

Mandak, Joe, Associated Press, Philly.com, March 6, 2012.

Ward Reed, Paula, *Pittsburgh Post-Gazette*, March 19, 2012.

Kerlik, Bobby, No Politics Permitted, Chief Clerk Tells Orie Jury, *Pittsburgh Tribune-Review*, March 9, 2012.

Kerlik, Bobby, Orie to Stay in Jail During Appeal, *Pittsburgh Tribune-Review*, June 19, 2012:

http://triblive.com/home/2057417-74/orie-prison-manning-county-judge-request-appeals-attorney-cambridge-comment

Kerlik, Bobby, Jeremy Boren and Brad Bumsted, State Supreme Court Justice Joan Orie Melvin Hit with Four Felonies, *Pittsburgh Tribune-Review*, May 19, 2012.

http://triblive.com/news/1824018-74/melvin-orie-court-state-charges-justice-judicial-jury-grand-supreme

Kerlik, Bobby, Orie's Attorney: Prosecution Has No Evidence Linking Her to Fraud, *Pittsburgh Tribune-Review*, February 29, 2012.

Boren, Jeremy, and Adam Brandolph, Orie Sentenced to Up to 10 Years in Prison, *Pittsburgh Tribune-Review*, June 12, 2012.

Judge Declares Mistrial in Orie Case, KDKA, CBS Pittsburgh, March 3, 2011.

Ward Reed, Paula, and Angela Couloumbis, PA Supreme Court Justice: I'll Fight Charges, Philly.com, May 20, 2012.

Information on the "Angel ladies": http://www.angel2ladies.com/

http://www.thewhisperingangels.com/index.html

Mandak, Joe, and Pete Jackson, 3 Political Sisters Convicted of Corruption Charges, Associated Press, AP.org., March 21, 2013:

http://bigstory.ap.org/article/3-political-sisters-pa-convicted-corruption

CHAPTER 26

Milliron Associates web page: http://www.millironassociates.com/

Bumsted, Brad, and Megan Guza, 7 years after late-night raises, reforms of legislature unsubstantial, *Pittsburgh Tribune-Review*, July 10, 2012.

Bumsted, Brad, Scandal doesn't shake lawmakers to reform, December 20, 2009.

Bumsted, Brad, political columns, *Pittsburgh Tribune-Review*, November 1, 2011 and May 18, 2012.

Couloumbis, Angela, Gov. Corbett turns testy on handling of Penn State, *Philadelphia Inquirer*, February 14, 2011:

http://articles.philly.com/2012-07-14/news/32664480_1_sandusky-case-corbett-sandusky-investigation

Bumsted, Brad, commentaries, *Pittsburgh Tribune-Review,* July 20, 2012; November 12, 2012; and January 22, 2013.

The Freeh Report: http://www.thefreehreportonpsu.com/REPORT_FINAL_071212.pdf

Fisher, Aaron, *Silent No More,* New York, Ballantine Books, 2012.

Fernandez, Bob, Hershey School's Purchase of Golf Course Helped Investors, *Philadelphia Inquirer,* October 3, 2010.

In the News, Milton Hershey School (mostly published pieces by Bob Fernandez on the Hershey Trust in *The Philadelphia Inquirer*), Philly.com:

http://articles.philly.com/keyword/milton-hershey-school

Ganim, Sara, *Patriot-News,* Harrisburg, Pulitzer.org: March 31; November 5, 8, 11, 14, 15, 17, 20; December 11, 20, 2011.

Ganim, Sara, Pulitzer.org pieces on the Sandusky case:http://www.pulitzer.org/works/2012-Local-Reporting

Ganim, Sara, Stories not included in Pulitzer collection: A *Patriot-News* Special Report: Who knew what about Jerry Sandusky? There were many missed chances to investigate as early as 1995, *Patriot-News,* Harrisburg, November 13, 2011; Mike McQueary told Joe Paterno he saw something 'extremely sexual' between Jerry Sandusky, young boy, *Patriot-News,* Harrisburg, December 16, 2011.

Collection of *Patriot-News* stories on Sandusky:

http://topics.pennlive.com/tag/tim%20curley/index.html

Krawczeniuk, Borys, Kane Says Corbett Probably Played Politics with Sandusky Case, *Scranton Times-Tribune,* September 27, 2012.

Bumsted, Brad, *Pittsburgh Tribune-Review,* November 25, 2011; July 12, 2012; July 21, 2012.

Ivey, Dejesus, *Patriot-News,* Harrisburg, November 12, 2012.

Kibler, William, *Altoona Mirror,* April 25, 2012.

Bumsted, Brad, *Pittsburgh Tribune-Review,* November 12, 2012:

http://triblive.com/news/allegheny/2912548-74/corbett-governor-state-gov-budget-cuts-kane-tom-office-popularity#axzz2HivjGkNY

Bumsted, Brad, and Mike Wereschagin, Is Corbett's Flip-Flop Start of 2014 Bid? *Pittsburgh Tribune-Review,* January 6, 2013.

Dawson, Mike, Mike McQueary files whistle-blower defamation lawsuit against Penn State, CentreDaily.com, State College, October 3, 2012.

Bumsted, Brad, AG Kathleen Kane appoints special Sandusky investigator, *Pittsburgh Tribune-Review,* February 4, 2013.

http://triblive.com/news/allegheny/2912548-74/corbett-governor-state-gov-budget-cuts-kane-tom-office-popularity#axzz2HivjGkNY

Ecenbarger, William, Kids for Cash: Two Judges, Thousands of Children, and a $2.6 Million Kickback Scheme, *The New Press,* October 2012.

CHAPTER 27

Empire Center webpage: http://www.empirecenter.org/html/legislative_salaries.cfm

Overall references:

Citizens Voice, Kids-for-Cash Timeline, May 28, 2010: http://citizensvoice.com/news/ kids-for-cash-scandal-timeline-1.818188#axzz1hSn2AoS3

New York Times, Sandusky Timeline, November 11, 2011: http://www.nytimes.com/ interactive/2011/11/11/sports/ncaafootball/sandusky.html

Pittsburgh Post-Gazette, Bonusgate Timeline: http://www.post-gazette.com/stories/local/state/ bonusgate-timeline-51945/

Eight Legislative Leaders Serving Time

Robert Mellow

Democrat

Former Senate
Minority Leader

■ Charged with
conspiracy

■ Sentenced to 16 months on Dec. 1, 2012;
prison assignment in Federal Correctional
Institution to be determined

Vincent Fumo

Democrat

Senator; ranking member
on Appropriations
Committee

■ Charged with mail fraud,
wire fraud and conspiracy

■ Sentenced to 55 months on July 14, 2009;
6 months added to earlier sentence in
Nov. 2011; in Federal Correctional Institution
in Ashland, Ky.

Mike Veon

Democrat

House Minority Whip

■ Charged with theft,
conspiracy and conflict of
interest

■ Sentenced to 6-14 years on June 18, 2010
and 1-4 years on June 9; in the State
Correctional Institution at Laurel Highlands

Brett Feese

Republican

House Majority Whip;
House GOP chief counsel

■ Charged with theft,
conspiracy and
conflict of interest

■ Sentenced to 4-12 years on Feb. 10; in the
State Correctional Institution at Waymart

John Perzel

Republican

House Speaker

■ Charged with theft,
conspiracy and conflict of
interest

■ Sentenced to 2½-5 years on March 21; in
the State Correctional Institution at Laurel
Highlands

Bill DeWeese

Democrat

House Speaker

■ Charged with theft,
conspiracy and conflict
of interest

■ Sentenced to 2½-5 years on April 24; in
the State Correctional Institution at Retreat

Jane Orie

Republican

Senate Majority Whip

■ Charged with theft of
services, obstruction,
forgery and tampering with
evidence

■ Sentenced to 2½-10 years on June 4;
in the State Correctional Institution at
Cambridge Springs

Steve Stetler

Democrat

Former House Democratic
Caucus chair

■ Charged with theft,
conspiracy and conflict
of interest

■ Sentenced to 1½-5 years on Sept. 25;
in the York County Prison

Source: Tribune-Review research

E. DENISE SHEAN | TRIBUNE-REVIEW